COMPILED BY ALAN ROBERTSON

HOWARD BOOKS
A DIVISION OF SIMON & SCHUSTER
New York Nashville London Toronto Sydney New Delhi

Howard Books
A Division of Simon & Schuster, Inc.
1230 Avenue of the Americas
New York, NY 10020

First Howard Books hardcover edition October 2013

Permissions acknowledgments appear on page 383.

Interior design by Davina Mock-Maniscalco

Manufactured in the United States of America

10 9 8 7 6 5 4 3 2 1

Library of Congress Cataloging-in-Publication Data is available.

ISBN 978-1-4767-5798-8 (pink camo)
ISBN 978-1-4767-4555-8 (ebook)

MEET THE ROBERTSON FAMILY AND FRIENDS

PHIL ROBERTSON: The patriarch of our family and *the* Duck Commander. Phil has been studying and teaching God's Word for the past thirty-eight years. He and Miss Kay attended and graduated from an intense two-year advanced Bible program associated with the seminary that Jase and Al studied at from 1988 to 1990.

MISS KAY ROBERTSON: The matriarch of our family and the glue that holds everything together. Miss Kay has taught children's classes at our church for years and led scores of women's Bible study groups for the past twenty-five-plus years.

SI ROBERTSON: Phil's younger brother and a faithful man of God. Si is known for his tall and colorful tales, but he is very serious about his commitment to God and his study of the Bible. You will always find Si in attendance when God's Word is being taught at our church.

AL ROBERTSON: The oldest of the four Robertson sons. Al worked for the family's church for twenty years after graduating from seminary. He is back at Duck Commander now, but continues to study, teach, and preach all around the country as well as at home. One of his main purposes in the family business is to remind everyone to stay true to God, His Word, and His mission for the Robertson family.

LISA ROBERTSON: Al's wife of twenty-eight years. Lisa worked with Al at the church for several different ministries there before joining him back at Duck Commander. She is a committed mother and grandmother and guides her family in the ways of Christ.

ANNA (ROBERTSON) STONE: Al and Lisa's oldest daughter. Anna has worked for Duck Commander for almost ten years since graduating from high school. She has been married for nine years and has two daughters, Carley and Bailey.

Jay Stone: Anna's husband of nine years, Jay coached and taught at a local middle school for twelve years before coming to work for Duck Commander a year ago. Jay works with the guys in the duck call room to fulfill the ever-growing demand for Duck Commander duck calls.

Alex (Robertson) Mancuso: Al and Lisa's youngest daughter. Alex went to Louisiana State University in Baton Rouge and graduated from the Louisiana Culinary Institute there as a pastry chef. She continues the family's love for cooking and has recently come home to work for Duck Commander to develop restaurant opportunities for the family. She recently married Vince Mancuso, who also works for Duck Commander.

Jase Robertson: The second oldest Robertson son. Jase went to seminary with Al after graduating from high school and actually worked in full-time ministry for five years before going back to Duck Commander in the mid-nineties. Jase shares God's Word in presentations all around the country.

Missy Robertson: Jase's wife of twenty-two years. Missy grew up in a minister's home, as her parents have been active doing evangelistic campaigns for forty-plus years. She is a talented singer and has participated as part of the church praise team for the past twenty years and led many children's choruses as well.

Reed Robertson: Jase and Missy's oldest son, who just turned eighteen. Reed will be a senior at Ouachita Christian School this year and is heavily involved there in athletics. Reed is a gifted singer and musician and speaks around the country about his family and faith.

Cole Robertson: Jase and Missy's second son, who is fifteen. Cole will be a sophomore at Ouachita Christian School this year and plays baseball there. He is very involved with the church youth group and speaks around the country about his family and faith.

Willie Robertson: The third brother of the Robertson sons. Willie is the CEO of Duck Commander and has grown the business and the brand to incredible heights. Willie went for one year to seminary before going to Harding University and then graduated from ULM in Monroe. He has worked with youth and college kids at the family church and ran Camp CH-YO-CA for a few years before returning to Duck Commander. Like the rest of his family, Willie speaks all around the country about faith, family, and ducks.

KORIE ROBERTSON: Willie's wife of twenty-one years. Korie's family had several successful businesses including a Christian publishing business that produced hymnals and Christian books for many, many years. Korie is a godly woman who continues the legacy of a great Christian upbringing.

JOHN LUKE ROBERTSON: Willie and Korie's oldest son, who is seventeen. John Luke will be a junior at Ouachita Christian School and is heavily involved at the school and in our church youth group. He speaks around the country about his family and faith.

SADIE ROBERTSON: Willie and Korie's oldest daughter, who just turned sixteen. Sadie will be a sophomore with Cole at Ouachita Christian School; she is a talented athlete and very involved in her school and friends there. She is popular on *Duck Dynasty* and speaks around the country about her family and faith.

WILL ROBERTSON: Willie and Korie's third child, who is eleven. Will was adopted as a newborn, but is probably more like his dad than any of his siblings. He has a great sense of humor and is also a talented singer and plays football as well.

BELLA ROBERTSON: Willie and Korie's youngest child, who is ten. Bella and Will are almost the same age, but she is about half his size. Like most girls her age, she is very active and loves horses.

JEP ROBERTSON: The youngest of the Robertson sons. Jep is the only son who completely grew up in a Christian home, and the family business encompasses all of his thirty-four years. Since graduating from high school, Jep has worked for the family business and has worked in film production for the past ten years filming and editing the Duck Commander hunting DVDs.

Jessica Robertson: Jep's wife of eleven years. Jessica is a busy mom with four children ranging from ten to four years old. She has a great smile and personality and is a fan favorite on *Duck Dynasty*. Jessica and Jep speak around the country about their faith and the family.

John Godwin: John was a big Duck Commander fan who befriended the Robertson family, was converted to Christ, and eventually came to work for the business about twelve years ago. He and his wife, Paula, have one daughter, Johanna, who recently started college. John speaks around the country about his faith and role in the duck call business.

Justin Martin: Martin, as he is known by most, has been with Duck Commander for about four years. He worked for a sporting goods store as he was attending college and befriended Willie, who eventually hired him. He appears around the country demonstrating duck calls on behalf of Duck Commander.

Jon Gimber: Jon is a first cousin to the Robertson clan; his mother, Judy, was Phil and Si's older sister. Judy passed away from cancer seven years ago. Like most Robertsons, Jon loves to cook and is an avid hunter. He came to work for Duck Commander almost a year ago and is a vital part of the company's growth and future.

Lynda Hammitt: Lynda is the voice of Duck Commander, as she works as the receptionist answering the phone every day. She has appeared on *Duck Dynasty* and has been with the company for several years. She and her husband worked as missionaries in Africa for many years before a car accident sent them home to the United States and eventually to West Monroe, Louisiana, and the Robertson family church.

Mountain Man: MM's real name is Tim Gurardy, and he started as Willie and Korie's air conditioner repairman. An appearance on the first season of *Duck Dynasty* has led to more appearances, and MM appears all over the country now signing and taking pictures with fans. Tim was converted to Christ after connecting with the Robertsons and attends the family church when he is not traveling and appearing.

Introduction

THE WORD OF God has been a constant in the Robertson home since Dad became a Christian almost forty years ago. Whether we were discussing and debating at the dinner table, teaching in a small-group setting, or sharing with someone who doesn't know the Lord, the Bible has been very near and dear to our family. Like every family, we get busy with life and need regular reminders to read, meditate on God's Word, and apply it to our daily lives. Because our family understands this need, we wanted to write a daily devotional book to help guide others to the life-changing power found in Scripture.

Dad's parents, Granny and Pa, helped us buy our home place on the river and lived next door to us when Dad became a Christian. They were retiring and wanted to fish, hunt, grow gardens, and be close to family in their later years. They also had a divine appointment to teach our family a lot of scripture. God knew that our family needed them nearby to help guide our young family in our Christian walk. They were totally committed to studying the Bible and shared so much of what they discovered with our whole family. Forty years ago, our two homes on the Ouachita River were guided by the Scripture, and that foundation has now grown to seven homes, with many more on the horizon as the Robertson family continues to grow. This book is really dedicated to Granny and Pa and the legacy they continue to grow in us concerning our love for the Bible.

We are all very excited about sharing some of our favorite passages and why they are special to us. You'll find that some of the chosen passages are repeated by other family members—that's because some of the same passages have significantly impacted different people in our family. If you have watched our television show, you know how much we like to talk and expound on things, and this devotional book is no different. You will find some lengthy passages that don't need a lot said about them because there isn't much to add to the power that God has instilled. You'll also find other passages that spark a memory from our past, a challenge for our present, or a hope for our future. It is our prayer that those sentiments will bless your day and your spiritual walk.

We encourage you to read through the passage, message, and prayer more than once during the day and allow God's Word to bless you and guide you in your daily walk with Him. We also challenge you to change whatever needs to be changed in your life to act in line with the truth of God's Word. God says that his Word is active and sharp and was written to impact, shape, and transform lives and lifestyles.

If ever there was a time in our world that we needed to be guided by the principles of the Bible, it is now. So many people in the world are struggling for answers to their life issues, and the best guide and most absolute truth available is still the Holy Bible. We invite you to spend a year with our family. As we walk through passages from God's holy words of truth and light, you will be blessed by the journey.

January

JANUARY 1

AN OBEDIENT WALK

Blessed are all who fear the LORD, who walk in obedience to him. You will eat the fruit of your labor; blessings and prosperity will be yours. Your wife will be like a fruitful vine within your house; your children will be like olive shoots around your table. Yes, this will be the blessing for the man who fears the LORD.

—PSALM 128:1–4

I DON'T KNOW OF a better description of what has happened to the Robertson family than this passage. Dad made the decision to make Christ his Lord in 1975, and that decision changed not only his eternal destiny but his earthly one, as well. The sober-minded decision to start a new company called Duck Commander led to a brand that would be respected and recognized by duck hunters all over the world. A video series led to a show on Outdoor Channel, which led to a juggernaut named *Duck Dynasty*. The whole phenomenon began with the fear of the Lord and an obedient walk, and it continues today with the blessings of a committed family around the dinner table.

Prayer

Father, we thank You for the ability to see a clearer path and the courage to seize it, by Your grace. Thank You for the blessings of our family and the mission set before us. In Christ we humbly pray, amen.

—Al

UNASHAMED

I am not ashamed of the gospel, because it is the power of God for the salvation of everyone who believes: first for the Jew, then for the Gentile.

—ROMANS 1:16

BEING ASHAMED IS feeling humiliated or embarrassed because we feel inadequate or inferior. It's feeling reluctant because we *fear* shame before anything even happens to us. To counter this feeling of being ashamed, we must remember at all times that we are *saved, rescued, redeemed, justified,* and *sanctified* by the Spirit of the living God. Over and over, Jesus said, "Do not be afraid." Read 2 Timothy 1:7 right now and read Romans 1:16 (above) again. Get the picture? The Hebrew writer said that Jesus is not ashamed to call us brothers. Therefore, we should not be ashamed of Him and the gospel about Him!

Prayer

Thanks, Father, for Your Spirit that empowers us. Help us through Your Spirit to love people more than we fear them. Amen.

—*Phil*

January 3

The Best Argument

But Christ has indeed been raised from the dead, the firstfruits of those who have fallen asleep.

—1 CORINTHIANS 15:20

MY FAMILY IS notorious for arguments. It is how we communicate, and it is not surprising to see someone stating your stance as their own days after they had the opposing view. I would suppose that's when you realize you won the argument. I believe one of the strongest arguments for Christ's resurrection is the fact that Christ's closest followers died in martyrdom because of their witness of a risen Lord (1 Corinthians 15:5–6). History books document that these men would rather die than deny the resurrection. It begs the question, "Who would die for a lie, knowing it was a lie, when the issue was life after death?"

Prayer

Lord, give me the confidence not only to share the death, burial, and resurrection of Jesus but to live and die in view of the risen Savior. Jesus is Lord.

—*Jase*

January 4

More Than We Imagine

Now unto him that is able to do exceeding abundantly above all that we ask or think, according to the power that worketh in us, unto him be glory in the church by Christ Jesus throughout all ages, world without end.

—EPHESIANS 3:20–21, KJV

I HAVE A FRIEND who is a missionary in the mountains of Mexico. He's in his eighties, and he sleeps in his car. One night, he was preaching in a remote village, and when the invitation was given, a lot of people came forward—including a man who was weeping and wanting salvation. He had left his family ten years earlier and was seeking reconciliation with them, so he asked Jesus to change him so he could be a good husband and father. After the man told the preacher all of this, a woman and a young boy stood up—his wife and child. Ever since she had accepted Christ five years earlier, the man's wife had been praying for her husband. Jesus not only saved him but had his wife and son waiting on him too. God did more than this man could have ever imagined.

Prayer

Jesus, I thank You for being able and willing to bless us. Help us to be appreciative of all You do to make our lives abundant; help us to count our blessings and give You the glory you deserve. In Christ we pray, amen.

—*Willie*

JANUARY 5

LIKE A ROARING LION

Be alert and of sober mind. Your enemy the devil prowls around like a roaring lion looking for someone to devour.

—1 PETER 5:8

WHEN I WAS in Vietnam, I stayed for about six months in a hotel and I would share a room for a couple of weeks at a time with guys who were coming back from the jungle on their way home. These guys were decompressing before they went home, but they sure had some wild tales to tell me. One guy said a tiger ate the arm off of one of his buddies after a firefight! It scared me enough that I was glad I wasn't out there in the jungle! Our enemy the devil is described like that in the verse above, and he scares me too! God is stronger, but I don't want to give that old devil any room to have at ole Si.

Prayer

Heavenly Father, I am glad You are stronger than the devil, and I ask that You watch out for me and my family. Help me to stay alert and keep watch. Through Jesus I pray, amen.

—Si

JANUARY 6

A Legacy of Wisdom

My son, if you accept my words and store up my commands within you, turning your ear to wisdom and applying your heart to understanding—indeed, if you call out for insight and cry aloud for understanding, and if you look for it as for silver and search for it as for hidden treasure, then you will understand the fear of the Lord and find the knowledge of God.

—PROVERBS 2:1–5

THE VERSE REMINDS me so much of my dad. I know I'm probably a little biased, but I think he is probably one of the wisest men on planet Earth. I was blessed to come into our family *after* Dad turned his life over to God. I got to see him at his best. Mom and Dad modeled a great marriage to me, and Dad taught me what it meant to be a godly man. Now that I have children of my own, I try to be wise and pass along wisdom to them. Like the scripture above says, we really do have to *seek* after wisdom and put our mind to living wisely. I know I have a long way to go, but I've been taught by the best, and I thank God for that teaching.

Prayer

Dear Lord, I pray for insight and cry aloud for understanding. Help me seek out wisdom in every decision I make. I want to seek out wisdom so that I can understand Your love and knowledge.

—Jep

January 7

The Gift of Cooking

Offer hospitality to one another without grumbling. Each of you should use whatever gift you have received to serve others, as faithful stewards of God's grace in its various forms.

—1 PETER 4:9–10

I HAVE ALWAYS ENJOYED cooking and learned a lot about it from my grandmother Nannie and from Phil's mother, Granny. When my boys were at home I always saw cooking as a gift that I could use to help share the gospel and also to provide a great atmosphere for my sons' friends, so they'd want to come into our home. Food continues to draw our family together, and I never want to lose the gift God has given me to open up our home and feed people delicious food.

Prayer

Father, I am so grateful for my gift of cooking and enjoying people in my home. I thank You for Phil's abilities, as well, and pray we never grow tired of having people in and feeding them. I pray that more people will learn this great art and use it to help people and expand Your kingdom. I pray all of this in Jesus' name, amen.

—Miss Kay

January 8

The Simple Way Out

So he went down and dipped himself in the Jordan seven times, as the man of God had told him, and his flesh was restored and became clean like that of a young boy.

—2 KINGS 5:14

WHEN TIMES GET difficult, we often ask God for the easy way out. Easy means that someone waves a wand and *poof,* it's done, fixed, no more trouble. While God doesn't always give us an *easy* way out, He does often give us a *simple* way out. But simple involves action on our part. In the scripture above, God told Naaman to dip himself in the Jordan seven times. Going to the river and dipping himself seven times was not something difficult, but Naaman wanted the easy way out. He didn't want to exert any effort at all. But God required more of him, and most of the time He requires something of us as well. Not because He can't perform the miracle, but because He knows exerting effort is what we *need.* So next time troubles comes your way, remember to look for the simple solution that God has for you. It may not be easy, but it very well could be simple.

Prayer

Dear Lord, please help me to rest assured that You are going before me and that when I call on You, You *will* help me. Thank You for growing me during these hard times.

—*Korie*

MAKING MUSIC

It is good to praise the Lord and make music to your name, O Most High.

—PSALM 92:1

I LOVE TO SING and make music. I love to sit at the piano and pound out new harmonies. And now that my kids are older, fewer things give me more enjoyment than having my teenage boys sit with me and sing. Often they'll play the guitar, the ukulele, or the piano, and we see what we can come up with. It's such a good feeling when we get all of the music to come together. And it's an even better feeling when we sing about our Savior and praise Him for what He's done for us. I'm sure it gives our Father in heaven even more enjoyment than it gives us. This is a good thing!

Prayer

Lord, thank You for Your gift of music. Thank You for the simple pleasure of melody and harmony. Thank You for the talents You have given my family and the enjoyment they bring to us. We praise You for Your mighty works and pray that we will always be able to sing to You and praise You through music.

—*Missy*

JANUARY 10

DO UNTO OTHERS . . .

In everything, do to others what you would have them do to you, for this sums up the Law and the Prophets.

—MATTHEW 7:12

AS A YOUNG girl I would hear my mother quote the above scripture to my sister and me. At the time, I remember thinking, *That's easier said than done!* But her words have always stuck with me. As I watched my mother being kind to others no matter how she was treated, her actions spoke even louder than words. I watched and learned from her example. She showed kindness even when kindness wasn't necessarily due. I always want to show the love of Christ to others, no matter how I'm treated.

Prayer

Lord, I ask that no matter how I'm treated, You help me always show love and kindness to everyone. I want my reaction to others, without hesitation, to be the right response.

—*Jessica*

January 11

Pleasing Him

May these words of my mouth and this meditation of my heart be pleasing in your sight, Lord, my Rock and my Redeemer.

—PSALM 19:14

I DON'T THINK MUCH about the words that come out of my mouth on a second-by-second or minute-by-minute basis, but if I read this scripture correctly, I should. Each and every word I say should be pleasing to God! Every thought or meditation in my heart should be pleasing to God! Oh, wow! Do I have a lot of work to do! I am better at this than I was in my younger days, but I need to be much better than I am now. To hold each thought and each word captive—that is my goal.

Prayer

Father, You know how we struggle. Just because we don't always say what we're thinking doesn't mean You aren't reading it in our hearts. Please, Lord, help me to think before I speak and pray before I think! I want You to be pleased with my thoughts and my words. Clean my heart, and put Your words there to dwell. In Jesus' name, amen.

—*Lisa*

WHY NOT ME?

Blessed is the one who perseveres under trial because, having stood the test, that person will receive the crown of life that the Lord has promised to those who love him.

—JAMES 1:12

MY WIFE, PAULA, and I were new Christians, and life was going well. She worked in the emergency room at the local hospital, and one day the unthinkable happened: she was stuck with a needle from a patient with the HIV virus. We were doing all the right things, and then this happened! I have to admit, "Why us?" did come to mind, especially because we thought we were finally living right. But Paula had an amazing reply: "Why not me . . . better me than someone who hasn't heard of Jesus." *Wow!* Woman, get off my toes. I was challenged that day to grow my faith up to that level. It's our unwavering faith that helps us persevere!

Prayer

Father, protect us from the evil one. Help us to be faithful and aware of Your presence at all times. Help us realize our shortcomings and help us to get back up when we fall. Help us to not take You for granted or the freedom we have in You. I thank You for my wife and her faith. In Your precious name, amen.

—*Godwin*

January 13

Doing Your Part

For to me, to live is Christ and to die is gain.

—PHILIPPIANS 1:21

THIS CONCEPT IS one of the coolest things about being a Christian. If we are still living on planet Earth, we get the opportunity to spread the Gospel of Jesus Christ, and when we die we get to spend eternity with Him! Talk about a no-lose situation! We are all put on this Earth for a reason. Your role may be as a planter of the seed of God's Word, or a seed waterer, or a seed picker. You can be any one of these, but most likely, you have been all three at some point. You may never know what a person needs to hear, so you might as well be prepared to do all three with equal enthusiasm as long as you're here on Earth. Then on that great day, you will hear the words we all long to hear: "Well done, my good and faithful servant!"

Prayer

God, we know that You sent Your Son here so that we may be saved and live eternally with You. Help us to know that while we are here we must continue to spread Your message until we are called home.

—*Martin*

January 14

The Full Life

The thief comes only to steal and kill and destroy; I have come that they may have life, and have it to the full.

—JOHN 10:10

SOMETIMES, AS TEENS, we might think that God is a rule-making God. But God is not about making rules, and being a Christian isn't about all the things we shouldn't do. Living for Jesus is about living free and understanding that you are here for a reason. The above verse tells us that Jesus came so we can live a full life. Full like a swimming pool when the water hose has been left on—full and running over. He wants us to experience it all! Following the thief, or Satan, will only lead to destruction, so why would we make that choice? The Christian life isn't boring. Let God use you. Do great things. Go live life to the fullest.

Prayer

Father, please use me as You want. I want a full life, even if I don't know where that will take me. I trust that You know what is best for me. Use me. In Jesus' name I pray, amen.

—John Luke

JANUARY 15

A Fire in My Heart

But if I say, "I will not mention his word or speak anymore in his name," his word is in my heart like a fire, a fire shut up in my bones. I am weary of holding it in; indeed, I cannot.

—JEREMIAH 20:9

WHEN MY BROTHER Jase and I went to seminary way back in 1988, this verse from the prophet Jeremiah became the motto for our entire class. We wanted to be men and women who never shrank back from an opportunity to be God's spokesperson when there was something that He wanted said. Jeremiah is called the weeping prophet because not many people ever wanted to hear what he had to say, and God kept giving him some tough sermons to preach. God always has something He wants done on this earth, and His people are the ones to do it. And they will be able to do it, if they keep that fire in their hearts burning bright. Don't hold back God's message today!

Prayer

Father, give us the courage to hold up when things don't go well and the people around us don't seem interested in what You have to say through us. Please keep our fire lit and our hearts burdened to be Your man or woman this very day. We humbly ask this through Christ, amen.

—Al

January 16

Only One Way Out!

Jesus answered, "I am the way and the truth and the life. No one comes to the Father except through me."

—JOHN 14:6

I'VE HEARD TOO many people say, "I'll take my chances without this Jesus. I'm not convinced He has anything that I need." Really? Now, think about this for a minute. In the end, we all end up six feet deep in the ground. We're buried under all that dirt, and we have no way to get out on our own. The only thing we have to look forward to is worms and decay. But there is a way out—in fact, there's only *one* way out. The only way out of that grave is Jesus! The truth is that Jesus offers us victory over the grave. It's up to you whether you take Him up on His offer. Jesus is our *life*. Without Him there is only death—forever! The choice is yours. What's it gonna be, friend?

Prayer

Father, we thank You for Jesus. He is our way, our truth, our life! We acknowledge that Jesus is our only chance to survive this existence. We understand that we have no hope beyond that cold grave without belief in Jesus' resurrection. It is because of Him and by His name that I pray to you. Amen.

—*Phil*

JANUARY 17

WE ARE THE REEL

We are therefore Christ's ambassadors, as though God were making his appeal through us.

—2 CORINTHIANS 5:20

AS A KID I was part of the bass-fishing craze. Everyone seemed to have a giant ski boat with a huge outboard motor. We were "river rats," and our boat was built for practicality and longevity. We still use it today. I remember asking my dad if we were going to upgrade. He explained to me the difference between "fishers" and "catchers." Despite my dad's beliefs and his idea of *making* trends instead of *following* them, I saved my money and bought myself a fancy Ambassador reel. I quickly realized that it's not about the name brand of the tackle or how it looks; it's about who is controlling it. We are all flawed, and some of us look a little rough around the edges, but God uses us anyway. The key is to realize we are the reel, Jesus is the lure, and God is in control.

Prayer

Lord, use me despite my flaws and weaknesses. Give me wisdom and insight to recognize the opportunities You give me to make You known.

—*Jase*

January 18

Clearing Our Hearts

Sow to yourselves in righteousness, reap in mercy; break up your fallow ground: for it is time to seek the Lord, *till he come and rain righteousness upon you.*

—HOSEA 10:12, KJV

When I was a kid, a neighbor cleared land for a new hayfield. They cut the timber and cleared the stumps with a dozer, then burned all the stumps and brush. Then we walked the ground and picked up chunks of wood before it could be plowed and planted. It took a lot of work before the field was suitable for planting. But the work didn't stop after that—it had to be kept up. A neglected field reverts back to brush and weeds. God is saying our hearts are like that field; they take a lot of clearing and burning of useless things before they are productive for His use. The good news is that when we are saved, God clears and plants His Spirit in us so we can be productive for Him. But without constant care and attention, the weeds and brush creep back into our lives. This Christian walk of ours is not a one-time decision—it is a lifelong commitment.

Prayer

Lord, help us submit to Your ways of righteousness and mercy, let Your Holy Spirit plow our hearts with conviction so we can be a fertile field for You. In Jesus' name, amen.

—*Willie*

JANUARY 19

We Will Be Content

But godliness with contentment is great gain. For we brought nothing into the world, and we can take nothing out of it. But if we have food and clothing, we will be content with that.

—1 TIMOTHY 6:6–8

WE GREW UP poor, okay, with not much more than the clothes on our backs as possessions. I didn't even wear clothes until it was time to go to school, and I still fought Mama over having to wear them then, so I had even less than everybody else! But no one ever told us we were poor, so we thought that everybody lived like we did. Some would say that it was ignorance, but I think it was contentment with what we had. We lived off the land and we did okay. I don't want any success to ever change my contentment.

Prayer

Heavenly Father, I pray for contentment and satisfaction in what You have blessed me with. I am grateful for my humble beginnings, and I don't want to ever be greedy. In Jesus' name, I pray, amen.

—*Si*

JANUARY 20

R-E-S-P-E-C-T

Show proper respect to everyone, love the family of believers, fear God, honor the emperor.

—1 PETER 2:17

WITH THE NEW footprint of Duck Commander, we are now engaging countless people in countless situations. Because of my selfish nature and foolish pride, there are times that I use my knowledge—rather than God's wisdom—and selfish desires to drive my decisions. During these times, I sometimes forget that there are more important factors than me. Reading the above scripture makes me remember to show respect to everyone and reminds me that I am in these situations because of a purpose—God's purpose. This is a simple little verse that carries a huge meaning, which God obviously intended us to live by.

Prayer

Father, I thank You for loving me, thank You for guiding me, and thank You for Your promises. Fill me with Your love, and let me show it to everyone I encounter, so that I am a living example of You. Fill me with respect; let my decisions always honor You. In Your Son Jesus' name I pray, amen.

—*Jon Gimber*

JANUARY 21

New Beginnings

Create in me a pure heart, O God, and renew a steadfast spirit within me. Do not cast me from your presence or take your Holy Spirit from me. Restore to me the joy of your salvation and grant me a willing spirit, to sustain me.

—PSALM 51:10–12

HAVE YOU EVER done something so bad that you thought it was just too much to be forgiven? David wrote the above words after a scandalous affair, the murder of a friend, and the loss of a child. He had a few issues! David felt desperate and without hope, thinking he was too far gone for God's love. But then he remembered the kind of God he served, and hope sprang up in his heart as he realized that God has the power to renew, restore, and rebuild the human heart. You, too, may sometimes feel that you are beyond God's reach—but the truth is that He is always ready to redeem. You, too, can once again find joy, even after devastating sin and consequence.

Prayer

Father, please restore our joy today and create purity in our lives. We humbly ask that Your Holy Spirit bear fruit through us today as we walk in this world. Thank You for Jesus and His ability to turn our messes into His message. It is through Him that we pray today, amen.

—*Al*

January 22

Pass It On!

Likewise, teach the older women to be reverent in the way they live, not to be slanderers or addicted to much wine, but to teach what is good. Then they can urge the younger women to love their husbands and children, to be self-controlled and pure, to be busy at home, to be kind, and to be subject to their husbands.

—TITUS 2:3–5

THESE VERSES ALWAYS remind me of my grandmother Nannie. I have tried to be like her for most of my life, and her voice is the one that gave me strength through the hardest times of my early life with Phil. She had taught me to fight for my man and my marriage, and that is exactly what I did. Her wisdom proved to be right, and now I try to share that wisdom with the younger generation. I teach multiple groups for young women and absolutely love it! Passing on what we know to those coming after us is not only commanded by God but is a true joy.

Prayer

Father, I am so grateful for my grandmother and the lessons she taught me. Please help me to be like her and teach younger women to hang tough when things get rough in a marriage. Thank You so much for Phil changing his life and for my boys and their families. I owe You everything. I pray this through Jesus, amen.

—Miss Kay

January 23

Peace of Mind and Heart

Do not be anxious about anything, but in every situation, by prayer and petition, with thanksgiving, present your requests to God. And the peace of God, which transcends all understanding, will guard your hearts and your minds in Christ Jesus.

—PHILIPPIANS 4:6–7

ANXIETY CAN BE a real struggle for me. One thing I've learned about anxiety is that I can't get rid of it on my own. But I can beat it with prayer and thanksgiving. It's amazing what simply talking to the Father can do—especially if we sprinkle in plenty of praise and thanks. I love what this verse says about the peace of God guarding our hearts. On my own, I don't always have an easy time keeping my heart in the right place, but when I ask God to "guard" my heart and my mind, I can feel confident and at ease, knowing that He's got my back. Next time anxiety tries to creep in your life, rejoice that you are a son or daughter of God Almighty and invite Him to guard your heart and mind.

Prayer

God Almighty, I pray that I will rejoice in You every day of my life. Please place a guard around my heart and mind so that it feels and thinks what You want me to feel and think. I pray this with peace and thanksgiving in my heart. Amen.

—*Jep*

January 24

Loving Difficult People

Dear friends, since God so loved us, we also ought to love one another. No one has seen God; but if we love one another, God lives in us, and His love is made complete in us. This is how we know that we live in him and he in us: He has given us of his Spirit. And we have seen and testify that the Father has sent his Son to be the Savior of the world.

—1 JOHN 4:11–14

LET'S FACE IT, people are sometimes hard to love. We have a big family, and we all work together and play together. This means we have many opportunities to grow in all the fruits of the spirit, because it can be difficult to always be kind, loving, and forgiving with those you are with daily. But with the help of the Holy Spirit, God's spirit, we can all do it. This is also true of loving our coworkers, our fellow church members, and our neighbors. The next time you are having a hard time loving someone, remember to call on the Holy Spirit—who lives in you—for help. You can love that person who aggravates you with God's help.

Prayer

God, first, help me to be lovable. And I also need the help of Your Spirit to love those around me. Guide my words and actions so that I don't hurt others but instead love them like You do. Amen.

—*Korie*

January 25

Let's Go to Work!

When the perishable has been clothed with the imperishable, and the mortal with immortality, then the saying that is written will come true: "Death has been swallowed up in victory." "Where, O death, is your victory? Where, O death, is your sting?" The sting of death is sin, and the power of sin is the law. But thanks be to God! He gives us the victory through our Lord Jesus Christ. Therefore, my dear brothers and sisters, stand firm. Let nothing move you. Always give yourselves fully to the work of the Lord, because you know that your labor in the Lord is not in vain.

—1 CORINTHIANS 15:54–58

WHAT A MOTIVATION to work for the Lord! We do not work to be saved. We work for the Lord because *we are saved.* Jesus has already done all the work for us—He did it on the cross. Then He proved He had the power to do it when He arose from the dead. No more sin for us—no more death! The victory is ours through our Lord Jesus! Let's go to work—*for others.* Remember this!

Prayer

Thank You, God, for the victory we have over sin and death. We know that this victory is not because of our works, but because of what Jesus did, is now doing, and will do in the end! Amen.

—*Phil*

FORGIVENESS GOES BOTH WAYS

Blessed is the one whose transgressions are forgiven, whose sins are covered. Blessed is the one whose sin the LORD does not count against them and in whose spirit is no deceit. . . . I acknowledged my sin to you and did not cover up my iniquity. I said, "I will confess my transgressions to the LORD." And you forgave the guilt of my sin.

—PSALM 32:1–2, 5

THESE VERSES ARE some of the most comforting that I've ever read in God's Word. Just like everyone else, I've made my share of mistakes—and have downright sinned. Although my life and my level of sin have changed drastically with age and wisdom, I still need to be reminded that when I do sin against my Lord, my sins are forgiven. My sins are not held against me. And as I remember that God quickly and lovingly forgives me, I also need to remember to extend that same love and forgiveness to others—even those who sin against me personally. I'm so thankful to know that the shame and the guilt of my sin are gone when I confess it to the Lord. What a blessing!

Prayer

Father, I thank You for Your forgiveness and the continual cleansing of my transgressions. Please, Father, remind me daily of the blessing You gave us when You sent Your Son to redeem us. Help us to offer this forgiveness to others as You have forgiven us. In His name, amen.

—*Lisa*

January 27

Speaking the Truth in Love

For lack of guidance a nation falls, but victory is won through many advisers.

—PROVERBS 11:14

OUR NATION IS in real need of good leadership, good information, and good decisions. But with good information comes the responsibility to be discerning and wise in how we communicate that information and how we translate it into good decision making and leadership. A wellspring of good information is readily available to us all in the timeless words of Almighty God. Another good source of good information is the well-studied, grace-loving people of God. As we seek to make our voices heard by the leadership of our great nation, it is important to speak the truth of God in love—ever mindful that our goal is to bring about good and that to do that, our delivery must be kind and thoughtful. Stay engaged as God's voice, but not enraged. To be heard, you must be worth listening to!

Prayer

Please give discernment to our leaders and bless them with wisdom and with ears that will hear what You have to say. We trust in You, as our ultimate leader, and we know that Your ways are always right and good. We pray this prayer in Jesus' name, amen.

—*Al*

JANUARY 28

BE AN INSPIRATION IN YOUR YOUTH

Don't let anyone look down on you because you are young, but set an example for the believers in speech, in conduct, in love, in faith and in purity.

—1 TIMOTHY 4:12

THE LORD TELLS us that it doesn't matter how old or young you are; what matters is that your life and actions be an example to all other believers. If you're a new Christian, you have a lot to learn from others who have been in their faith for a long time. However, they also can learn from and be inspired by your growing strength and faith. Even if you're not new to Christianity, remember that everyone's faith can teach you something. Try to see young faith as a way to rekindle the newness and feelings of excitement you had when you first met Christ. As the scripture above says, "Don't let anyone look down on you because you are young." This means that our life and example must exemplify the goodness of God.

Prayer

Dear Lord, please help me to learn from the faith of others. I know that there is always room to grow in my faith, no matter my age. Please help me to recognize all the opportunities You present to me on a daily basis. Thank You, Jesus, amen.

—Alex Robertson Mancuso

January 29

Loving God's Enemies

But God demonstrates his own love for us in this: While we were still sinners, Christ died for us.

—ROMANS 5:8

As we watch the current events in the news, we see all kinds of chaos and violence. We see not only the threats of other nations but also individuals engaging in violence against each other. Sadly, there is a lot of hate in the name of religion. But in the above verse, we see God's love and grace for the people He created. The amazing truth is that while we were His enemies, He *died* for us. If Jesus did this for us while we were His enemies, aren't we obligated to treat His enemies with the same love and compassion? But instead, in taking our political stances—correct though they may be—we slander and strike out against the enemies of God's truth. This is not God's way of dealing with His opposition. We serve God well when we follow His example.

Prayer

Father, thank You for the great love You have for us and the great sacrifice You made for us. Help us to be mindful of that when we are dealing with others. Help me to love as You love—unconditionally and purposefully. We pray this in Jesus' name, amen.

—*Willie*

When the Storms Come

"Therefore everyone who hears these words of mine and puts them into practice is like a wise man who built his house on the rock. The rain came down, the streams rose, and the winds blew and beat against that house; yet it did not fall, because it had its foundation on the rock. But everyone who hears these words of mine and does not put them into practice is like a foolish man who built his house on sand. The rain came down, the streams rose, and the winds blew and beat against that house, and it fell with a great crash."

—MATTHEW 7:24–27

I AM NOT A fan of storms. They make me feel unsettled and unsure—definitely unsafe. I think all of us want to feel safe and secure. But, unfortunately, storms come, lives are changed, and things get broken that can't be fixed. It is the way with this world. But thanks be to God, we can always know that He is faithful and true. He is the foundation that will keep you through the storm—the only foundation that is fail-safe. No matter what the storm brings, we can be sure that our mighty God is right there with us and will bring us through whatever we face.

Prayer

Beloved Father, I hate storms! They hurt, and I get so scared. Open my eyes to Your comfort and shelter. I ask You to make your presence and comfort a reality in my life.

—Lynda Hammitt

January 31

Our Powerful Predator

Free yourself, like a gazelle from the hand of the hunter, like a bird from the snare of the fowler.

—PROVERBS 6:5

When I go into the woods or the duck blind, I have one thing on my mind: "How do we get 'em today?" To be a successful hunter, you have to think, see, and hear like your prey. We do our best to outwit the animals, but sometimes they elude us. I wonder if they are as excited about escape as we are about taking them.

But the thing of it is, *we* are being hunted by a powerful predator every day of our lives. The devil is out there hunting for our souls and hearts. A good thing for us is that we've learned lessons in nature that can assist us in being elusive. To escape a snare, you have to trust your spiritual instincts, you have to be ready to move quickly, and you have to stay out of the captor's range.

Prayer

Help us escape the snares of the devil and trust in Your ways of providing escape and awareness. Forgive us when we willingly fall into traps set by the devil. When we're caught, we end up crying out for Your help. We praise You for always hearing our cries and delivering us—even when we don't deserve it. All glory to You through Jesus, amen.

—*Jase*

February

FEBRUARY 1

YOU ARE DEFINED BY YOUR FATHER

If anyone is in Christ, the new creation has come: The old has gone, the new is here!

—2 CORINTHIANS 5:17

ANYONE WHO WAS around me the first twenty-eight years of my life quickly knew that I was no son of God. They could tell by my speech, my attitude, and my actions. I could not hide my evil ways, nor did I try to. I did what I pleased, when I pleased, and my whole world revolved around me and my selfish whims. Now that I am a new creation, anyone who is around me knows it immediately. I make it a point to make sure they know—by my speech, my attitudes, and my actions. You, too, are known to those around you by what they see in you. You have a choice to make—will you be a son of God or a son of the devil? There are no other options. Your life is yours to live, and your choices are yours to make. My advice is that you choose to honor God with your life.

Prayer

Father, thank You for creating the "new me"! I was dead—now I'm alive. I was lost, now I'm found—all by Your hand. Thank you. Amen.

—*Phil*

FAMILY MAKES IT A HOME

For every house is built by someone, but God is the builder of everything.

—HEBREWS 3:4

MY FAMILY MOVED to the banks of the Ouachita River when I was eight years old, just prior to my third-grade school year. We had driven as a family to our potential new home to check it out, and I remember coming over the hill and seeing a spectacular view of the river on our left. That's when my dad decidedly stated, "We'll take it!" We had not even seen the house, and my mom thought Dad had ruined any chance of our getting the best deal possible. We bought the place, and I really believe the only requirement needing to be met for my dad was that the house be upright. The house is just a building. The people that dwell there make it a home. The place we resided gave us not only a great backdrop of God's creation but the perfect place to enjoy life together as a family.

Prayer

God, I thank You for being our Father and being the architect of family. Help us to build relationships with our families based on each other instead of where we are located.

—*Jase*

FEBRUARY 3

PASSING THROUGH THE STORM

A furious squall came up, and the waves broke over the boat, so that it was nearly swamped. Jesus was in the stern, sleeping on a cushion. The disciples woke him and said to him, "Teacher, don't you care if we drown?" He got up, rebuked the wind and said to the waves, "Quiet! Be still!" Then the wind died down and it was completely calm.

—MARK 4:37–39

LIKE IN THIS passage, storms often arise quickly in our lives—seemingly coming out of nowhere. The trials in life are often sent to test us in a way that results in new confidence and strength. The commands of our Lord are always accompanied with empowerment. Jesus didn't promise that the trip would be easy. He just wants us to hold our heads up and keep on keeping on—no matter what. As we put our trust in Him, we will find that even the worst storms will bring us new wisdom and, ultimately, unflinching hope—*if* we cooperate with Him and trust that He is working in us. Even through the storm, we can be assured that Jesus is right there beside us, offering His hand of comfort and always a way out.

Prayer

Help me to remember that all storms in my life must pass through Your hands first and that You are a faithful and loving God.

—*Willie*

Faith to Meet the Challenge

Then the Lord said to Satan, "Have you considered my servant Job? There is no one on earth like him; he is blameless and upright, a man who fears God and shuns evil."

—JOB 1:8

HAVE YOU EVER been sitting in an audience and some performer starts pulling people onstage for whatever reason? Am I the only one who wishes I could turn invisible at that moment? God called out Job and brought him to Satan's attention and offered him as a testing ground—because he trusted his heart and his strength. Job ended up facing a lot of trials and tribulations, but through it all, he never lost his integrity. When trials come into your life, remember that God is in control. Perhaps—just perhaps—He has allowed this trial because He trusts your faith and knows your strength. And though the trial may hurt like the dickens and weaken you with its intensity, always know that God will provide a way out and that He's with you every step of the way.

Prayer

Father, we pray for strength and peace as we face the difficulties of this life. When we are called out, please bless us with what we need to be Your man or woman. In Jesus, we ask this prayer, amen.

—Al

February 5

Rest Assured

For it is by grace you have been saved, through faith—and this not from yourselves, it is the gift of God—not by works, so that no one can boast. For we are God's handiwork, created in Christ Jesus to do good works, which God prepared in advance for us to do.

—EPHESIANS 2:8–10

KNOWING THAT SALVATION can't be earned, but it is a gift through my faith in Jesus, shows me how much God loves me. When I make a bad decision, I know that God's grace is sufficient. Knowing this humbles me because I know that even though I've blown it, God still loves me. And it makes me confident because I know that Jesus willingly died on the cross, and that His death is more than sufficient to pay for my sin. It's interesting that the apostle Paul (who wrote the words above) follows his assurance of God's grace with a reminder that we are created to do good works. God's grace is free, but He does require something from us—a life of service and outreach. Can we meet the challenge? I think we can—by God's grace.

Prayer

Dear Lord, I thank You so much for Your precious grace that saved us through faith. We know we don't deserve it but are so accepting of this gift. Help us to do good works in Your precious name. Amen!

—Jep

FEBRUARY 6

THE DNA OF TRUE LIFE

If we claim to have fellowship with him and yet walk in the darkness, we lie and do not live out the truth. But if we walk in the light, as he is in the light, we have fellowship with one another, and the blood of Jesus, his Son, purifies us from all sin.

—1 JOHN 1:6–7

ONE DAY I had to give blood to check and see if I had a hereditary illness. After the doctor reviewed the test results, he actually showed me my DNA. There were two strands: my mother's and my father's. After checking them all, he said I was clear of the disease. Of course I was relieved, but I told that doc that he was one strand shy. "That's crazy!" he said. "You don't know what you're talking about." But I said, "You are the crazy one, Jack! There's one more strand in there, and it's the most important one of all!" I told him the strand he was missing was the blood of Jesus Christ, because that was part of my DNA, as well. I don't know if I convinced him or not, but it's the truth!

Prayer

Heavenly Father, we are grateful for the blood of Your Son that gives us life. We walk in the light, and we love each other because it's in our blood. Thank You for dying for us and saving us. Amen.

—*Si*

FEBRUARY 7

A FATHER'S LEGACY

My son, do not forget my teaching, but keep my commands in your heart, for they will prolong your life many years and bring you peace and prosperity.

—PROVERBS 3:1–2

AFTER PHIL FOUND the Lord, he was all about teaching our sons what they needed to know as they grew to manhood. He taught them about hunting, nature, being a man, and most important, about being a Christian. Like most children, our boys grew to appreciate his wisdom as they got older and wiser themselves. And like most children, many of their lessons were learned by ignoring dear old dad and beating their heads against the wall of their own stubbornness—some of the boys were more stubborn than others. Now, as adults and spiritual peers, they are passing on what they learned to my grandchildren and great-grandchildren. They are following this scripture's teaching—and now they are paying that teaching forward.

Prayer

Father, I thank you with all my heart that You helped Phil to find You. His life change has affected not only our boys but generations to come. Heavenly Father, thank You for putting Your commands in their hearts. I pray that we all continue to listen and learn until we leave this world. I pray all these things through Christ, amen.

—*Miss Kay*

FEBRUARY 8

THE POWER OF SALTINESS

"You are the salt of the earth. But what good is salt if it has lost its flavor? Can you make it salty again? It will be thrown out and trampled underfoot as worthless."

—MATTHEW 5:13, NLT

DID YOU KNOW that just by being a Christian, you are going to irritate some folks? Not that you'll do it on purpose, but unbelievers don't understand why Christians act as they do. But the good news is that salt has many great qualities. Just as salt can irritate, it can also preserve, heal, and spice up life. Salt seasons, it gives flavor—zest. As you love Jesus and follow Him, the flavor of Jesus will come out in you, if you let it. Hurting people will seek you out, and you will—with God's help—show them the path to healing. Another trait of salt is that it makes you thirsty. Does the way you live make others thirsty for Jesus (John 4)? As you keep your eyes on Jesus and focus on living for Him, people will be drawn to the water—the living water.

Prayer

Dear Jesus, help me to be the salt of the world. Help me to get out of the shaker and change the world around me for You. Help me not to lose my flavor, but instead to draw others to the living water that is You. Amen.

—*Korie*

February 9

Shine Like Stars

Do everything without grumbling or arguing, so that you may become blameless and pure, "children of God without fault in a warped and crooked generation." Then you will shine among them like stars in the sky.

—PHILIPPIANS 2:14–15

Wow, if I could accomplish just this one thing every day, I could be a huge influence on my family and my friends. Why is it that sometimes our first response is to complain when something doesn't satisfy our immediate want or need? We all know that positive person, that one who shines when he or she walks into a room, the one who can find the good in every single person or circumstance and never says a negative word. I want to be that person. God wants me to be that person, that shining person. I want to shine like a star in the sky—how fun would that be!

Prayer

Lord, You see the good in every person. You see the good in me and know the outcome of each and every circumstance long before I am confronted with it. Help me to be slow to react so that I can make wise decisions—decisions that will have a positive influence on the people closest to me. Thank You for the example of Your Son and His ultimate sacrifice for me.

—Missy

FEBRUARY 10

TRUSTING GOD'S ANSWER

Trust in the Lord with all thine heart; and lean not unto thine own understanding. In all thy ways acknowledge him, and he shall direct thy paths.

—PROVERBS 3:5, KJV

MANY TIMES I'VE asked for guidance from God, only to think that He wasn't giving me an answer. Looking back now, I can see that He always answered—just not always in the way I wanted. I remember telling Him that I trusted Him with all my heart, but I discovered that I really only trusted Him if the answer was what I wanted it to be. I lived for the now; God saw my life as a whole—how the situation or choice would impact me and/or others in the future. Whether it would hinder people from coming to know the Lord or help people to do so. I am newly committed to acknowledging Him in everything I do, whether I feel like it's the right thing or not.

Prayer

Dear Lord, I'm sorry that I haven't acknowledged You in all my decisions or in the roads I've gone down. I do love You with all my heart. Even if I don't always understand the path You are leading me down, I pray that my trust in You will never falter. I pray that I will see Your will clearly and not hesitate to follow.

—Jessica

FEBRUARY 11

OUR FATHER'S LOVE

The LORD is compassionate and gracious, slow to anger, abounding in love. . . . For as high as the heavens are above the earth, so great is his love for those who fear him. . . . As a father has compassion on his children, so the LORD has compassion on those who fear him.

—PSALM 103:8–13

HAVE YOU EVER loved someone so much that all you wanted for them is blessings? This is how I feel about my children and grandchildren. I want their path in life to be smooth, and I want them to always be safe from harm. I want them to be happy and to feel secure and loved—but most of all, I want them to know Christ. God's expression of love in the scripture above is quite mind-blowing. As a parent and grandparent, we get just an inkling of how God feels about us. This kind of love is a blessing beyond words! And just as we have to allow our children to learn from mistakes and from the hard knocks of life, Christ allows us to learn from ours. But even when our road is difficult, we can be assured that "the Lord has compassion on those who fear him."

Prayer

Father, I thank You for allowing us to be parents and to know in a small part how much You love us. In your Son's name, amen.

—*Lisa*

Payback—Jesus Style

Blessed are those who are persecuted because of righteousness, for theirs is the kingdom of heaven.

—MATTHEW 5:10

NAYSAYERS WILL COME and go, but always remember to hold on to your faith and beliefs. My grandfather, who is a minister, used to say that the biggest compliment he could get was being called a "holy roller." He also said that these days, that term stood for someone whose alarm went off on Sunday morning and then he rolled over and went back to sleep. If people are going to persecute you, it might as well be over something great like the love of Jesus Christ. When they do, treat them just as Jesus did, and love them anyway. Being made fun of, or persecuted, for your faith is one of the most difficult aspects of the Christian walk, but trust me, there is nothing more rewarding than seeing the look in people's eyes when the kind of "payback" you give them is the love of Jesus.

Prayer

Father, please bless me, but bless my persecutors as well. When I am ridiculed for my faith, fill me with the strength to "pay them back" with the love of Jesus. Through my actions, help me show them the love You have for all of us.

—*Martin*

FEBRUARY 13

LESSONS ON KINDNESS

Make sure that nobody pays back one wrong act with another. Always try to be kind to each other and to everyone else.

—1 THESSALONIANS 5:15, NIRV

MY GRANDMOTHER, MY mother's mom, always tells us that kindness is a fruit of the spirit, so it's something we want in our lives. But being kind isn't always a kid-friendly activity. Kids watch other kids on TV talk mean to each other or make fun of others, and they think it's okay to act like that in real life. But it's never okay to treat someone unkindly. My mama always says she learned from her grandmother that nothing is more important than the feelings of someone else. I think our grandmothers are pretty smart ladies, plus the verse above makes it very clear how we are to treat others. Whether it's your friends or your family, treating them kindly will make everyone happy, including God.

Prayer

Father, help me to see where I might not be treating others as I need to treat them and to change my ways. Help me to always treat others with kindness, and forgive me when I've failed in this area. In His name I pray, amen.

—Sadie

FEBRUARY 14

NAKED AND UNASHAMED

This is why a man leaves his father and mother and is united to his wife, and they become one flesh. Adam and his wife were both naked, and they felt no shame.

—GENESIS 2:24–25

IF YOU'VE EVER watched *Duck Dynasty,* you know that Miss Kay and I enjoy each other physically. The gift of physical intimacy and the ability to build a brand-new family is one of the greatest gifts the Creator gave to husbands and wives. But any couple that develops true intimacy does so by being faithful to each other, maintaining their unity, and embracing God's gift of oneness. When differences of opinion come up—and believe me, they will—you've got to work through them together until you're once again united. To make a marriage last and to enjoy the physical relationship God gave you, you must commit to each other through the good and the bad times. God has given married couples a reason to celebrate their union—so enjoy!

Prayer

Thank you, Creator, for all that we see, hear, and sense and for giving us the gift of relationships here on planet Earth. Help me in my commitment to stay unified with Miss Kay, to work on myself, and to build more intimacy. All these things I pray in the name of Jesus, amen.

—*Phil*

FEBRUARY 15

(FEBRUARY 15–21 IS A SPECIAL SERIES ON PSALM 23)

1: MEDITATION ON PSALM 23

The LORD is my shepherd, I lack nothing. He makes me lie down in green pastures, he leads me beside quiet waters, he refreshes my soul. He guides me along the right paths for his name's sake. Even though I walk through the darkest valley, I will fear no evil, for you are with me; your rod and your staff, they comfort me. You prepare a table before me in the presence of my enemies. You anoint my head with oil; my cup overflows. Surely your goodness and love will follow me all the days of my life, and I will dwell in the house of the LORD forever.

—PSALM 23

MOST OF US instantly recognize the poetry and grace of the twenty-third Psalm. You might want to read it again to allow its richness to soak into your soul. David's picture of a shepherd and his sheep has provided comfort and guidance for thousands of years. May it bless us today and this week as we meditate on it.

Prayer

We trust You, our great Shepherd and Father, to guide our steps today and provide for all of our needs. Bless us, Lord, and lead us to greater understanding of Your ways and Your words. We pray this in Jesus' name, amen.

—Al

FEBRUARY 16

2: EMBRACE YOUR INNER SHEEP

The LORD is my shepherd, I lack nothing.

—PSALM 23:1

MOST OF US don't really like to be thought of as sheep, do we? When have you ever seen a sheep as a school mascot? Maybe a fighting ram, but never a mewing sheep! Sheep don't do a whole lot except wait to be shorn or slaughtered. They are very timid animals who depend on provision to survive. David was given the role of shepherd by his father and spent many days and nights taking care of sheep. It is with that personal insight that he compared himself to this helpless animal when it came to his dependence on God. David depended on his own shepherd, the Almighty God, so that he would be fulfilled. Jesus would use the same analogy later in John 10. Embrace your inner sheep today and depend on the Chief Shepherd for your personal fulfillment.

Prayer

To our great Shepherd we lay down our lives today and accept that we cannot be fulfilled without You, O Lord. In submission and recognition of weakness, we offer our lives to You, and we pray for a great harvest of blessing. Thank You, Father, for fulfilling and shepherding each one of us. In Jesus we pray, amen.

—*Al*

FEBRUARY 17

3: SPIRITUAL NOURISHMENT

He makes me lie down in green pastures, he leads me beside quiet waters.

—PSALM 23:2

THE ROBERTSON FAMILY loves to eat! A dinner table loaded with Miss Kay's food always provides some of the best times for our family to visit, unwind, and catch up on what is going on in our worlds. Sitting around the table together always provides nourishment way beyond just physical food; it nourishes our very souls. That is the image I get when David shows nourished sheep gaining more than just the physical blessing; they are gifted with an emotional and spiritual blessing, as well. Community, family, and relationships are a big part of our lives and should be combined into the physical needs of food and drink.

Prayer

Lord, thank You for community and family and the fulfillment that comes from them. Thank You for providing our physical needs like food, water, and shelter. Forgive us when we take our daily bread and drink for granted, and help us share that honored blessing with family and friends as much as possible. We love You and honor You today through the name of our Lord Jesus, amen.

—*Al*

February 18

4: Safe Passage

He refreshes my soul. He guides me along the right paths for his name's sake.

—PSALM 23:3

THOUSANDS OF YEARS ago, when David guided his sheep through the foothills around Bethlehem, his sheep had to maneuver through countless slippery paths and treacherous passageways. As David meditated on those perilous paths, he wrote of the soul guidance of his own Shepherd. If we want our own souls to be restored and refreshed like David's, we need to know and follow the correct path in order to maintain spiritual nourishment and not grow weak and weary. Our heavenly Father has always promised to show a path of safety—as long as we are willing to trust Him and walk in His path.

Prayer

Today, Father, we pray for refreshment and restoration of our souls. We humbly ask You to guide our steps in the right direction and trust in Your wisdom and vision to lead us away from danger and temptation. Please allow Your grace to guide us and Your love to sustain us. We pray this because of our risen Savior, Jesus, amen.

—*Al*

FEBRUARY 19

5: NO FEAR

Even though I walk through the darkest valley, I will fear no evil, for you are with me; your rod and your staff, they comfort me.

—PSALM 23:4

I GREW UP IN the isolated countryside on the banks of the Ouachita River. Dad once famously said, "Where I live we don't call 911, I am 911!" We were so far out that there was truth in those words, so when my brothers and I were young and Dad was gone selling duck calls, the nights were scary without his presence. Every sound in the woods or on the river seemed ominous without our father there to protect us. But when he was home, we felt safe. Our heavenly Father's presence gives us the same assurances and feeling of protection. Yes, there will be dark and scary moments for all of God's children, but confidence to walk through them, under the watchful eye of the ultimate protector, is what gives us true comfort.

Prayer

We humbly ask for protection from the dark forces that are at work against us today. We pray for comfort in difficult hours, strength in weak moments, and light for the shadows that befall us. Thank You for being our guide, our comforter, and our protector. We love You and give You all the praise you deserve. We pray in Jesus' name, amen.

—*Al*

6: Undeserved Generosity

You prepare a table before me in the presence of my enemies. You anoint my head with oil; my cup overflows.

—PSALM 23:5

My dad fished the Ouachita River commercially when we were first establishing Duck Commander as a business. The money made from fishing sustained our family and helped pay the early equipment notes for our start-up company. We viewed thieves stealing fish from our nets as enemies of our well-being. Whenever we heard a boat motor near one of our nets, we would jump in our boat and roar up on the unsuspecting thieves with shotgun in tow for a discussion about why they shouldn't be there. But because of something Dad read in the Bible, he began giving thieves the fish they were attempting to steal and inviting them to come to him when they wanted fish and he would freely give it to them. This offering of grace and blessing to those who would take our livelihood changed people's view of Dad, but it also changed Dad. He realized that this is what our Father in heaven does for His sons and daughters every single day.

Prayer

Father, we thank You for the blessings that we do not deserve and for Your overflowing kindness to us. We ask for opportunities to bestow blessings on others. In the name of Jesus, amen.

—Al

February 21

7: The Secret to Your Purpose

Surely your goodness and love will follow me all the days of my life, and I will dwell in the house of the Lord forever.

—PSALM 23:6

David concludes his masterpiece by highlighting the two greatest sustainers of a blessed life: goodness and love. He then lays out the ultimate goal for all of humanity: an eternal destiny. All people strive for a good life here on earth, but far too few understand that loving others and striving for what is good is the real secret to obtaining purpose and meaning in the day-to-day struggle of living. That kind of life will help us gain insight into the true meaning of our existence—which is to have an eternal relationship with the Creator of humanity. May this day lead to the next in a good and loving way, and may we never forget our purpose is to live with God for all eternity.

Prayer

We humbly ask for a spirit of love and goodness as we walk the steps You have laid out before us this day. We ask for a glimpse of eternity in the finite world in which we live, and we pray that our actions this day will reflect Your presence that lives within us. Thank You for the hope that is found in Jesus Christ. We pray through Him, amen.

—Al

FEBRUARY 22

How Will They Know?

How, then, can they call on the one they have not believed in? And how can they believe in the one of whom they have not heard? And how can they hear without someone preaching to them?

—ROMANS 10:14

I AM SO THANKFUL for good friends. One of my best friends, Tony, wasn't worried about what I would think of him if he shared his faith with me; he just wanted me to know the hope that he had and the peace that came with it. He wanted me to know about a loving God and what He did for me. And I'm so thankful he told me. Sometimes we worry so much about what people think of us that we can't share our faith. I was glad to hear it, and there are a lot more people out there ready to hear it. As the verse above says, people can't believe in Someone they haven't heard of—someone has to tell them. You could be that person.

Prayer

Father, help us to think of others more than ourselves. Let us take advantage of every opportunity that comes our way; use us as Your instruments for Your glory. In Your name I pray, amen.

—Godwin

FEBRUARY 23

SHARING THE LOVE

Love is patient, love is kind. It does not envy, it does not boast, it is not proud. It does not dishonor others, it is not self-seeking, it is not easily angered, it keeps no record of wrongs. Love does not delight in evil but rejoices with the truth. It always protects, always trusts, always hopes, always perseveres. Love never fails.

—1 CORINTHIANS 13:4–8

OUR FAMILY HAS always loved people. We would never have hosted all of the events, bought and cooked all the food, and kept all of the kids we did through the years if we didn't love people. We especially love seeing people come to Christ. Phil is always the one to teach and share and I am usually the one to counsel, cook, and wrangle the kids while the parents' lives are about to be changed. Phil says we have to love people more than we fear them, and I believe that's true. I always want to live a life of love.

Prayer

Father, I love You and Jesus and the Holy Spirit so much. I am grateful that You planted love in me, Phil, and our family. Please give us strength to keep loving others and sharing the message of love with the lost. In Jesus' name I pray, amen.

—Miss Kay

No Matter What

Shadrach, Meshach and Abednego replied to him, King Nebuchadnezzar, we do not need to defend ourselves before you in this matter. If we are thrown into the blazing furnace, the God we serve is able to deliver us from it, and he will deliver us from Your Majesty's hand. But even if he does not, we want you to know, Your Majesty, that we will not serve your gods or worship the image of gold you have set up.

—DANIEL 3:16–18

THESE BOYS HAD been forcefully taken from home to a strange and foreign land. During their stay in this new land, they showed great faith and were placed in positions as overseers of the foreign nation they were deported to. But even in their success, they were unwilling to compromise their faith in the one true God. When commanded to bow down to a false god, they refused, knowing their refusal would put their lives in danger. They had confidence in their God and knew He could save them if He chose to. But even in their powerful display of faith, they made no demands on God; they simply trusted in Him. What an example for us!

Prayer

Lord, help us to trust and be faithful to You like these Hebrew boys were. Help us to leave the outcome in Your hands.

—*Willie*

February 25

The Unchanging Nature of Jesus

Jesus Christ is the same yesterday and today and forever.

—HEBREWS 13:8

MY DAD HAS never owned a watch. I followed in his steps and have yet to purchase a timepiece. My dad uses words such as "daylight," "midday," "dusk," and "dark" to convey his schedule. Taking this view of time brings a certain sense of freedom, but it also creates a lot of chaos and confusion when trying to plan a meeting. Time itself conveys a beginning, a middle, and an end—which also happen to be the key ingredients of a good story. But Jesus is much more than a good story; He is a real being and is eternal. He does not change. He *is,* no matter the circumstances, no matter the time, and because of this fact, everything in our lives is better.

Prayer

Lord, thank You for giving us hope of life everlasting. Help us to constantly make changes for the better because of Your unchanging nature.

—*Jase*

WHAT'S WRONG WITH JESUS?

The Son is the image of the invisible God, the firstborn over all creation. For in him all things were created. . . . He is before all things, and in him all things hold together. And he is the head of the body, the church; he is the beginning and the firstborn from among the dead, so that in everything he might have the supremacy. For God was pleased to have all his fullness dwell in him, and through him to reconcile to himself all things, whether things on earth or things in heaven, by making peace through his blood, shed on the cross.

—COLOSSIANS 1:15–20

THE ABOVE PASSAGE says it all. Now, after reading those verses, ask yourself this question: *What is wrong with Jesus?* What is wrong with the perfect God—the perfect man? What else could He offer us? What more could He be? And finally, what other chance is there for escaping planet Earth alive? To my way of thinking, the answer is obvious: Jesus is our all in all. He's the way, friend; there is no other.

Prayer

Father, we thank You today for Jesus—the perfect one who made us perfect by Your love and grace and by His sacrifice on a cross. In the name of the perfect one—Jesus—I pray, amen.

—Phil

FEBRUARY 27

MORE THAN ENOUGH

For you have spent enough time in the past doing what pagans choose to do—living in debauchery, lust, drunkenness, orgies, carousing and detestable idolatry.

—1 PETER 4:3

WHEN I WOULD go up to the rooftop of the hotel I lived in for half my tour in Vietnam, I would see my buddies walk out the front door of the hotel, and then a few hours later, they'd stagger back in. I told myself I would never do that, but after being there for a while, I walked out and staggered back, just like the rest of them. The more I missed home, the more I drank to make me not think about it. When I finally did make it home, I decided I had drunk enough whiskey in Vietnam to last me a lifetime, and I decided that tea would be the strongest thing I would drink from then on. Almost fifty years later, I am still holding to that good decision. Drunkenness is not the way to go, Jack!

Prayer

Heavenly Father, I want to thank You for helping me quit drinking all of those years ago. I am glad that I have had a clear mind and want to keep it that way. I am grateful for Jesus, and I pray through Him. Amen.

—Si

FEBRUARY 28

TAKE A BREATH

Do not be anxious about anything, but in every situation, by prayer and petition, with thanksgiving, present your requests to God. And the peace of God, which transcends all understanding, will guard your hearts and your minds in Christ Jesus.

—PHILIPPIANS 4:6–7

EVERYBODY I KNOW has worried at one time or another. Some things in this life are almost impossible not to worry about—like the safety of our spouse and children. But the Lord says we shouldn't even worry about that. So the next time you find yourself worrying that your daughter might not make the cheerleading squad or that you might not be able to pay that bill on time, take a deep breath and put things in their proper perspective. Pray to the Father that His will be done, and thank Him for the hope we have in Jesus.

Prayer

I thank You, Father, for the peace that only You can provide. I pray that You protect my family and that we honor You with all we do. I know Your plan for us on this earth will be seen through, so please ease my worries and help me focus on my walk with You. I thank You most of all for Jesus and our salvation, and I pray in His name, amen.

—Jay Stone

March

MARCH 1

GIVING WITHOUT JUDGMENT

"Do not judge, and you will not be judged. Do not condemn, and you will not be condemned. Forgive, and you will be forgiven. Give, and it will be given to you. A good measure, pressed down, shaken together and running over, will be poured into your lap. For with the measure you use, it will be measured to you."

—LUKE 6:37–38

MY WIFE IS really awesome about giving money or food to anybody she sees on the side of the road, and I used to get upset about it. I would tell her, "They are just going go buy alcohol or drugs with that." She would reply, "It's not our place to judge, but to show them kindness just as Christ has done to us." And you know what? She was right! The way Jesus lived and His message while here on Earth had much to do with our hearts toward other people—especially the downtrodden. It's always better to err on the side of generosity than to withhold kindness because we are unsure of how our gift will be used. Our job is to follow Jesus' example; He will worry about the rest.

Prayer

Heavenly Father, help us to give with joyful and nonjudgmental hearts to those who are in need. Lord, we expect nothing in return, only that You be pleased with our faithfulness. Amen!

—*Jep*

March 2

Imprinted on Our Hearts

Train up a child in the way he should go: and when he is old, he will not depart from it.

—PROVERBS 22:6, KJV

BEING A MOM of four children, I try so hard to instill God's Word in their little hearts. We're blessed to also have a family that lives by God's Word. It's very daunting to know that Jep's and my influence on our children could hinder or help them in knowing our Lord and Savior. It's a huge responsibility! But I trust that if we share God's Word with them and live our lives by His Word, it will forever be imprinted on their hearts. Whenever I fall short of my goals, God's Word is there in the back of my mind, calling me to repentance and guiding me to wisdom. The truth is that as we train our children, we are also being trained ourselves. Growing in God's Word is a lifelong process. I'm thankful that our family travels this road together.

Prayer

Lord, I thank You for Your Word, which guides us and teaches us Your ways. I pray that Jep and I will stay committed to sharing Your Word with our children every day. I pray that it will be imprinted on all of our hearts and never leave. Even if our children go astray, I pray that the Word they have learned will pierce their heart, calling them back to You.

—Jessica

March 3

Three Licks

Whoever spares the rod hates their children, but the one who loves their children is careful to discipline them.

—PROVERBS 13:24

When we four boys were growing up, the "Robertson Rule" for misbehavior was three licks (meaning a belt on the posterior three times) per transgression. Dad says that there were only three grounds for those three licks: (1) disrespecting Mom, (2) fist-fighting with one another, and (3) tearing up perfectly good equipment—meaning *his* equipment. The "Robertson Rule" had some built-in boundaries that kept discipline from going too far. The limit was three licks, and the offenses were few and well defined. It is never acceptable for parents to hit their children out of anger or without restraint. I respected my dad then for what he was doing, and I respect him now for what he did to help bring discipline to our lives. My parents loved us enough to discipline us, and I have tried to do the same with my children and grandchildren.

Prayer

Father, please guide us in the ways of discipline and help us to be consistent and loving as we guide our families. We pray this prayer through Him, amen.

—Al

MARCH 4

THE BONDS OF LOVE

But Ruth replied, "Don't urge me to leave you or to turn back from you. Where you go I will go, and where you stay I will stay. Your people will be my people and your God my God. Where you die I will die, and there I will be buried. May the LORD deal with me, be it ever so severely, if even death separates you and me."

—RUTH 1:16–17

I JUST LOVE THE story of Ruth, don't you? The most amazing thing about the above words of Ruth is that she said them not to her husband, but to her mother-in-law! I was blessed to have a wonderful mother-in-law. We called Phil's mother Granny, and she lived on our land for many years. Much of what I know and believe about hospitality and cooking I learned in her kitchen. Even though they were very poor, Granny made sure her children never went hungry for food, but she always wanted them to be hungry for God's Word—and they all are to this day. Ruth and Naomi teach us about the power of family and the bonds of love. You can cultivate this same kind of love with your in-laws.

Prayer

Father, bless us today with the ability to commit ourselves to those who love us. Help us to carry on the legacy of those who have gone before us or to create a new legacy for future generations. Amen.

—Miss Kay

MARCH 5

OUT OF THIS WORLD!

Do not be yoked together with unbelievers. For what do righteousness and wickedness have in common? Or what fellowship can light have with darkness? . . . Therefore, "Come out from them and be separate," says the Lord.

—2 CORINTHIANS 6:14–17

LIVING IN THIS world is unavoidable, but we do have a choice about *how* we live. And Scripture is clear about the kind of lifestyle God's people are to live. Although we have to live in this world, we are called not to be *of the world*. There should always be a stark difference between the godly and ungodly; if there isn't, then there's no difference between darkness and light. *We* are the light of the world—and our light must be very visible to everyone we come in contact with.

Prayer

Father, I lived in darkness for twenty-eight years. What I did in those years is shameful to even mention. I praise You for delivering me from darkness and bringing me into the light. May we all walk in the light as we interact with our fellow man. I pray this through the light of the world, Jesus. Amen.

—*Phil*

STRONG AND COURAGEOUS

"Be strong and courageous, because you will lead these people to inherit the land I swore to their ancestors to give them. . . . Be careful to obey all the law my servant Moses gave you; do not turn from it to the right or to the left, that you may be successful wherever you go."

—JOSHUA 1:6–7

JOSHUA WAS A strong and courageous kind of guy, but God knew he needed even more strength and courage in order to lead the men and women under his charge. In reality, the most courageous thing any leader can do is face his weakness. Understanding our weaknesses helps us think through possible life scenarios and how we can react courageously, in spite of our weakness. Good leaders are born from discipline, which is born from consistent response to structure—and the very best structure around is the Word of Almighty God. To listen, not swerve, and be humble in success takes courage and strength. Joshua led like he'd been taught and became one of the greatest leaders in the whole Bible.

Prayer

Father, please strengthen my resolve to go neither left nor right, but to stay on the correct and straight path. Thank You for those who have guided and led me through the years. Through Jesus, amen.

—Willie

March 7

He Who Struggles

Then the man said, "Your name will no longer be Jacob, but Israel, because you have struggled with God and with humans and have overcome."

—GENESIS 32:28

THE BIBLE TELLS an interesting story about a wrestling match between Jacob and an angel. After Jacob wrestled all night with this guy, he received a blessing and a name change. "Jacob" means "deceiver," and that word had described the tone of Jacob's life from a very young age. His brother, Esau, was the primary victim of his deceit, and there had been bad blood between them for most of their lives. In fact, their feud became so intense that Jacob fled for his life and was away from his family for many years. It is no coincidence that Jacob's heart was changed, along with his name (it was changed to Israel, which means "he who struggles with God"), on the eve before a surprise face-to-face meeting with his brother. Esau forgave his brother, and a new relationship was born that day.

Prayer

We repent of our deceit and pray for honesty as we face those we have harmed or hurt. We ask all of these things in Jesus' name, amen.

—Jase

MARCH 8

THE BEST I HAVE TO GIVE

Let the message of Christ dwell among you richly as you teach and admonish one another with all wisdom through psalms, hymns, and songs from the Spirit, singing to God with gratitude in your hearts. And whatever you do, whether in word or deed, do it all in the name of the Lord Jesus, giving thanks to God the Father through him.

—COLOSSIANS 3:16–17

MY FAMILY IS always kidding me about how loud I sing at church. I am just trying to make a joyful noise, okay, and I do love to sing praises to God. I may sing just a little off key—okay, maybe a lot—but I figure if that's the voice the good Lord gave me, then that's the voice He wants me to belt out my praise with. What else am I gonna do? I figure He saved me and gave me all of the good things I have, so He deserves the best I have to give when it comes to worshipping Him. And the voice I have is the best I got, Jack!

Prayer

Dear Father, I am thankful for what You have done for me, and I want to always praise You. Thank You for giving me a voice so I can sing for You. You are the one true God, and I worship You and I always will. In Jesus' name I pray, amen.

—*Si*

March 9

God Meets Our True Needs

And my God will meet all your needs according to the riches of his glory in Christ Jesus.

—PHILIPPIANS 4:19

I CAN'T TELL YOU how many times the kids have come up to me and said, "Mom, I need . . ." I laugh. Today, we all have so many things we "need." We need a cell phone, a new car, our favorite food, our friends to hang out with—the list is endless. Our family has taken many trips to the Dominican Republic to work with an orphanage and feed the hungry. This helps us stay grounded in what is really important in life. My children understand that their "needs" are really "wants" and that we have to help those who are really in need. If you and your family have not found a place that really *needs* you to help them with their real *needs,* then contact your local church congregation. I'm sure they will point you in the right direction. Your family will be truly blessed.

Prayer

God, thank You for not always giving us the things we think we need, but for supplying our needs according to Your riches and the glory of Jesus. Please sustain those around the world who depend so heavily on You to survive. In Jesus' name, amen.

—*Korie*

PERSEVERING IN CONFIDENCE

Do not throw away your confidence; it will be richly rewarded. You need to persevere so that when you have done the will of God, you will receive what he has promised.

—HEBREWS 10:35–36

OUR DAUGHTER, MIA, was born with a cleft lip and palate. Over the years, she has had multiple surgeries and procedures and has seen many doctors, nurses, and surgeons. The one thing I hear most from these professionals is how impressed they are at her confidence. Even at a young age, Mia knows who she is and where she belongs. She is not self-conscious about her condition. She has her moments of discouragement, but she perseveres! These circumstances have shaped her into who she is: a friendly, caring, witty, sometimes sassy, and very confident kid. I've learned so much just from watching her indomitable spirit. She teaches me as much as, if not more than, I teach her.

Prayer

Thank You, Lord, for the example of my child and what she shows me every day. Her confidence comes from You, Lord, and I pray that she continues to look to You always. You've promised that You will never leave or forsake us—and You never have. We can't wait to be in heaven with You, where we will live forever with imperishable bodies.

—*Missy*

March 11

Who's a Man?

Jesus wept.

—JOHN 11:35

WE WERE RAISED under the mantra of "Who's a man?!" I always viewed tears as a sign of weakness and the opposite of manhood until I read this passage and had a daughter with special needs. The most difficult time I experienced in life was having a child born with a cleft lip and palate. I have to admit that hearing an ultrasound tech say, "Uh-oh," at the sight of our daughter on the monitor filled me with fear. Then a month later, when a nurse handed that little baby over after the first of many surgeries, I didn't feel like a macho man. The tears just came. Somewhere in the process, I realized the helplessness of my role and decided that God alone is in control. Submission to God and the situation allowed me to ask, "Why not?" instead of "Why?" Our daughter is an amazing trouper—an example to us all—and her situation has allowed us to be used by God to help other families. Maybe manhood doesn't mean that we never shed a tear or feel fear but that we know Who our true strength comes from—and rely fully on Him.

Prayer

Help us to persevere because we know that one day we will experience an everlasting, pain-free dwelling with You.

—*Jase*

March 12

Bone Deep

For the word of God is alive and active. Sharper than any double-edged sword, it penetrates even to dividing soul and spirit, joints and marrow; it judges the thoughts and attitudes of the heart.

—HEBREWS 4:12

WE HAVE STUDIED the Bible with many people, and out of all those people, God's Word was only rejected one time. For some, it takes a while to penetrate, but usually after a few days, they are back to hear more or to obey His commands. God's Word gets up inside me each time I hear a class, lesson, or sermon. It penetrates my mind, soul, and spirit. It even gets into my bones and joints and down into the marrow. I cannot hear and disregard what it says because it cuts me each time. I am grateful for this. It means my heart has not hardened. It means His spirit is alive and active in my life. Though His Word is sometimes sharp, it has brought nothing but countless blessings into my life.

Prayer

Dear God and Father, please keep Your Word active and living in our lives. Prick our hearts, Lord, when we start to become tired of your living Word. This I pray with the help of your Spirit and in Your Son's name. Amen.

—*Lisa*

MARCH 13

A LIGHT ON THE RIVERBANK

Do not forget to show hospitality to strangers, for by so doing some people have shown hospitality to angels without knowing it.

—HEBREWS 13:2

FROM A YOUNG age, I can remember my grandparents opening their home to complete strangers. Kay would always have a delicious meal prepared, and Phil would share a story that had the power to change their lives forever. He would share his life as a broken man and then as a humble man after he was baptized into Christ. I can remember shining the car lights on the river at night after these storytelling sessions, so Phil and his guests could see. Kay would be there holding a warm towel for them once they came out of the water, lives renewed through their new birth. We would always sing a song of praise and have a prayer of thanksgiving on the riverbank. As I grew older and got married, I have opened my home up to new friends and potential forever family, as well. I have a sign in my kitchen that says BLESS THIS HOME AND ALL WHO ENTER IT, and I take that sign to heart in my quest for hospitality.

Prayer

Father, help us to show Your hospitality and be salt and light in this dark world. Let our light shine brightly so that we may make new friends and share the Good News about You. In Jesus' name, amen.

—*Anna Robertson Stone*

March 14

A Rolling Stone

Whoever digs a pit will fall into it; if someone rolls a stone, it will roll back on them.

—PROVERBS 26:27

ABOUT THIRTY YEARS ago, there was a zealous official who made some claims that Korie's family's company owed a lot of taxes to local municipalities. Of course, our local media went wild because the business was very high-profile and successful, and her great-uncle, who helped run the business, had been the mayor of our town. Her grandfather was also a partner, and he ran the business; he was one of our elders at our church. He was mortified that there was so much bad local publicity, so he personally oversaw the accounting to make sure their company found out what they owed and paid it in full. Well, it turned out the company was *owed* a large sum of money because they had actually *overpaid* their taxes! Korie's grandpa held a local news conference and informed the public of the situation. He then suggested that the official should read Proverbs 26:27. A reporter then read it on air. That was one of the coolest things that I had ever heard, and it has never left me.

Prayer

Father, help me to never be vindictive or envious. I know it will always come back to haunt me. Through Jesus I pray, amen.

—Al

MARCH 15

COUNTING TIME

Jesus said to her, "I am the resurrection and the life. The one who believes in me will live, even though they die; and whoever lives by believing in me will never die. Do you believe this?"

—JOHN 11:25–26

JESUS PUTS THE same question to us that He put to the woman at the well: *Do we believe Him?* He laid out who He is and the promise of never dying to those who believe, and then He demanded an answer: *Do we believe?* Whether we realize it or not, we all base our daily transactions on the assumption that Jesus *did* live. For we all count time by Jesus—even the atheist. It is 2013 *anno Domini,* a Latin phrase that means "in the year of the Lord." How did we all end up counting time by Jesus? Read the verse again! It's because He's the "resurrection and the life"! Many historical figures have impacted life on this planet, but humanity only counts time by one!

Prayer

Father, we thank You for Jesus, Who guarantees our resurrection from the grave. We thank You for the impact that came from His coming; His life; His death, burial, and resurrection; and His return to Your right hand. We vow to continue to remind our fellow human beings about why we count time by Your Son and our Lord. It is through Him that I pray, amen.

—*Phil*

March 16

Grow Where You're Planted

The man from whom the demons had gone out begged to go with him, but Jesus sent him away, saying, "Return home and tell how much God has done for you." So the man went away and told all over town how much Jesus had done for him.

—LUKE 8:38–39

In the scripture above, Jesus delivered a man from a multitude of demons. This man's life had been restored, and he was so grateful that he begged Jesus to allow him to go with Him. But Jesus had other plans. Jesus had a mission for this man to stay right where he was and preach the gospel at home. This man had an undeniable testimony that he could share right where he was. He was obedient to what his Savior asked, even though it wasn't what he wanted or where he wanted to be. Korie and I travel all around the world doing God's work, but earlier in our lives, most of our impact was done right here in West Monroe. I've learned the valuable lesson to grow where God plants me!

Prayer

Lord, help me be a missionary wherever You desire me to be. At home or abroad, I want to tell others the good news of what You have done for me. Thank you, Jesus, amen.

—*Willie*

March 17

The Truth of God

The fool says in his heart, "There is no God." They are corrupt, their deeds are vile; there is no one who does good.

—PSALM 14:1

ONE OF THE things I learned in Vietnam is that without God, there is no end to the evil men and women can do. Hey, I didn't even have to go to Vietnam to learn that! History has shown us that when people try to govern and rule without God, the results are disastrous and murderous. Without exception, every atheistic philosophy has been marked by the murder of people and enslavement of idealism. Hey, some people have even done horrible things in the name of Christianity, perverting God's truth. When truth is misused or downright ignored, bad things happen. In the verse above, the psalmist speaks truth in pure and simple terms—when we deny the reality of God, bad things happen. Today, I want to recognize God in my life, in my family, in my community, in my country, and in my world. May He forever rule, so there will be good for all!

Prayer

Father, we recognize Your greatness, Your rule, and Your place of honor over the human race and all of the governments of this world. May Your name be glorified today among the nations! We pray through Jesus Christ, amen.

—*Si*

March 18

Identify the Source!

Now the serpent was more crafty than any of the wild animals the L*ORD* *God had made. He said to the woman, "Did God really say, 'You must not eat from any tree in the garden'?"*

—GENESIS 3:1

WE DON'T KNOW all of the background as to why Satan landed on planet Earth to be a thorn in our flesh, but we all sure feel his impact and his influence. Sneaking around like a serpent, he feigned innocent ignorance by questioning Eve about the one rule God had given her and her husband. It reminds me of the old saying "Curiosity killed the cat"! This menacing whisper in Eve's ear put a chain of events into action and humanity's destiny was set toward sinful rebellion. When I hear a whisper that asks me to doubt God's wisdom, I know exactly who it's coming from! Praise God for *His* voice, which answers my doubts!

Prayer

Father, forgive us when we hear what our itching ears want to hear and when we ignore Your voice of reason. We pray for protection in dealing with the evil one who still tempts and torments us. Thank You for the Christ, who has dealt with our treacherous enemy once and for all. It is in His name we pray, amen.

—Jep

March 19

The Search for Wisdom

"So give your servant a discerning heart to govern your people and to distinguish between right and wrong. For who is able to govern this great people of yours?"

—1 KINGS 3:9

WHEN I STUDY the Bible, my goal is always to learn something that will make me think more like Christ. The Lord asked Solomon what he wanted. Solomon's answer was recorded here, but it was the spirit of this request that is so important. Solomon was asking God for wisdom—true wisdom, that is: the ability to know right from wrong. Solomon did not ask for wealth or power, just for the ability to know the difference between right and wrong as he ruled. God was so pleased with this request that in addition to giving Solomon what he wanted, he gave him also *everything* he didn't ask for—health, long life, wealth, and respect. This shows us God's attitude toward our search to know right from wrong and using what we learn in our lives.

Prayer

Lord, open my mind and eyes to know right from wrong. Allow me to search for the truth in wisdom. Let this wisdom guide my thoughts and actions as I go through my walk. Teach me to ever search for Your truth in all that I do. In Jesus' name, amen.

—*Jon Gimber*

March 20

Endeavor to Persevere

Not only so, but we also glory in our sufferings, because we know that suffering produces perseverance.

—ROMANS 5:3

COMMON SENSE TELLS us that the last thing we should do in a time of suffering is think of it as glorious, but the Word tells us we must. It seems that all we want to do is gripe and complain when we struggle, but even during those times, we must still thank and praise God. I have had struggles in my life when it felt like it was pointless to continue on, but I finally stopped and looked at all the blessings around me and realized just how bad things really could be. Perseverance is a must-have skill in the Christian walk because our enemy is relentless. He will never stop coming. I always think of Chief Dan George in *The Outlaw Josey Wales* when a struggle comes my way, and I "endeavor to persevere."

Prayer

God, we know times of struggle are headed our way, but let us not forget that You are in control of our lives.

—Martin

MARCH 21

CHANGING YOUR WAYS

Although they know God's righteous decree that those who do such things deserve death, they not only continue to do these very things but also approve of those who practice them.

—ROMANS 1:32

HAVE YOU EVER woken up with that voice in the back of your mind that says, "Boy, I didn't do right last night"? You look back at the night before and are stung with regret and new resolutions to do better next time. Then it gets dark again, and you meet up with the same friends, and your regrets and resolutions melt away because you're with friends, and they're doing the same things you are—nothing changes. After I became a follower of Jesus, I put those old ways behind me. Not that I'm perfect now—far from it! But my heart is now set on God and I'm walking in His direction, not my old paths.

Prayer

Father, keep us humble by letting us remember not only what You've done for us but where we came from. Let us walk in Your paths so we can help others follow You too. In Your name, amen.

—*Godwin*

A SECRET TO MARITAL SUCCESS

Be kind and compassionate to one another, forgiving each other, just as in Christ God forgave you.

—EPHESIANS 4:32

PHIL AND I have counseled many couples through the years, and we've found that this verse solves most of the problems married people face. I learned to live this verse the hard way because Phil was not always kind, compassionate, and forgiving, and so I had to be all those things for both of us! Carrying that burden was tiring at times, but because I was able to live it, Phil eventually became that kind of person too. And now, together we help others get there earlier in their marriage than we did. I have also seen this perseverance work in my boys' marriages, as well, and I'm thankful to say, all their marriages have held together because of this great principle.

Prayer

Father, we thank You for forgiving us of our sins and being so kind and compassionate in spite of our weaknesses. Help us to live this way and impact everyone we meet. Through Jesus I pray, amen.

—Miss Kay

March 23

Getting Our Priorities Straight

Therefore God exalted him to the highest place and gave him the name that is above every name, that at the name of Jesus every knee should bow, in heaven and on earth and under the earth, and every tongue acknowledge that Jesus Christ is Lord.

—PHILIPPIANS 2:9–11

EXALTED TO THE *highest place*—wow! Someday, every knee will bow and every tongue will confess that Jesus is Lord, but what about right now? Do you give Jesus the highest place in your life? We are busy people. Just thinking about all of the activities that go on in our lives makes me tired—appearances, filming, writing, sports, doctor's appointments, church, Bible studies . . . the list goes on and on. I learned something about balancing all this from watching a great example: my mom knows how to accomplish what is needed without losing focus on Christ. How do you make sure Jesus is given the highest place? Ask God to help you to make Him top priority.

Prayer

Lord, please help me to prioritize my life. Help me remember that we don't have to do everything that comes our way. Help me to be still and to listen for Your voice. Thank You for the example of my parents in never forgetting You. Amen.

—*Korie*

MARCH 24

GROWING OUR CHILDREN'S FAITH

Love the LORD your God with all your heart and with all your soul and with all your strength. These commandments that I give you today are to be on your hearts. Impress them on your children. Talk about them when you sit at home and when you walk along the road, when you lie down and when you get up.

—DEUTERONOMY 6:5–7

WITH TWO TEENAGE boys trying to find their way, Jase and I have made the decision to watch them closely in their behavior and attitudes while letting them grow in their independence. However, when we see the potential for bad decision making, we begin a nightly roundup. Everyone meets in the living room with their Bible and notebook, and instruction begins straight from the Word. It is our responsibility to grow our children into godly, faith-filled men and women. Our ultimate goal is to equip them with the skills needed to make godly decisions that will affect them and their future spouses and children in order to get them to heaven.

Prayer

Dear Lord, thank You for giving us Reed, Cole, and Mia, who are such blessings to our lives. I pray that as I give them over, You will use them to further Your kingdom. Please help me as I guide them in the right direction and teach them about Your love and sacrifice.

—Missy

MARCH 25

THE VERY BEST BLESSING

See what great love the Father has lavished on us, that we should be called children of God! And that is what we are! The reason the world does not know us is that it did not know him.

—1 JOHN 3:1

OUR FAMILY HAS been blessed with a lot over the past couple of years, with notoriety and money. But, really, the greatest blessing in our lives is God's love for us—even when we do wrong. *You* have been blessed with this very same thing. No matter who you are or how much money you have, you are always a child of God. The things we have in this world mean nothing when compared to our eternal salvation. We are all the same in God's eyes.

Prayer

Dear Lord, thank You for blessing me with another day when I can share Your love. Help me, today, not be of this world but to live as a child of Yours. In Your Son's name I pray. Amen.

—*Reed*

March 26

The Overflow of My Heart

"No good tree bears bad fruit, nor does a bad tree bear good fruit. Each tree is recognized by its own fruit. . . . A good man brings good things out of the good stored up in his heart, and an evil man brings evil things out of the evil stored up in his heart. For the mouth speaks what the heart is full of.

—LUKE 6:43–45

WHEN I LOOK at my friends and family, I love that I see good fruit coming from their lives. I think a good deal about what fruit I bear. I look at my mom, how she takes such great care of my grandparents in their later years. I watch Kay and see how giving she is—not only monetary giving, but the great love she has for people. I see many men and women around me who are overflowing with goodness. I will always strive to have God's goodness in my heart so that what comes out of me is good too.

Prayer

Lord, thank You so much for the Holy Spirit Who lives in me. I pray that I always bear good fruit. I never want to have evil stored up in my heart. Please, keep Your goodness in me, for Your glory and not mine.

—Jessica

March 27

Representing Christ in Love

"A new command I give you: Love one another. As I have loved you, so you must love one another. By this everyone will know that you are my disciples, if you love one another."

—JOHN 13:34–35

THE MOST COMMON response we hear from people after visiting our congregation is that they felt welcomed and loved. This is something we have really worked on over the years. A church gathered together should never feel cold, unfriendly, or unloving. We want visitors to feel like this is where they belong. When someone visits your church, you never know if they are Christians who just moved to your area and are looking for a new church home, or if they are seeking a new family because of hurt from where they used to be, or if they simply are seeking Christ for the first time. We want to represent Christ in every action. People can tell if we are truly disciples of Jesus in the way we love one another and the way we love those who walk in for the first time.

Prayer

Father, we ask for Your guidance and wisdom each time we meet someone for the first time. Help us to reflect Your light, love, and acceptance to each person—the same way, every day. In Jesus' name, amen.

—*Lisa*

March 28

Trying to Out-Give God

"Bring the whole tithe into the storehouse, that there may be food in my house. Test me in this," says the Lord Almighty, "and see if I will not throw open the floodgates of heaven and pour out so much blessing that there will not be room enough to store it."

—MALACHI 3:10

A LOT OF THINGS are written, preached, and taught about tithing. My old preaching partner Mike Kellett always said that he and I "would preach at the drop of a hat . . . and then we would pass the hat for a love offering!" Malachi was speaking to an entire nation when he challenged them about giving, but the application works one person at a time. I have found the best challenge for me—one guy with a lot of blessings—is to do just what this scripture says: test God by trying to out-give Him! Giving involves more than just my money; I also try to out-give God in time, mercy, forgiveness, and love, as well. According to this verse, I will receive more of what I try to out-give God in. But I can't hold on to those blessings, because I just keep giving them away.

Prayer

Father, I pray today that I will make every attempt to out-give You with my money, my time, my love, my mercy, and my goodness. I thank You for the gift of Christ, and it's in His name I pray, amen.

—Al

March 29

Of First Importance!

Now, brothers and sisters, I want to remind you of the gospel I preached to you, which you received and on which you have taken your stand. By this gospel you are saved, if you hold firmly to the word I preached to you. . . . For what I received I passed on to you as of first importance: that Christ died for our sins according to the Scriptures, that he was buried, that he was raised on the third day according to the Scriptures.

—1 CORINTHIANS 15:1–4

DID YOU HEAR that, brothers and sisters?! First importance! The gospel is of first importance! The death, burial, and resurrection of Jesus is what everything else revolves around! Since this gospel is of first importance, nothing else is as important as the gospel. Don't argue with people about faith; simply tell them about Jesus—the most important thing there is on the earth!

Prayer

Father, we thank You for the gospel of Jesus! Through the gospel, our sins were removed and forgotten by You. Through the gospel, our bodies will be raised from the dead. Our problems are solved, and You did it all *for us* and it is *free*! Thank you! Thank you! Amen.

—Phil

March 30

Wise Warnings

One evening David got up from his bed and walked around on the roof of the palace. From the roof he saw a woman bathing. The woman was very beautiful, and David sent someone to find out about her. The man said, "She is Bathsheba, the daughter of Eliam and the wife of Uriah the Hittite."

—2 SAMUEL 11:2–3

BOREDOM AND BEING awake when others are asleep can cause us a lot of problems. King David should have been off with his army, but instead he stayed home and got bored, which led to a lot of sin and a lot of misery for his family and for him. The servant's reply to David carried a warning—he identified the object of David's lust as another man's wife. Whose voice will God put in my ear today to warn me before I walk down a dark path? I pray that I listen and avoid trouble!

Prayer

Father, I ask for wisdom and discernment this day as I walk the path set before me. Please give me voices of reason as I may be unreasonable and unaware of the evil one's schemes against me. If I am that voice today for someone else, help me to be clear and bold as Your servant. I ask this prayer through Your Son, Jesus, amen.

—Jase

March 31

As for Me and My House

"If serving the Lord seems undesirable to you, then choose for yourselves this day whom you will serve, whether the gods your ancestors served beyond the Euphrates, or the gods of the Amorites, in whose land you are living. But as for me and my household, we will serve the Lord."

—JOSHUA 24:15

JOSHUA LAYS OUT a simple and stark choice for his fellow Israelites in this passage: choose the false gods of this culture around you, or choose the one God who delivered you and led you to glory. Joshua made his choice proudly and proclaimed it for all to hear, and then he laid out the simple and profound charge to follow his example. Today and every day, I want to live my life choosing *the* God over false gods, proudly proclaiming it and inviting others to follow my example. *As for me and my house, we will serve the Lord today and every day!*

Prayer

Please bless me today, Father, as I proudly choose to follow You and humbly ask that my choice and my example will bring You glory. I ask this in Jesus' name, amen.

—*Willie*

April

April 1

The Source of All

From him and through him and for him are all things. To him be the glory forever! Amen.

—ROMANS 11:36

NOW, I KNOW that I'm a slow-talking fellow. But the good thing about talking slow is that I have time to think before I speak—and that can be a good thing. Here, I want to speak about the God I have chosen to follow. This God is the source and the sustainer of all things; He is the rightful end of everything that exists. God spoke the world into existence. By His words alone, He created everything that exists. And now He graciously allows us to walk the face of the world. He's given us the air we breathe, the water we drink, the food and nourishment for our bodies. But most important, He gave His only Son to die on the cross for our sins so we can be forgiven of our sins by accepting Jesus Christ as our Savior. He loves us all. No matter how fast or slow you say it, it's the truth. He loves us!

Prayer

Dear Lord, God our Savior, I thank You for this world You have created for us to walk and live on. Thank You for sending Your only Son to die for all our sins. I pray, Lord, that You will give me the wisdom to spread Your message so others can know what a loving God You are. You will always come first in my life. Amen.

—Mountain Man

APRIL 2

JUSTICE IN THE END!

Vindicate me, my God, and plead my cause against an unfaithful nation. Rescue me from those who are deceitful and wicked.

—PSALM 43:1

HEY, JACK, SOMETIMES you just get done wrong! When a man or woman of God lives and works with deceitful and wicked people, there are going to be times when goodness and innocence are just flat taken advantage of. Even if there is no justice or vindication from the authorities on earth, relief can always be found in God. God promises that *His* kingdom is governed by a higher cause and by immutable justice—even though we may not experience that justice here on earth. God's bigger-picture philosophy shows us an end to troubled times as we trust in His ultimate justice and vindication.

Prayer

We pray today, Father, for a greater vision of who You are and how powerful You are. When we are wronged, help make it right by granting us justice and rescue from the clutches of evil people. We look forward to the day when we will be with You in heaven, forever. We have hope because of Christ, and it is because of His sacrifice we pray, amen.

—Si

April 3

(April 3–9 is a special series on Joseph)

1: Jealousy Destroys Relationships

Now Israel loved Joseph more than any of his other sons, because he had been born to him in his old age; and he made an ornate robe for him. When his brothers saw that their father loved him more than any of them, they hated him and could not speak a kind word to him.

—GENESIS 37:3–4

WHAT IS IT with younger brothers being so favored and spoiled? We always kid our youngest brother, Jep, about his "favored status" being the baby of the Robertson brothers. Kay tries to deny her favoritism, but somehow it sneaks out. Jep was definitely raised in a different home and environment than the older boys were. It is easy to see how sibling jealousy can arise and destroy a family's unity. Our kidding of Jep is always good-natured—we know we're all loved. Don't let the sin of jealousy spread in your heart and damage your love to those who are closest to you.

Prayer

Father, please guide us away from jealous tendencies and bless us with a gracious spirit toward those in our families. We ask this in Jesus' name, amen.

—*Willie*

April 4

2: Our Big-Picture God

So when Joseph came to his brothers, they stripped him of his robe—the ornate robe he was wearing—and they took him and threw him into the cistern. The cistern was empty; there was no water in it. . . . So when the Midianite merchants came by, his brothers pulled Joseph up out of the cistern and sold him for twenty shekels of silver to the Ishmaelites, who took him to Egypt.

—GENESIS 37:23–24, 28

The jealousy of Joseph's brothers grew to the extent that they actually *sold* their own brother into slavery. This terrible tragedy brought brokenness to their father's heart and birthed a terrible lie that would shame and divide Joseph's ten older brothers for the next thirteen years. But God always provides a door to escape, in spite of sinful schemes designed to utterly destroy His people. God had a plan for Joseph, and this separation was necessary to implement it. We serve a big-picture God who works all things out for His children in His own time.

Prayer

We thank You, Father, for protecting us, especially when we are unaware that You are doing it. Please give us the vision to see Your hand at work in the big pictures of our lives.

—*Willie*

APRIL 5

3: It All Starts with Trust

Now Joseph had been taken down to Egypt. Potiphar, an Egyptian who was one of Pharaoh's officials, the captain of the guard, bought him from the Ishmaelites who had taken him there. The LORD was with Joseph so that he prospered, and he lived in the house of his Egyptian master. When his master saw that the LORD was with him and that the LORD gave him success in everything he did, Joseph found favor in his eyes and became his attendant. Potiphar put him in charge of his household, and he entrusted to his care everything he owned.

—GENESIS 39:1–4

WE HAVE ALL known people who just seem to find success in everything they do. The "Midas touch," we often call it. This passage clues us in to the fact that God provides the successes we enjoy when we trust in Him, no matter the circumstances. Joseph was a teenage boy, separated from his family in a strange place thousands of miles from home, but he continued to believe in his heart and God kept blessing him. And others noticed.

Prayer

We praise You today, Father, for our successes and give You glory for the great blessings we receive from Your bounty. Help us never to forget that You are our wellspring of success. Through Jesus, we receive and pray, amen.

—Willie

April 6

4: Maintaining Purity

Now Joseph was well-built and handsome, and after a while his master's wife took notice of Joseph and said, "Come to bed with me!" But he refused. . . . "No one is greater in this house than I am. My master has withheld nothing from me except you, because you are his wife. How then could I do such a wicked thing and sin against God?" And though she spoke to Joseph day after day, he refused to go to bed with her or even be with her.

—GENESIS 39:6–10

You gotta love this guy! To me, the most amazing thing about this scenario is that a teenage boy would have enough awareness of his relationship with God that he would deny his natural impulses and rely on his spiritual awareness. Joseph realized at a young age that immorality is a sin against God, even before it is a sin against someone else or against yourself. To maintain purity because of a relationship with God, rather than fear of consequence, is the highest level of nobility and morality.

Prayer

Father, we thank You for our relationship with You and pledge to maintain it before all others in our lives. We want to honor You with our bodies, our minds, and our hearts, and we ask Your forgiveness for the times we fall short of this pledge. We ask this because of the sacrifice of Jesus Christ, amen.

—*Willie*

APRIL 7

5: Life Isn't Always Fair

When his master heard the story his wife told him, saying, "This is how your slave treated me," he burned with anger. Joseph's master took him and put him in prison, the place where the king's prisoners were confined. But while Joseph was there in the prison, the LORD was with him.

—GENESIS 39:19–21

HAVE YOU EVER wondered why things turned out bad even when you did the right thing? When dealing with people of the world, we have no guarantee that reward follows doing the right thing. I surmise that Potiphar knew what kind of woman his wife was and that this wasn't the first time she had engaged in this lurid behavior. But he took out his disappointment on Joseph to save face. Normally, a slave would have been executed for such an accusation, but instead he was put in the king's prison. Yet again, God's providential hand was there to protect Joseph's life, as he continued to work out His plan and mature Joseph for his ultimate destiny.

Prayer

We ask Your blessing today, Lord, especially for when we are treated badly for making the right decisions. We know this world is not fair, but we trust You to guide us and use us to accomplish our purpose and fulfill our personal destinies. We pray this through Jesus, amen.

—*Willie*

April 8

6: From Tribulation to Triumph

So Pharaoh said to Joseph, "I hereby put you in charge of the whole land of Egypt." Then Pharaoh took his signet ring from his finger and put it on Joseph's finger. He dressed him in robes of fine linen and put a gold chain around his neck. He had him ride in a chariot as his second-in-command, and people shouted before him, "Make way!" Thus he put him in charge of the whole land of Egypt.

—GENESIS 41:41–43

JOSEPH'S GIFT OF interpreting dreams finally came back to bless him when he was able to interpret the king of Egypt's dreams about an impending famine. After thirteen years of slavery and prison, Joseph emerged as the number-two man in all of Egypt, the world's superpower of that era. Not bad for a boy thought dead by his father! God works things out on his timetable to bring the best results for us too. Can we trust Him through tribulations to gain the blessing of triumph?

Prayer

Our great God and Father, we ask for wisdom as we navigate the trials of this life to see Your hands at work in us. We ask for protection through the famines of our walk and humility through the bountiful times. We ask these things through Christ, our Lord, amen.

—Willie

7: Grace over Vengeance

Then Joseph said to his brothers, "Come close to me." When they had done so, he said, "I am your brother Joseph, the one you sold into Egypt! And now, do not be distressed and do not be angry with yourselves for selling me here, because it was to save lives that God sent me ahead of you. For two years now there has been famine in the land, and for the next five years there will be no plowing and reaping. But God sent me ahead of you to preserve for you a remnant on earth and to save your lives by a great deliverance."

—GENESIS 45:4–7

THE ULTIMATE FINALE for Joseph was the divine appointment to reunite with his brothers, who had plotted to kill him, sold him into slavery, and lived a lie that tormented their family for more than twenty years. The cleansing power of forgiveness and trust in God was displayed by Joseph, in spite of his powerful position. He could have gotten full revenge on his broken brothers, but instead he told them not to be angry with themselves for what they had done. To give grace over vengeance is the foremost thing we can do to mirror our Divine Maker!

Prayer

We thank You for grace and forgiveness, O Lord. We deserve death, but You gave us life through Christ, and we praise You for it through Him, amen.

—*Willie*

DIVINE POWER TO DEMOLISH ARGUMENTS

For though we live in the world, we do not wage war as the world does. The weapons we fight with are not the weapons of the world. On the contrary, they have divine power to demolish strongholds. We demolish arguments and every pretension that sets itself up against the knowledge of God, and we take captive every thought to make it obedient to Christ.

—2 CORINTHIANS 10:3–5

WE HAVE BEEN given divine power! We have weapons that are not of this world—the most powerful on earth. While discussing any issue with the worldly people you come in contact with, make sure, during your conversation, that the gospel truth and its power to set them free comes from your mouth into their ears. Even if they don't respond immediately, the Word of God has entered their hearts and will yield its fruit. When the gospel is preached, you unleash divine power upon the ones who hear. Use your weapons wisely.

Prayer

Father, You have given us divine power to demolish evil strongholds. You are the omnipotent one! Guide us on earth and be our God by helping unleash this power upon the evil one who lives in the hearts of men. Through Jesus, amen.

—*Phil*

APRIL 11

TRUSTING GOD OVER EARTHLY LEADERS

But when they said, "Give us a king to lead us," this displeased Samuel; so he prayed to the LORD. And the LORD told him: "Listen to all that the people are saying to you; it is not you they have rejected, but they have rejected me as their king."

—1 SAMUEL 8:6–7

SAUL WAS THE first king of Israel, but he came to power by the will of the people and not by the will of God. The Israelites looked to the nations around them and wanted to be just like them but never asked what God wanted for them. This sentiment is still around in the modern world, as well. Trusting that government has the power to sustain us rather than the hand of Almighty God still blinds the hearts of billions around the world. While we are commanded to respect our leaders, let us never choose them over our Creator in any matter.

Prayer

We humbly ask the architect of our existence to lead us in every aspect of our lives today. We ask for a blessing on the men and women elected to lead us, but we also ask that their hearts be in tune with Your ways to lead, Your ways to govern, and Your ways to live. We accept Your rule through Jesus Christ, our Lord, amen.

—*Al*

APRIL 12

THE GIFT OF SEX

Marriage should be honored by all, and the marriage bed kept pure.

—HEBREWS 13:4

MY FAMILY HAS always been open to discussions about sex. God is the architect of marriage, and sex between a male and female inside of marriage is a recipe to a guilt-free, adultery-free, STD-free society. As a kid, there were a few embarrassing moments thinking about our parents in this way, but not only would I not be here without it, it is a lot easier to believe than "A stork dropped you from the sky." I'm thankful my parents gave me good advice, and their candid information was a contributing factor in my decision to wait for marriage. Abstinence before marriage gives you and your partner a strong foundation for all the trials of marriage. As in all aspects of life, God gives us grace and second chances, but this doesn't negate that God's way is always ideal.

Prayer

God, I thank You for the gift of marriage. Help us keep the marriage bed pure as we strive to trust You with our marriages and lives.

—*Jase*

APRIL 13

SCRUBBED CLEAN

Blessed is the one whose transgressions are forgiven, whose sins are covered. Blessed is the one whose sin the LORD does not count against them and in whose spirit is no deceit.

—PSALM 32:1–2

THERE IS NO greater freshness and feeling of renewal than when the burden of sin has been lifted from our soul. The hiding, the shame, and the weight are lifted when God's healing power is allowed to do its scrubbing and cleansing. There is no human alternative for this divine gift and no mystical substitute. Today I want to embrace forgiveness, counting myself among the blessed and feeling alive in truth.

Prayer

Heavenly Father, forgive my sins and cleanse my heart and spirit. Please allow me to be washed in Your sacrifice and bathed in Your love. I give You every thought and every dishonest impulse to be returned in purity and wholesomeness. I pray this prayer through Jesus, amen.

—Jep

April 14

The "If" of Forgiveness

For if you forgive other people when they sin against you, your heavenly Father will also forgive you. But if you do not forgive others their sins, your Father will not forgive your sins.

—MATTHEW 6:14–15

CHRIST IS SPEAKING directly to us in the verse above. And in this verse, He offers a wonderful promise—*forgiveness*! But this promise comes with an "if," and the "if" all depends on our hearts. He will forgive us *if* we forgive others. We can choose to forgive and be forgiven, or we can hold bitterness in our hearts and not be forgiven. If we hold on to bitterness, anger, and envy, we only hurt ourselves further. Our selfish focus leaves Christ on the cross and our sins still with us. But when we live by Christ's words and forgive others, healing, repair, and love are ours, and we can live in freedom. Here is your personal challenge: pick that person, right now, who needs your forgiveness, and put them at the top of your prayer list.

Prayer

Dear God who forgives, open my heart to let go of the wrong done to me. Free me from the bitterness that grows so quickly, and help me enter into the freedom of the wide open spaces of Your love.

—*Lynda Hammitt*

April 15

God's a Lot Smarter Than Me

"For I know the plans I have for you," declares the Lord, "plans to prosper you and not to harm you, plans to give you hope and a future."

—JEREMIAH 29:11

BECAUSE I'M A little kid, most of my days are planned for me. I get up and go to school during the school year, and in the summer I go to summer camp or on vacation or play around the house. But one day I will be in charge of what I do each day. I know that making the choices for my life will be easier when I depend on God to plan my life. I'm sure that what He plans for me will be way better than what I can plan for myself. That doesn't mean I won't work toward going to college or getting a job or being a good wife and mother, because I will, but I know that God will direct the path I will take *if* I put my path in His hands. And why wouldn't I? He's a lot smarter than me—a fifth grader!

Prayer

Father in Heaven, please continue to direct my steps and show me the way You want me to go. Help me to always keep my eyes open to Your plan for my life, amen.

—*Bella*

APRIL 16

BLESSINGS ON PURE HEARTS

Everything is pure to those whose hearts are pure.

—TITUS 1:15, NLT

BECAUSE OF THE large audience for our television show, we have had many opportunities to visit children who have severe illnesses. Just bringing smiles to faces and joy—even though they are in pain—is such a great blessing to our family. We also enjoy having the opportunity to pray for healing and hope for these families. Television, radio, and the social media are full of impurities. We can get pulled into the things that are not pure quickly. For us, seeing the hearts of these children is like seeing the heart of God—true pureness. Be sure your family has plenty of opportunities to see and understand pure hearts. Read to them from God's Word and have them bind it on their hearts.

Prayer

Lord, please help me to be more pure in heart. At some point in our lives, we start judging the outside of people. We forget that each man or woman is someone's son or daughter, a child of God. When I see someone who is different than I am, whether because of clothing style, skin color, religion, or something else, I pray I will be more childlike in my heart. I pray for all of those struggling with illness and difficulty. I pray this through Jesus, amen.

—Korie

APRIL 17

PROUD OF OUR BOYS

Like arrows in the hands of a warrior are children born in one's youth. Blessed is the man whose quiver is full of them.

—PSALM 127:4–5

I HAVE ALWAYS BEEN proud of my boys and the men they have become. They have never been perfect, and they still make mistakes (just like their mama!), but they have honored and respected me and their dad for most of their lives. I am proud that all four of them still have a close relationship with their dad and me. They all married godly women, as well, and the love you see on our show is the real thing. We have learned to love, forgive, and be there for each other, and I wouldn't trade anyone for anybody. As the verse above says, we are truly blessed!

Prayer

Father, I thank You for my sons, my daughters-in-law, my grandchildren, and my great-grandchildren. You blessed us with men and women who love and fear You and that is all Phil and I could ever have asked for. Please protect them from the devil, and keep our love and teaching ever before them. All of this I pray through Jesus, amen.

—*Miss Kay*

April 18

God Is Waiting

Do not be anxious about anything, but in every situation, by prayer and petition, with thanksgiving, present your requests to God.

—PHILIPPIANS 4:6

WHY IS IT that so many times we go to prayer as a last resort? I catch myself doing this quite often. My theory for myself is that, as a mom, I've learned to make all of the day-to-day decisions that need to be made for my house, my job, my kids, and myself without giving any of them a second thought. Then I become overwhelmed with all the stress that it brings. However, when I start each day by giving everything over to my God in prayer, thanking Him for all of the opportunities this day will bring me, it's astounding how the stress begins to dissipate. Isn't that amazing how that happens? My God is there . . . waiting. He's waiting for you, too.

Prayer

Father, how awesome it is that You are there for me at every turn in my life and in every one of my days. Please help me to start each day with a conversation with You. You know my heart. You know my needs. Give me those moments in each day when I may stop and look to You for guidance. I know You want what's best for me and my family. Thank You for Your continued presence in my life.

—Missy

APRIL 19

THE TONGUE IS A FIRE

The tongue is a small part of the body, but it makes great boasts. Consider what a great forest is set on fire by a small spark. The tongue also is a fire, a world of evil among the parts of the body. It corrupts the whole body, sets the whole course of one's life on fire, and is itself set on fire by hell.

—JAMES 3:5–6

THIS VERSE REMINDS me that everything I say matters, whether I think it's insignificant or not. It's a little scary to know that the very smallest of comments can have a large impact or that a little gossip or remark against someone's character can have an enormous impact on that person. I am working on biting my tongue and not being one who has to have the "last word." Thinking of my tongue as a "fire" that can set a whole forest ablaze reminds me that I need to work on this daily.

Prayer

Lord, please guard my tongue and help me not to be a person who tears others down, but rather a person who encourages and lifts others up. I pray You will help me have good stored up in my heart, that You will get rid of any evil in me. I want to be the woman of God You want me to be so that I can impact my friends and family for the good for Your glory!

—Jessica

Growing Trust

Trust in the LORD with all your heart and lean not on your own understanding; in all your ways acknowledge him, and he will make your paths straight.

—PROVERBS 3:5–6

NOW, THAT VERSE is *filled* with challenge. The first word, "trust," is probably one of the biggest things we struggle with. To trust someone you know with all your heart is extremely difficult. To completely trust someone you can't even see seems nearly impossible. The key to this verse is faith. When we have faith in something or someone, we overcome the impossible and head toward the incredible. We are sometimes scarred by hurts in our lives and feel we can't ever trust again. But when we are healed by Jesus, faith takes over and we can believe the unbelievable; we can trust the things that seem untrustable. Jesus Christ can and will create that faith and trust in your heart and mine. Call on Him to show you what real trust looks like. He will make your path straight!

Prayer

Father, I never knew what true joy was until You changed my life and gave me faith and trust. I thank You, Father, for this incredible gift. Please, Father, touch our lives so that we know what true love, true faith, and real trust is. In Your Son's name, amen.

—*Lisa*

April 21

Passing on the Blessing

" ' "The Lord bless you and keep you; the Lord make his face shine on you and be gracious to you; the Lord turn his face toward you and give you peace." ' "

—NUMBERS 6:24–26

Lisa and I have many great memories of raising our two daughters, but two of the most memorable are the family blessings we had for each of them when they were sixteen. We gathered our earthly family and some of our church family and asked for God's richest blessings on them as they entered that crucial period of becoming young women. We have always felt that it is important to say, not just think, words of blessing to and over your children, and now grandchildren. We need to be blessed, and we need to pass on blessings to others, as well.

Prayer

Father, we thank You for the blessing You give us every day by sustaining and maintaining our very lives. We ask that we will pass along those rich blessings to the important people in our lives and that they, in turn, will pass along those blessings to their important people. We are blessed in Jesus' love and by His name, amen.

—Al

WHEN JESUS COMES AGAIN

We believe that Jesus died and rose again, and so we believe that God will bring with Jesus those who have fallen asleep in him. . . . The Lord himself will come down from heaven, with a loud command, with the voice of the archangel and with the trumpet call of God, and the dead in Christ will rise first. After that, we who are still alive and are left will be caught up together with them in the clouds to meet the Lord in the air. And so we will be with the Lord forever. Therefore encourage each other with these words.

—1 THESSALONIANS 4:14–18

IF YOU'VE EVER wanted to know what will happen when Jesus comes again, you just found out as you read the previous passage. Those who die "in him" are guaranteed to be raised with Him, and those believers who are still alive when He returns will be "caught up" in the clouds with Him. You can believe it because Jesus died and rose again! You can stand on it, you can live by it, and you can look at your upcoming death with a smile. Your death is not the end—it is the *beginning*!

Prayer

Father, we thank You for the death, burial, and resurrection of Jesus. We have no fear of death because of Jesus and His resurrection. We praise and thank You for this assurance! Through Him, amen.

—*Phil*

APRIL 23

A Gentle Whisper

The LORD said, "Go out and stand on the mountain in the presence of the LORD, for the LORD is about to pass by." Then a great and powerful wind tore the mountains apart and shattered the rocks before the LORD, but the LORD was not in the wind. After the wind there was an earthquake, but the LORD was not in the earthquake. After the earthquake came a fire, but the LORD was not in the fire. And after the fire came a gentle whisper. When Elijah heard it, he pulled his cloak over his face and went out and stood at the mouth of the cave. Then a voice said to him, "What are you doing here, Elijah?"

—1 KINGS 19:11–13

THOSE OF YOU who know me know that I don't come off as a real quiet guy. But when God spoke to Elijah on the mountain, He came in a "gentle whisper." The lesson for Elijah—and for all the rest of us cats—is that God does some of His best work in the quieter moments. He sometimes moves in ways that go unnoticed by our busy selves. Everybody notices the fireworks display, but how many of us listen in the darker, quieter moments? But if we'll be still and pay attention, we just might have an encounter with God that changes our lives.

Prayer

Father, help us to be quiet and listen for Your presence. Speak to us today, and instruct us in the task You have set for us.

—*Si*

APRIL 24

HE GETS US!

I pray that the eyes of your heart may be enlightened in order that you may know the hope to which he has called you, the riches of his glorious inheritance in his holy people.

—EPHESIANS 1:18

AS THE APOSTLE Paul wrote the above verses, he was *praying* for us—for you and for me—praying that we would truly understand the richness of what God has given us. I don't know about you, but I *need* that kind of prayer. Paul was reminding us of what a great God we have! Our God is excited about our having our "hope" fulfilled and about our receiving the "inheritance" He has waiting for us in heaven. He gets us!! He understands that we need help grasping how much He loves us. Sometimes, I think He isn't getting much of a bargain in having us as His children, but this verse reminds us that He couldn't be happier to call us His children and that He has our reward ready and waiting.

Prayer

Father, I thank You for loving us enough to not give up on us. Thank You for allowing us—through Your words of encouragement—to know for sure the hope that we have. In Your name I pray, amen.

—*Godwin*

APRIL 25

GODLESS CHATTER

Timothy, guard what has been entrusted to your care. Turn away from godless chatter and the opposing ideas of what is falsely called knowledge.

—1 TIMOTHY 6:20

THESE DAYS, THERE is a lot of "godless chatter" going on. Twitter, Facebook, Instagram, apps, CNN, Fox News—the list goes on and on. There are so many things in our lives that say, "Listen to me! I'll tell you what's right!" But who really decides right from wrong? God tells us that all this "chatter" is "falsely called knowledge." It's okay to use social media, but keep in mind who is really in control, and who, above all else, lets us know what is good, right, and wholesome. Beware of all the avenues that Satan uses to plant evil in our minds and hearts. Don't allow the "chatter" of our modern lives to make you deaf to the voice of God, which is the only truth in the universe.

Prayer

Dear Lord, allow me to hear You over the noise of my everyday life. Help me to avoid false knowledge and listen to Your words, which are the ultimate truth. Help me to not be deceived by all the ideas, opinions, and lies of the world. You are my only true compass. With the help of Christ I pray, amen.

—Alex Robertson Mancuso

APRIL 26

HAND-WOVEN MASTERPIECES

From one man he made all the nations, that they should inhabit the whole earth; and he marked out their appointed times in history and the boundaries of their lands.

—ACTS 17:26

MY GRANDMOTHER WOULD set an extra place at our dinner table. I always thought that was odd until an actual stranger was invited in at suppertime and enjoyed a meal with us. That extra place would host many, and the spirit of my grandmother's tradition was passed on to my parents as our home was always filled with strangers. My parents seemed to bring out the best in people, mainly because of their lack of prejudice and their desire to point people to God. When people embrace God as their Maker, you realize that God doesn't make junk, mistakes, or accidents. We are all hand-woven masterpieces worth the price of God's Son.

Prayer

God, I thank You for making us in your image. Lord, help me not to judge anyone based on outward appearance but to view everyone as created by You on purpose. In the name of Jesus, amen.

—*Jase*

APRIL 27

All the Same!

So in Christ Jesus you are all children of God through faith, for all of you who were baptized into Christ have clothed yourselves with Christ. There is neither Jew nor Gentile, neither slave nor free, nor is there male and female, for you are all one in Christ Jesus.

—GALATIANS 3:26–28

ONE OF OUR favorite days at our church is a yearly outreach day we call Duck Commander Day. There are always several who wear camouflage clothing on any given Sunday, but on this particular Sunday, everyone is asked to wear camo, and most do! I know of several older ladies (older than me!) who went down to the sporting goods store on a Saturday to buy their first camo outfit! It makes us so proud! The best thing about this is that we are all clothed the same. There's no rich or poor, upscale or downscale, good or bad; we're all the same. This is a great illustration of what we are when we are clothed with the blood of Jesus Christ. We're all one!

Prayer

Our gracious God, we are so blessed to be able to find unity and equality in the blood of Your Son, Jesus Christ. Forgive us when we think more highly of ourselves than we should and when we look down on our fellow Christians. Through Christ we pray, amen.

—Miss Kay

April 28

Renewed Love

Place me like a seal over your heart, like a seal on your arm; for love is as strong as death, its jealousy unyielding as the grave. It burns like blazing fire, like a mighty flame. Many waters cannot quench love; rivers cannot sweep it away. If one were to give all the wealth of one's house for love, it would be utterly scorned.

—SONG OF SONGS 8:6–7

I LOVE TO USE this verse at weddings just before the rings are exchanged. In this passage Solomon paints such a great picture of the power of love and the symbols that represent that love. When my wife and I renewed our vows a few years back, we exchanged new rings, as well, to symbolize a new beginning in our marriage. Sometimes love can get lost and has to be found again and renewed and recommitted. The power of human love is one of the greatest forces found on earth, and when nurtured, it can bring joy that would never seem possible.

Prayer

Father, we thank You today for those we love. Give us the ability to forgive those we love and help those whom we have hurt forgive us, as well. Thank You for being and inspiring love in us. Thank You for sending Your Son to save us. Through Him we pray, amen.

—Al

APRIL 29

HONEST LIPS

An honest answer is like a kiss on the lips.

—PROVERBS 24:26

FIFTEEN YEARS AGO, this verse came to mean a lot to me and my husband, Alan. Through hard times in our past, I had learned a bad habit (sin) of being dishonest. I had so many skeletons in my closet, and I didn't want to or know how to clean them out. One day while I was meditating on God's Word, I came across this verse. It showed me that when I was honest with Alan, it was as refreshing as a kiss on his lips. It also reminded me that if I want to be physically kissed, I must be honest with him—because who wants to kiss lying lips? My life completely turned around when I decided to be honest with myself, with God, and with my husband. It really is refreshing to kiss "honest" lips.

Prayer

My God and Father, You know that dishonesty was a struggle for me for many years, but You gave me the courage to stand up and face my sin and embrace honesty. While we all struggle with our sinfulness, we know You are always honest with us and that we must strive to be honest with You and others. Thank You for Your forgiveness. In Jesus' name, amen.

—*Lisa*

April 30

Jesus All the Time!

We have renounced secret and shameful ways; we do not use deception, nor do we distort the word of God. On the contrary, by setting forth the truth plainly we commend ourselves to everyone's conscience in the sight of God. . . . The god of this age has blinded the minds of unbelievers, so that they cannot see the light of the gospel that displays the glory of Christ, who is the image of God. For what we preach is not ourselves, but Jesus Christ as Lord, and ourselves as your servants for Jesus' sake.

—2 CORINTHIANS 4:1–5

WHAT CAN I say? Tell your neighbor about Jesus at work, at play, in the duck blind, in the boat, on the archery range, on the shooting range, on the open range, or in your apartment. Jesus is number one—all the time! Every time! We all together as God's people represent Jesus wherever each of us is.

Prayer

Give us boldness with no retreat, Father. It is a wicked world we live in. It always has been. Give us power, give us strength, give us courage, give us one mind—*Yours*! Amen.

—*Phil*

May

May 1

Football Lessons

I can do all this through him who gives me strength.

—PHILIPPIANS 4:13

I AM PRETTY TALL for my age, so all the football coaches at school really wanted me to play football. At first I didn't like football because it's a lot of hard work and it gets very hot in Louisiana. When I get tired and discouraged, I remember this verse, and it gives me strength to keep practicing and working hard. I know that as I get older, I might get in situations that will be even harder than football, like friends who might tempt me to do things I know I shouldn't do. When that happens, I will be able to find the strength to say no because God will be on my side cheering me on. This verse promises me that. Whether it's football, schoolwork, or standing strong against sin, God will give me the strength.

Prayer

Father, I thank You for standing beside me and helping me to be strong. I want to be able to stand up for You and to tell others about what You have done for me. Help me to always look to You, amen.

—*Will*

Blessings of Adoption

But we must always thank God for you, brothers loved by the Lord, because from the beginning God has chosen you for salvation through sanctification by the Spirit and through belief in the truth.

—2 THESSALONIANS 2:13, HCSB

I LOVE THE REMINDER that God chose us from the beginning and that He is going to complete His transformation process through the Holy Spirit. He adopted us as children, and our job is to believe the truth. Our decision to adopt Will has been one of the greatest decisions of our lives. Adoption is not an easy process, and the fear of the unknown is always an issue, but the blessing far outweighs the burden. God feels the same way about us and knew all of this from the beginning, and yet, He still chose us. Decide today that you are going to accept God's gift of salvation and live it out to completion and become a co-heir with Christ. Choose truth, and live the abundant life that is promised.

Prayer

Dear Lord, thank You so much for adopting us even though we are not always grateful children. Help us to keep our eyes on You, our heavenly Father, instead of looking back into the ways of the world. We appreciate the blessings of our children and ask You to watch over them today. In Jesus' name, amen.

—*Korie*

MAY 3

FAITH IS AN INDIVIDUAL CHOICE

After that generation died, another generation grew up who did not acknowledge the Lord or remember the mighty things he had done for Israel. The Israelites did evil in the Lord's sight and served the images of Baal.

—JUDGES 2:10–11, NLT

THIS VERSE IS a powerful reminder that we can't live on the faith of other people. Our relationship with God is personal. I've had many godly role models in life, but I had to choose for myself to put my faith in Jesus. Even though I had great parents who loved God, I could not rely on their faith. These verses remind Korie and me of the tremendous responsibility of teaching our children the right things to help them build their own faith in God.

Prayer

Father, we thank You for our parents and grandparents and the faith they have passed on to us. Please help Korie and me, Lord, to be believers who pass on the wonderful faith we have in You. I pray for all five of my children and ask that You strengthen them as they develop their faith in You. In Jesus' name, amen.

—*Willie*

May 4

True Beauty

Charm is deceptive, and beauty is fleeting; but a woman who fears the LORD *is to be praised.*

—PROVERBS 31:30

AS I AGE, I am more aware of this verse than ever before. As a woman, I see wrinkles, crow's-feet, laugh lines, age spots, weight gain, etc. As a daughter of the Almighty, I am seen as beautiful, because I live for the Lord. Charm only lasts till someone gets to know the real you. Outward beauty is for the young or those who "get a little help" with the aging process. But a kind spirit, a servant heart, a respectful life—those are characteristics of the real "beauties." These beauties love the Lord, their families, and those who are less fortunate. They fear the Lord and keep His commandments. Seek to be this kind of beauty, not the kind you see on television or in magazines. Pattern your life after those you read about in the Bible or see living for Christ each day.

Prayer

Father, please help me heed my own words. Lord, I am guilty of caring more about my outward beauty than what You see in my heart. Help us to remember this verse and find our beauty in the things You place in our hearts and minds. In Your Son's name, amen.

—*Lisa*

MAY 5

MY BEST DECISION

I have been crucified with Christ and I no longer live, but Christ lives in me. The life I now live in the body, I live by faith in the Son of God, who loved me and gave himself for me.

—GALATIANS 2:20

TO DIE TO myself and to live for Christ is the most incredible thing I have accomplished in my forty-eight years on this earth. I made that decision when I was eighteen, and I have been living for Christ ever since. I wish I could say that every action was worthy of Him, but that would be a lie. But because of His life and death, I have the comfort of knowing that I don't have to be perfect, because He is!

Prayer

Father, I am so blessed to have lived in You for thirty years, and I consider it an honor to have died and been raised in Christ to live for Him. I pray for continual growth and for opportunities to help others find this new life. Through Christ I pray, amen.

—Al

MAY 6

Modesty Is a Two-Way Street

I also want the women to dress modestly, with decency and propriety, adorning themselves, not with elaborate hairstyles or gold or pearls or expensive clothes, but with good deeds, appropriate for women who profess to worship God.

—1 TIMOTHY 2:9–10

MANY MAY SEE this verse as being directed only at women. However, this verse also holds meaning for men, as well. Ladies, your bodies are gifts for your husbands, or eventual husbands if you're unmarried. Instead of flaunting or agonizing over your body, clothe yourself with righteousness and goodness. It will serve you better than fancy or skimpy clothes, as all men of God will recognize the attractiveness of a godly woman. Gentlemen, this verse also gives you an idea of what to look for in a wife, as well as how your daughters should present themselves. Eve was a gift to Adam, as wives are gifts to their husbands. Think of women not as objects of lust, but as vessels of God's love for you. Don't forget, women are made in God's image as well, an image that deserves respect. Modesty is a two-way street and requires cooperation and respect on both sides.

Prayer

Father, clothe me in Your love. Help me see myself and others in Your image, so that one day I may see Your face. In Jesus' name I pray, amen.

—*Alex Robertson Mancuso*

MAY 7

IF CHRIST HAS NOT BEEN RAISED . . .

For if the dead are not raised, then Christ has not been raised either. And if Christ has not been raised, your faith is futile; you are still in your sins. Then those also who have fallen asleep in Christ are lost. If only for this life we have hope in Christ, we are of all people most to be pitied. But Christ has indeed been raised from the dead, the firstfruits of those who have fallen asleep.

—1 CORINTHIANS 15:16–20

WHAT GOOD WOULD it do you or me if Jesus removed our sins but didn't solve our grave problem? If there is no resurrection—if there is no life with Him after death—all hope is lost! Listen . . . if there is no resurrection from the dead, I'd be going to duck hunt . . . a lot! I would probably neglect the important people in my life, thinking only of myself. If there is no resurrection, you could do whatever you want—as for me, I'd be staying in the woods! But as the scripture above proclaims, Christ *has* been raised. And that changes everything.

Prayer

Thanks, Father, for the glorious resurrection of Your Son and for the promised resurrection of all those whose faith is in Him! I live my life as a reflection of my faith in that fact. Amen.

—*Phil*

May 8

Godly Moxie

Jephthah the Gileadite was a mighty warrior. . . . Jephthah fled from his brothers and settled in the land of Tob, where a gang of scoundrels gathered around him and followed him. Some time later, when the Ammonites were fighting against Israel, the elders of Gilead went to get Jephthah from the land of Tob. "Come," they said, "be our commander, so we can fight the Ammonites."

—JUDGES 11:1–6

YOU MIGHT THINK the story above is a strange one for me to write about, because our son Jeptha (Jep) may not seem to have a lot in common with this fellow. But when you take a closer look, there are some real similarities. Both Jeps ran around with a "gang of scoundrels" for a while, and both stepped up to the plate to do the right thing when challenged. Even though our Jep came from a Christian home, he had some rough years. Now he's a godly man, a great husband, and a loving father. Judge Jephthah had the right moxie when Israel needed a warrior who would lead them. No matter how strong or weak our family heritage may be, our ability to continue the spiritual battle will make us a valuable commodity when the fur flies.

Prayer

Lord, grant all my boys and their families—and all these readers—the ferocity to fight for You. Through Christ, amen.

—*Miss Kay*

May 9

Return Blessing for Insult

Do not repay evil with evil or insult with insult. On the contrary, repay evil with blessing, because to this you were called so that you may inherit a blessing.

—1 PETER 3:9

As I've mentioned before, our Mia was born with a cleft lip and palate and has scarring on and above her lip. But she is surrounded by close family and friends who treat her like everyone else. One time, there was a child from another school who made fun of Mia in front of her friends, and she ran to us in the bleachers, buried her head in my lap, and cried. When her friends saw her reaction, they came to her rescue, telling me exactly what they were going to say to this girl and how they were going to say it. I appreciated their protection of my daughter, but I instructed them to let it go. They realized that if they were mean to this girl, they would be doing the same thing to her that she did to Mia. This was a poignant moment for all of us.

Prayer

Lord, please help quench the desire I have to lash out at people who insult me or my child. I know that You had to look the other way so many times when people insulted, laughed at, made fun of, and ultimately killed Your Son. Let me always look to You and Your example of mercy and forgiveness.

—*Missy*

MAY 10

"FACIAL" PROFILING

"The Son of Man came eating and drinking, and they say, 'Here is a glutton and a drunkard, a friend of tax collectors and sinners.' But wisdom is proved right by her deeds."

—MATTHEW 11:19

MY FAMILY HAS always been targets of judgments and "facial" profiling. It comes with our wardrobe and beards. We have been viewed as homeless, caveman-commercial stars, dangers to society, and country music singers. You realize that Jesus had a similar problem because he constantly hung out with nonreligious people and obviously had a reputation based on innuendo and judgments. It is difficult not to respond to negative chatter, but you have to realize that right actions speak louder than wrongful words and profiles. Jesus proved that more than anyone else by always doing what was right, and His unselfishness saved the world and gave us hope.

Prayer

God, I thank You for giving Your Son for us. Your holiness and ability to know the heart surpass our understanding. Help us not to sit in Your chair but focus on actions that bring You glory.

—*Jase*

MAY 11

COURAGEOUS LIVING

"Be strong and courageous, because you will lead these people to inherit the land I swore to their ancestors to give them. Be strong and very courageous. . . . Then you will be prosperous and successful."

—JOSHUA 1:6–8

FEAR ENSLAVES AND confines us. Anxiety and worrying can devour our minds and take over our thoughts. But God tells us not to fear and to be strong and courageous. God wants us to lay our fears aside so we can have a life filled with things that are pleasing to Him. Don't think of being strong and courageous as being a hero or saving someone's life, think of it as doing the little things. Like maybe paying for someone's coffee at Starbucks or helping an elderly lady at the gas pump or saying hello to someone in the hallway at school or the office. God needs you to be strong and courageous through the little things day by day.

Prayer

Lord, help us to focus on You today and not live in fear. Help me to realize that through You, I can be strong and courageous. Help me to see that Your love towers over all fears and dangers of this life. I love You. Amen.

—Cole

May 12

Liberty and Law

It is for freedom that Christ has set us free. Stand firm, then, and do not let yourselves be burdened again by a yoke of slavery.

—GALATIANS 5:1

WE AMERICANS LOVE our liberty! But we love our laws too. It is an interesting twist. We want to be "law-abiding citizens," but we also want to be free from the tyranny of too much government. Hey, liberty was the battle cry of our founding fathers. But we gotta remember that the struggle between law and freedom is also found in our spiritual walk. Christians love their freedom, but they also love their rules. We want to honor the laws of God, but we want freedom from the burden of trying to keep them flawlessly on our own. In Christ, we have the answer to both. Jesus sets us free from the burden of perfect obedience through His perfection, and He guides us to a better life by challenging us to live honorably, like He lived.

Prayer

We thank You, O God, for freedom and for law. Your laws are good, and we want to live by them, but sometimes we fall flat on our faces. We thank You for Your Son's perfect life. Through Him, amen.

—*Si*

May 13

(May 13–15 is a special series on Job)

1: "Take Your Best Shot!"

One day the angels came to present themselves before the Lord, and Satan also came with them. The Lord said to Satan, "Where have you come from?" Satan answered the Lord, "From roaming throughout the earth, going back and forth on it." Then the Lord said to Satan, "Have you considered my servant Job? There is no one on earth like him; he is blameless and upright, a man who fears God and shuns evil."

—JOB 1:6–8

THE ONLY THING more frightening to me than knowing the devil is prowling around looking for people is the idea that God sometimes points out His guys that the devil may have missed! Satan never went for Job because he didn't think he had a shot with him, but God put so much trust in Job that He basically said, "Take your best shot!" Do you think God would say "Take your best shot" with you or me? Probably should make us think . . .

Prayer

Father, we pray for integrity and recognition as Your children. Forgive us when we aren't easily recognized as Your followers. We pray for patience as we allow You to complete Your work in us as You did in Job, so many years ago. We pray this through Christ, amen.

—*Jep*

2: THE LORD GIVES AND TAKES AWAY

At this, Job got up and tore his robe and shaved his head. Then he fell to the ground in worship and said: "Naked I came from my mother's womb, and naked I will depart. The LORD gave and the LORD has taken away; may the name of the LORD be praised." In all this, Job did not sin by charging God with wrongdoing.

—JOB 1:20–22

AFTER GOD'S GLOWING review of Job, Satan attacked him by stealing all of his possessions and killing his children in three separate incidents. Can you imagine getting hit with all that bad news at one time? What's even more amazing is Job's response. He responded by mourning his losses, worshipping and praising God, and not blaming God for his calamities! No wonder God trusted him so much!

Prayer

Father, I am humbled by Job's faith and perseverance. Please help me to trust You in my life, no matter what comes my way and no matter how Satan attacks me or my family. Blessed be Your name, O Lord. We worship You in good times and bad. We pray this through Jesus, our Lord, amen.

—Jep

May 15

3: Maintaining Integrity

"Skin for skin!" Satan replied. "A man will give all he has for his own life. But now stretch out your hand and strike his flesh and bones, and he will surely curse you to your face." The Lord said to Satan, "Very well, then, he is in your hands; but you must spare his life." So Satan went out from the presence of the Lord and afflicted Job with painful sores from the soles of his feet to the crown of his head. . . . His wife said to him, "Are you still maintaining your integrity? Curse God and die!" He replied, "You are talking like a foolish woman. Shall we accept good from God, and not trouble?" In all this, Job did not sin in what he said.

—JOB 2:4–10

When Job continued to praise God, Satan took it up a notch. He attacked Job's health and damaged his relationship with his wife—who was certainly still crushed over losing all ten of her children. But Job *still* maintained his integrity and endured the ridicule and sermonizing of his "friends."

Prayer

Father, I am amazed at Job's response in such horrible circumstances. I pray I will keep my troubles in the proper perspective and live up to his example. Through Jesus I pray, amen.

—*Jep*

May 16

A Merciful Heart

Who is a God like you, who pardons sin and forgives the transgression of the remnant of his inheritance? You do not stay angry forever but delight to show mercy.

—MICAH 7:18

I WANT TO BE that person who can show mercy and be happy while doing it. When someone does me wrong, it's sometimes hard to forgive and let go of the bitterness. But then I am quickly reminded of my own sins and how even though I didn't deserve forgiveness, I was given it. Time and time again my walk has faltered, and I am so grateful God doesn't keep a record of my sins. All sins are washed clean by His blood!

Prayer

Lord, please help me to show everyone the mercy You have shown to me. Help me to be quick to forgive. I pray that my heart is never hardened; please help me to show love and compassion to others.

—*Jessica*

May 17

Let God Take Control

Humble yourselves, therefore, under God's mighty hand, that he may lift you up in due time. Cast all your anxiety on him because he cares for you.

—1 PETER 5:6–7

THIS VERSE SOUNDS so easy but is oftentimes a very difficult thing to do. It is human nature to want to control everything in your life because it gives you a sense of security. I can say from personal experience that life gets much easier once you give in and let God take control—not only in the difficult times but in the good times as well. Let Him control *everything* in your life, and all of a sudden the stresses and burdens of everyday living disappear, and a peace comes over you. How awesome it is that we serve a God Who actually wants us to lay all of our burdens on Him? It is truly something we all take for granted.

Prayer

God, I give everything in my life to You, for I know You know the plans You have for me. I pray that I will be humble and not try to be in control and that I will lay all my burdens at Your feet—and leave them there.

—*Martin*

MAKING THE CHANGE

Submit yourselves, then, to God. Resist the devil, and he will flee from you.

—JAMES 4:7

AFTER I OBEYED the Gospel, Aunt Kay told me that if I wanted to change my life, I needed to change my friends. What she was really telling me in a nice way was that I had to get the sinful temptations out of my sight. It seems simple, but it takes some distance and a lot of time. Now the sinful temptations of my youth are becoming either less tempting or easier to avoid. Because I loved and trusted her, I did what she said. It took me some years, though, to understand the reasons for the changes she was pushing for. Now I live more of a submissive life, I recognize temptation and evilness more quickly, and the answers for the times of temptation seem easier to find.

Prayer

God, I thank You for Your love and guidance. Let me continue to know when I am tempted, and give me the strength and wisdom to resist the devil's charm. Keep Your spirit strong in me. Amen.

—*Jon Gimber*

May 19

Empowered by the Gospel

"Fellow Israelites, listen to this: Jesus of Nazareth was a man accredited by God to you by miracles, wonders and signs, which God did among you through him, as you yourselves know. This man was handed over to you by God's deliberate plan and foreknowledge; and you, with the help of wicked men, put him to death by nailing him to the cross. But God raised him from the dead, freeing him from the agony of death, because it was impossible for death to keep its hold on him."

—ACTS 2:22–24

The message of Christ was first proclaimed in the first century. This same message is our message in the twenty-first century. The sins are the same; the gospel message is the same. Read on from this text and see what the people who heard this message were told to do after they heard it (Acts 2:37–41). Go and do the same!

Prayer

Father, I thank You for the glorious gospel of Your Son. What a great act of kindness and love You provided for us through Jesus. Empower us through Your spirit to go forth with the message. Amen.

—Phil

MAY 20

TRUE TO OUR WORD

When Jephthah returned to his home in Mizpah, who should come out to meet him but his daughter, dancing to the sound of timbrels! She was an only child. Except for her he had neither son nor daughter. When he saw her, he tore his clothes and cried, "Oh no, my daughter! You have brought me down and I am devastated. I have made a vow to the LORD that I cannot break."

—JUDGES 11:34–35

JUDGE JEPHTHAH MADE a vow to God that he would sacrifice whatever came out of his door first, if God would grant him victory over his enemies. He held true to his word, even though it cost him something so dear. What a great reminder of the importance of integrity as well as caution. We should be very careful when making vows and always be prepared to maintain our integrity, especially when it costs us something that is important.

Prayer

Father, we want to be trustworthy men and women of our word. We take every vow set before You very seriously and we pray for integrity, honesty, and courage to fulfill every promise we make. We thank You for always keeping Your word and for sending Your Son to provide us with salvation. It is through Him we pray, amen.

—*Al*

May 21

Whatever It Takes

When they could not find a way to do this because of the crowd, they went up on the roof and lowered him on his mat through the tiles into the middle of the crowd, right in front of Jesus. When Jesus saw their faith, he said, "Friend, your sins are forgiven."

—LUKE 5:19–20

OUR WORLD IS full of people in need. This man's friends cared enough about him and his needs to bring him to the one person they knew of who could help their friend. They cared so much about him they would not be deterred when they couldn't get in the door; they figured out a way to get to Jesus. There are a lot of people who are just like this paralytic—and we need to be a friend who will grab a corner of a mat and get them to Jesus, whatever the cost. Jesus is still the great physician and is still in the healing business, both physically and spiritually!

Prayer

Lord, help me to be a friend who is willing to do what it takes to bring people to You and to care for the people in need all around me. Help me have a faith that makes a difference. In Jesus' name, amen.

—Willie

May 22

Blessings in Burdens

As you know, it was because of an illness that I first preached the gospel to you, and even though my illness was a trial to you, you did not treat me with contempt or scorn. Instead, you welcomed me as if I were an angel of God, as if I were Christ Jesus himself.

—GALATIANS 4:13–14

THE APOSTLE PAUL had a strange way of looking at illness! He seemed to think it was normal that his illness is what God used to put him in contact with the Galatian church. I'm not sure I've gotten to that mind-set yet. I'm a pretty healthy guy, but I did have a heart attack a few years back, and I didn't like it very much. And another thing I find interesting here: the Galatians seemed to be okay with whatever burden came with Paul's illness because his illness is what allowed them to receive his message. This scripture gives me something to shoot for so that I can seek to share God's message through the difficulties of my life.

Prayer

Father, please help me see life like You see it, and help me be open to the message You have for me to share or receive from others. I know there are blessings in burdens that we bear, and I want to find them and rely on them to help make a difference in this world. I have this hope because of my Lord Jesus. In Him I pray, amen.

—Si

MAY 23

NOT BY MY POWER

But the fruit of the Spirit is love, joy, peace, forbearance, kindness, goodness, faithfulness, gentleness and self-control. Against such things there is no law. Those who belong to Christ Jesus have crucified the flesh with its passions and desires. Since we live by the Spirit, let us keep in step with the Spirit.

—GALATIANS 5:22–25

MY FAVORITE THING about this passage is the wonderful truth that the fruit that pleases God doesn't come from me, but from His Spirit who lives in me! Many times in my life—especially when Phil was in his wild days—I felt like everything was on me and I had to do everything alone. But when I became a Christian, I began to learn that all I need to do is stay out of the Spirit's way and follow His lead and I am going to see all kinds of good things come from my life. What blessings we have in Christ!

Prayer

Father, I thank You so much for doing all the hard work in my life. Your Spirit can do amazing things through me when I get out of the way and follow His lead. I am honored to house Him and ask forgiveness for when I stubbornly don't listen to Him. It is through Jesus I pray, with the help of the Spirit, amen.

—Miss Kay

A GOD OF RELATIONSHIP

Then the man and his wife heard the sound of the LORD God as he was walking in the garden in the cool of the day, and they hid from the LORD God among the trees of the garden.

—GENESIS 3:8

HOW COMFORTING IT is to know that we have a God who wants to have a relationship with us. He wants this relationship so much that He took evening walks with some of our ancestors—Adam and Eve. People, we are here on *purpose*. God wants to be with us! Why do we keep hiding from Him?

Prayer

Father, help us realize that it's no accident that we are here and that You love us and want us near You. Help us to seek You out and not hide from You. In Your name, amen.

—*Godwin*

May 25

Put Anger Away

Get rid of all bitterness, rage and anger, brawling and slander, along with every form of malice. Be kind and compassionate to one another, forgiving one another, just as God in Christ forgave you.

—EPHESIANS 4:31–32

WE'VE ALL HAD our issues with anger. Some more intense than others, but we still deal with anger, no matter to what degree. What God says is simple: "Let it be put away from you." The best remedy that I have found for anger is prayer. Pray for God to take it away every chance you get. Pray for the person who made you angry and forgive them for their transgressions. God has forgiven us and He expects us to forgive others.

Prayer

Father, I pray You take this anger from me and help me to keep from getting angry in the future. I know that You despise it, and I want to please You on a daily basis. I pray for those who have wronged me and that You grant me strength to forgive and love them as You command. Thank You for forgiving me and for the hope of eternal life through Jesus, in whose name I pray, amen.

—Jay Stone

MAY 26

JESUS IS THE WORD

In the beginning was the Word, and the Word was with God, and the Word was God. . . . Through him all things were made; without him nothing was made that has been made. In him was life and that life was the light of all mankind. The light shines in the darkness, and the darkness has not overcome it.

—JOHN 1:1–5

JESUS HAS BEEN with God since the very beginning. And in the passage above God explains His Son by saying that He is the *Word.* By this Word the world and all that's in it was created. By this Word, we are sheltered from the darkness—by Him we live. And now, we have the Word in a tangible form—the Bible. God has given us His written Word so that we can understand the very heart of God. The contrast between God's gift of Jesus and our selfishness in killing Him unfolds all too clearly in the Word. We all have the choice to live either in the light of God or in dark ignorance. We take our own power away when we keep our Bibles on a dusty shelf.

Prayer

Beloved Father, I want to live in Your light. Reveal the message of Your Word to me; shelter me in Your safety. Keep me from ignorance and darkness. I choose You!

—Lynda Hammitt

May 27

Armed for the Battle!

Put on the full armor of God, so that when the day of evil comes, you may be able to stand your ground, and after you have done everything, to stand. Stand firm then, with the belt of truth buckled around your waist, with the breastplate of righteousness in place, and with your feet fitted with the readiness that comes from the gospel of peace. In addition to all this, take up the shield of faith, with which you can extinguish all the flaming arrows of the evil one. Take the helmet of salvation and the sword of the Spirit, which is the word of God.

—EPHESIANS 6:13–17

LOOK AT OUR armor! We've been equipped with truth, righteousness, readiness, faith, salvation, and the Spirit—what more do we need? Once we are suited up, all God asks us to do is *stand.* If God is for us, who can be against us? Answer—*no one*! Every one of us is in a spiritual war every day of our lives! Arm yourselves fully, and go forth in the fight!

Prayer

Father, we thank You for heavily arming us. We need all the weapons You have given us. We always win because of You! Amen.

—*Phil*

May 28

Two for the Journey

Two are better than one, because they have a good return for their labor: If either of them falls down, one can help the other up. But pity anyone who falls and has no one to help them up! Also, if two lie down together, they will keep warm. But how can one keep warm alone? Though one may be overpowered, two can defend themselves. A cord of three strands is not quickly broken.

—ECCLESIASTES 4:9–12

One of the greatest blessings of marriage has been the friendship I have with Lisa. Our marital road has had a few bumps and potholes, but the journey has been sweet and fulfilling. My home is my refuge—mainly because my best friend lives there with me to share my ideas, laugh at my jokes, and protect me from the evil one.

Prayer

Father, I am grateful for all my friends, but especially my best friend and wife, Lisa. I thank You for guiding us both to a better relationship with You and for the strength the three of us share in our marriage. I am grateful for Christ. In His name, amen.

—*Al*

May 29

Knowing the Good

If anyone, then, knows the good they ought to do and doesn't do it, it is sin for them.

—JAMES 4:17

THIS IS A kind of catchall verse. When we don't know exactly where in the Bible to go for answers about how to live, this verse helps us see the light. Most people, even those of new or little faith, can spit out at least part of the Ten Commandments—and those give us a lot of guidance. But there are times when none of the ten or even the commands to "love your neighbor" and "love God with all your heart" seem to apply. These are the times that I go back to James 4:17. Knowing what good I need to do can involve anything—giving money; giving time; helping someone out; volunteering for something at work, church, or whatever. When I know what I should do and I don't do it, I am sinning. Tough to swallow, maybe, but this doesn't make it any less true.

Prayer

Father, keep me strong. Allow me to set aside my ambitions and justifications and simply keep You in my focus as I walk in this world. Let me see past my boundaries and know that I am serving You even when my service seems trivial. Focus my mind, my actions, and my future. In Christ, amen.

—*Jon Gimber*

MAY 30

What Does the Lord Require?

He has shown you, O mortal, what is good. And what does the LORD *require of you? To act justly and to love mercy and to walk humbly with your God.*

—MICAH 6:8

MICAH WRITES THIS simple truth in a context of worship and in the midst of a whole laundry list of what people bring to God to offer as sacrifices in worship of Him. It is very typical of human beings to want to impress by bringing a myriad of gifts to wow onlookers. What Micah so rightly challenges us to do is to bring God that which makes the most impact on the worshipper, as well as intended glory to the one Who is worshipped. To do the right thing, while treating people the right way, and the whole time maintaining humility in a walk with God is the simplest form of worship with the most profound impact on our lives and those we come in contact with.

Prayer

Today, God, we worship You with humble hearts and we pray for strength to live justly in our decisions and actions. Help us to be merciful and to walk as You would have us walk this day. We love You and thank You for Your gracious gift of Your Son, through Whom we pray, amen.

—*Jase*

May 31

We All Have the Same Origin

"The God who made the world and everything in it is the Lord of heaven and earth and does not live in temples built by human hands. And he is not served by human hands, as if he needed anything. Rather, he himself gives everyone life and breath and everything else. From one man he made all the nations, that they should inhabit the whole earth; and he marked out their appointed times in history and the boundaries of their lands. God did this so that they would seek him and perhaps reach out for him and find him, though he is not far from any one of us. 'For in him we live and move and have our being.' As some of your own poets have said, 'We are his offspring.' "

—ACTS 17:24–28

WELL, WE NOW know from this text who God is and who He not is. All of us, together, came from Adam, and I do not know what color he was. Never judge a man by the color of his skin. We all together are God's offspring. Love God and love your neighbor—all of them!

Prayer

Lord, help us to love all men as You do. Help us to love each other as You have loved us.
Amen.

—*Phil*

JUNE

JUNE 1

God Is Our Refuge

He that dwelleth in the secret place of the most High shall abide under the shadow of the almighty. I will say of the Lord, He is my refuge and my fortress: my God; in him will I trust.

—PSALM 91:1–2, KJV

I HAVE A FRIEND who leads a Bible-based drug recovery ministry in his church, and he based the ministry on these verses. He was an addict himself who received salvation and deliverance in a similar program. It has been a great privilege and blessing to see God become a refuge for men and women in addiction. People who come in broken and destroyed by drugs and alcohol find a place where they can be sheltered. Then when they are taught the Word of God, it takes hold in many of their lives, they accept Him as Savior, and He becomes their refuge. Sometimes friends of theirs come to the program when they see how God has given them that refuge and fortress. It's an amazing thing to witness.

Prayer

Father, thank You for being that safe place for us, a fortress we can run to when we are overwhelmed. Thank You for making a place for us that we can put all our trust in. Amen.

—Willie

June 2

In Your Anger, Do Not Sin

"In your anger do not sin": Do not let the sun go down while you are still angry, and do not give the devil a foothold.

—EPHESIANS 4:26–27

You can be angry (some things we need to be angry about!). Just because you get angry doesn't mean you have to sin! Say someone curses you unjustly. Anger rises up. If you then curse the one who cursed you, you sin. If you hold your tongue, even though you are angry, you haven't sinned yet. But if you are insulted and maligned and in your anger you lash out with your fists—you sinned. What you need to do is hold your tongue and hold your fists. When you're cursed, don't lash out with your tongue or your fists—just walk away. However, if you walk away and you are still bitter toward that person, you have sinned. Do none of these things. Be angry, but *do not sin*! What is the solution? *Forgive* the one who cursed you. Forgive him and love him anyway. The weak lash out when offended. *The strong forgive.* Be strong in the Lord.

Prayer

Lord, help us to forgive. Amen.

—*Phil*

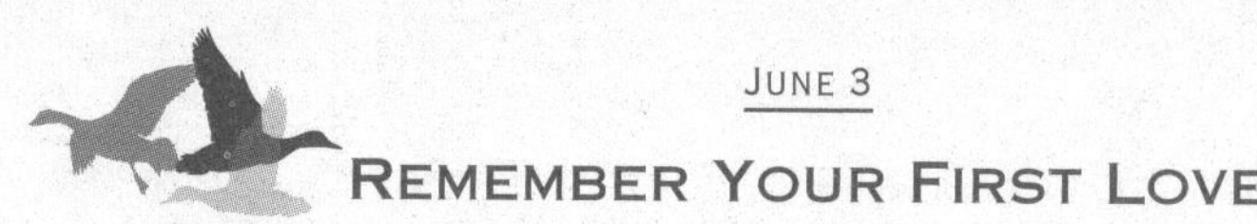

JUNE 3

REMEMBER YOUR FIRST LOVE

You have forsaken love you had at first. Consider how far you have fallen! Repent and do the things you did at first. If you do not repent, I will come to you and remove your lampstand from its place.

—REVELATION 2:4, 5

IN THE BOOK of Revelation, Jesus reveals seven challenges for seven churches to John, and those challenges are great reminders for churches today. In the first challenge to the Ephesians' church, Jesus challenges the church to remember their first love. It is so easy to forget what first brought us the greatest blessings. When Lisa and I were first married nothing seemed to matter except that we were together. As normal burdens, having children, and other things began to happen, we forgot that first love and our commitment. Repentance, renewal, and restoration brought us back and grounded us again. Churches are like that when they get away from the gospel message and start majoring in minors.

Prayer

Father, we ask for a constant reminder of our first love, especially the loving message of Jesus Christ. Forgive us, Father, when we forget and lose our way. We thank You for Jesus. In His name, amen.

—Al

June 4

Keeping It Simple

The acts of the flesh are obvious: sexual immorality, impurity and debauchery; idolatry and witchcraft; hatred, jealousy, discord, fits of rage, selfish ambition, dissensions, factions and envy; drunkenness, orgies, and the like. I warn you, as I did before, that those who live like this will not inherit the kingdom of God.

—GALATIANS 5:19–21

HEY, JACK, I'M kind of a simple guy, and I like it when things are spelled out in plain English. The passage above has always helped me, because of its simple description of sin. Some people try to "build a case" for why certain behavior is sinful, out of line, or wrong. They use a "connect the dots" kind of approach to show that this brother or that sister is out of line and needs to be corrected. Paul simply says sin is obvious, and then he lists the sins for us! That helps keep me on the straight and narrow.

Prayer

Father, thank You for being so clear about the kind of life You want us to live. Forgive me for the times I have ignored Your teachings and done things my own way. I want to be like You, and I want to help others do the same. In Jesus, I pray, amen.

—Si

JUNE 5

(JUNE 5–11 IS A SPECIAL SERIES ON PETER)

1: SNAP DECISION

[Jesus] said to Simon, "Put out into deep water, and let down the nets for a catch." Simon answered, "Master, we've worked hard all night and haven't caught anything. But because you say so, I will let down the nets." When they had done so, they caught such a large number of fish that their nets began to break. . . . When Simon Peter saw this, he fell at Jesus' knees and said, "Go away from me, Lord; I am a sinful man!" . . . Then Jesus said to Simon, "Don't be afraid; from now on you will fish for people." So they pulled their boats up on shore, left everything and followed him.

—LUKE 5:4–8, 10–11

AS WE GET to know Peter in this short series, we'll see that Peter was quite the impetuous fellow. He reacted to situations quickly—often without thinking—and he usually made snap decisions. His impetuous nature frequently got him into trouble, but the snap decision to leave all behind and follow Jesus was a good one. Peter's life would change forever because of this meeting with Christ.

Prayer

Father, help us in the decisions we are faced with daily, and help us to choose wisely—even when we have to choose quickly. We thank You for our appointment with Jesus that changes our destiny forever. Through Him, amen.

—*Jase*

JUNE 6

2: Heavenly Understanding

"But what about you?" he asked. "Who do you say I am?" Simon Peter answered, "You are the Messiah, the Son of the living God." Jesus replied, "Blessed are you, Simon son of Jonah." . . . From that time on Jesus began to explain to his disciples . . . that he must be killed and on the third day be raised to life. Peter took him aside and began to rebuke him. "Never, Lord!" he said. "This shall never happen to you!" Jesus turned and said to Peter, "Get behind me, Satan! You are a stumbling block to me; you do not have in mind the concerns of God, but merely human concerns."

—MATTHEW 16:15–17, 21–23

THIS EXCHANGE SUMS up Peter's years with Jesus. So loyal and insightful one minute and so led by worldly standards the next. Peter thought Jesus was bringing an earthly kingdom, with all the power and control that comes with it. We, too, sometimes expect Jesus to give us things He never intends for us. His vision for us is a heavenly one, and in the end far exceeds the vision we have for ourselves. We're a lot like Peter, aren't we? On fire one minute and then as cold as ice the next . . .

Prayer

Father, we ask for Your patience with us as we run so hot and cold. Forgive us our misconceptions and enlighten us to Your purposes. Through Jesus, amen.

—*Jase*

JUNE 7

3: Jesus Knew His Divine Purpose

So Judas came to the garden, guiding a detachment of soldiers and some officials from the chief priests and the Pharisees. They were carrying torches, lanterns and weapons. . . . Then Simon Peter, who had a sword, drew it and struck the high priest's servant, cutting off his right ear. . . . Jesus commanded Peter, "Put your sword away! Shall I not drink the cup the Father has given me?"

—JOHN 18:3, 10–11

PETER WAS ALWAYS ready to act, and you just know that the sight of his fellow disciple Judas betraying Jesus to the authorities had to stoke his impetuous fire. The fact that he was armed and struck one of the authorities showed that he was ready to die in a fight to defend Jesus. How shocked he must have been when Jesus gave up without a fight and even healed the wounded "enemy." To be like Christ, we have to give up our natural impulses, and that is not easily done. Jesus didn't come to this earth to overthrow, but to overcome by yielding to the divine plan of sacrifice, salvation, and servitude!

Prayer

Father, forgive us when we think we know better than You how to live our lives and battle the evil one. We thank You for Jesus' serving life and sacrificial death, and we pray through Him, amen.

—*Jase*

June 8

4: The Temptation of Cowardice

"You aren't one of this man's disciples too, are you?" she asked Peter. He replied, "I am not." . . . Meanwhile, Simon Peter was still standing there warming himself. So they asked him, "You aren't one of his disciples too, are you?" He denied it, saying, "I am not." One of the high priest's servants . . . challenged him, "Didn't I see you with him in the garden?" Again Peter denied it, and at that moment a rooster began to crow.

—JOHN 18:17, 25–27

THE VERY MAN who was ready to defend Jesus when he was apprehended now denied being His follower—just a few hours later. What happened? Fear has a way of ambushing us with little warning. Boldness can turn cowardly in the blink of an eye. Jesus had told Peter he would do this, but Peter vowed that he never would. What a lonely, shameful feeling to realize you have become what you vowed you never would be.

Prayer

Father, please forgive us when we deny being Your followers by our words, our actions, or our thoughts. We feel so ashamed when we give in to fear, and we pray for confidence and boldness to declare our allegiance to You. In His name, amen.

—*Jase*

JUNE 9

5: Bewildered and Confused

Mary Magdalene went to the tomb and saw that the stone had been removed from the entrance. So she came running to Simon Peter and the other disciple, the one Jesus loved, and said, "They have taken the Lord out of the tomb, and we don't know where they have put him!" So Peter and the other disciple started for the tomb. Both were running, but the other disciple outran Peter and reached the tomb first. He bent over and looked in at the strips of linen lying there but did not go in. Then Simon Peter came along behind him and went straight into the tomb.

—JOHN 20:1–6

WHAT A MISERABLE three days Peter must have had after he denied knowing Jesus. Can you imagine hearing that crowing rooster—the one that Jesus predicted—and then seeing Jesus' disappointed face across a courtyard? His Lord had died and he was lost, lonely, and empty. When he got the word that Jesus' body was not in the tomb, he must have been both hopeful and bewildered. What did it all mean and what would Jesus say to him, after what he had done?

Prayer

Father, we pray that You lift the burdens we carry when we are bewildered and afraid. We ask for vision to see Your plans. Through Jesus we pray, amen.

—Jase

JUNE 10

6: The Blessing of Restoration

"I'm going out to fish," Simon Peter told them, and they said, "We'll go with you." So they went out and got into the boat, but that night they caught nothing. Early in the morning, Jesus stood on the shore, but the disciples did not realize that it was Jesus. He called out to them, "Friends, haven't you any fish?" "No," they answered. He said, "Throw your net on the right side of the boat and you will find some." When they did, they were unable to haul the net in because of the large number of fish. Then the disciple whom Jesus loved said to Peter, "It is the Lord!" As soon as Simon Peter heard him say, "It is the Lord," he wrapped his outer garment around him (for he had taken it off) and jumped into the water.

—JOHN 21:3–7

JUST LIKE THE first time Peter met Jesus, a miraculous catch of fish reminded Peter who he was destined to follow. Peter had lost his way, but our gracious and loving Lord restored their relationship, and Peter rededicated his life to Him. Once reengaged, Peter would fulfill his destiny in Christ!

Prayer

Father, we thank You for second and two hundred twenty-second chances! We are so sorry we lose our way, but we praise You for using weak vessels to deliver Your message of hope. Through Christ, amen.

—*Jase*

JUNE 11

7: PURPOSE FULFILLED!

Peter stood up with the Eleven, raised his voice and addressed the crowd: "Fellow Jews and all of you who live in Jerusalem, let me explain this to you; listen carefully to what I say. . . . Jesus of Nazareth was a man accredited by God to you by miracles, wonders and signs, which God did among you through him, as you yourselves know. This man was handed over to you by God's deliberate plan and foreknowledge; and you, with the help of wicked men, put him to death by nailing him to the cross. But God raised him from the dead, freeing him from the agony of death, because it was impossible for death to keep its hold on him."

—ACTS 2:14, 22–24

I CAN'T HELP BUT think that Jesus was very proud up in heaven when Peter stood up on the Day of Pentecost and proclaimed the very first gospel sermon. All of the doubts, triumphs, fears, and defeats combined to make Peter a passionate spokesman for Christ. Peter wasn't perfect, but he allowed Jesus to redeem him and release him on a mission of proclaiming the gospel! The example of Peter gives all of us hope for restoration and fulfillment of our divine purpose—even though we are very human and extremely flawed.

Prayer

Father, we thank You for our mission to embrace, live, and share the good news of Your Son, Jesus. Through Him we pray, amen.

—*Jase*

JUNE 12

ROOTED IN GOD'S TEACHINGS

So then, just as you received Christ Jesus as Lord, continue to live your lives in him, rooted and built up in him, strengthened in the faith as you were taught, and overflowing with thankfulness. See to it that no one takes you captive through hollow and deceptive philosophy, which depends on human tradition and the basic principles of this world rather than on Christ.

—COLOSSIANS 2:6–8

THIS IS A great reminder to hold fast to our roots, which are in Christ Jesus. This reminds me not only of my dad but also my grandpa, who used to read me Bible stories when I was a child. He would teach me about Christ and was also guarding me against the world's empty and deceptive philosophy. We have to stay on guard against the evils of this world and be thankful that Jesus chose us to be *His* children.

Prayer

Dear God, help us to be overflowing with thankfulness as we live our lives. I want people to know I'm a son of Yours and not caught up in the human traditions of this world. I pray that my family and I remain firmly rooted in You and Your principles and continue to be built up in Christ Jesus.

—*Jep*

JUNE 13

THE CHOICE TO PROTECT

For you created my inmost being; you knit me together in my mother's womb. I praise you because I am fearfully and wonderfully made; your works are wonderful, I know that full well. . . . Your eyes saw my unformed body; all the days ordained for me were written in your book before one of them came to be.

—PSALM 139:13–16

THIS IS ONE of the greatest pro-life passages in the Bible. Here, David reminds us that God had his hand in our development from the moment of conception and that the safest place for any human being should be in his or her mother's womb. I am so very thankful for every one of my children and grandchildren and can't imagine life without a single one of them. God's hand was creatively involved with those "unformed" little bodies as He carefully "wove" them together in the safety of their mothers' wombs. God has a special plan for every one of us, and that plan began when our life began.

Prayer

Father, I am grateful for the protection I received in my mother's womb and for the life I have led to this point. I pray for those struggling today with the life-changing choice between abortion and protection. Please guide them to protect. I humbly ask Your blessing on all those folks today, through Jesus, my Lord, amen.

—*Miss Kay*

JUNE 14

SPIRITUAL HUNGER PANGS

Jesus answered, "It is written: 'Man shall not live on bread alone, but on every word that comes from the mouth of God.' "

—MATTHEW 4:4

AROUND OUR HOUSE, we love to eat a great meal. And as you have seen on *Duck Dynasty,* there is always a spread of food at our family table. I have to admit that Willie is the main reason for the spreads at our house! At the end of the meal, when everyone pushes back, there are usually only crumbs left. What about you? Do you and your family love to eat? Well, one thing we love even more than a traditional family meal is when we eat from the Bread of Life. Worship of God is the most important part of our week. Our busy days are just like your busy days; we have to make it a point to feast on the Word of God, to attend worship services, to sing praises to God. No, we do not live on bread alone; we live on God's Word.

Prayer

Jesus, thank You for giving us food to eat and allowing us to enjoy it, but we thank You even more for the Word that fills our spiritual hunger. Continue to give us hunger pains for Your Word. In Your precious name I pray, amen.

—*Korie*

June 15

Sharing Grows Understanding

I pray that your partnership with us in the faith may be effective in deepening your understanding of every good thing we share for the sake of Christ.

—PHILEMON 1:6

FOR A LONG time, I thought that I must become super wise in the Word, memorize lots of scripture, and understand Christ on so many levels—all before I could even begin to share my faith. But this scripture tells us the opposite. The more I share, the more I understand. We don't have to be Bible scholars to share Jesus. All we have to know is the story of His sacrifice and what it means to us. Once I realized that and started sharing that story with people, so much became clear to me. Relying on the power of His story and loving people enough to share it with them brings much clarity.

Prayer

Lord, the simple story of Your Son's sacrifice for me when I was such a sinner is so powerful. Help me to remember that the power is in that message and not in my speaking ability. Help me to look for opportunities to share that powerful message. I look forward to more and more understanding of You through Your Spirit.

—*Missy*

JUNE 16

LOVING DISCIPLINE

Whoever spares the rod hates his children, but the one who loves their children is careful to discipline them.

—PROVERBS 13:24

JEP AND I tried to discipline our children from the moment they could talk or walk. First it was a spat on the hand to keep them from doing anything dangerous, like putting their finger in a light socket. As they got older, it was to put a stop to little tantrums. Now the ages of our children are ten, eight, six, and four, and we work daily on treating each other kindly, showing love to each other, and when wronged by another, showing forgiveness. The key to effective discipline is doing it out of love for our children and a vision for who God wants them to be.

Prayer

Lord, I ask that Jep and I never waver in disciplining our children. Help us to always do this in a loving way, explaining the reason why they got in trouble in the first place. Help us to be quick to show forgiveness to our children. Help me to gratefully accept discipline from your hand in my own life. I thank you, Lord, for loving me and forgiving me.

—Jessica

June 17

Beautiful Words

. . . speaking to one another with psalms, hymns and songs from the Spirit. Sing and make music from your heart to the Lord, always giving thanks to God the Father for everything, in the name of our Lord Jesus Christ.

—EPHESIANS 5:19–20

I ALWAYS INTERPRET THIS verse to mean that we should use words that are praiseworthy to God. When I speak to someone, especially my brother or sister in Christ, I should use words that encourage, lighten their burdens, and promote godliness. I'm sure you've had conversations with people whose words were negative. No one likes to be around people whose words are not uplifting. When I speak, I want to speak with boldness, truth, and love. When difficult things need to be said or when sin needs to be addressed, it should be done out of love, not revenge or spite. Give thanks to God even for those we feel less inclined to love. Having an attitude of gratitude will shape the words that come out of our mouths.

Prayer

Lord, please remind each of us every day that You died for *everyone,* that You love everyone—even those difficult to love—and that Your eternal life is for everyone. Help us speak Your word to one another beautifully and in songs.

—*Lisa*

June 18

Do What It Says

Do not merely listen to the word, and so deceive yourselves. Do what it says.

—JAMES 1:22

A SIMPLE VERSE THAT describes a simple concept. Many ungodly people—people who are not doing what God says—can quote scripture. If getting into heaven was just a matter of rote memorization, there would be no purpose for faith, love, joy, gentleness, or any other spiritual fruit. The book of James goes on to tell us that one who hears the Word but doesn't live by it is like a man who looks at himself in the mirror, then goes away and immediately forgets what he looks like. Do you know what you look like? Of course you do! Do you know what your faith looks like? That's a harder question. We must not lack the courage of our convictions! The Bible is not just a book of stories; it is a book of instructions. We must follow them or the structure of our faith will fall to pieces.

Prayer

Father, please grant me the courage to act on the principles that I find in Your Word. Grant me the power and wisdom to do what You have told me is righteous and good. Thank You for laying it out for me and for making it easy for me to understand what I must do to spread Your love and mercy. Because of Jesus I pray, amen.

—Alex Robertson Mancuso

JUNE 19

A New Me

You were taught, with regard to your former way of life, to put off your old self, which is being corrupted by its deceitful desires; to be made new in the attitude of your minds; and to put on the new self, created to be like God in true righteousness and holiness.

—EPHESIANS 4:22–24

AFTER I WAS born again, my old friends came calling. "Come on, Phil. Let's go drink a beer," they would say. What was my reply to them? I told them, "The one you boys are looking for is dead and he's been buried. This Phil is the *new* Phil." They looked at me like I was crazy. Why? They didn't understand that I was speaking of my new birth that occurred when I was baptized (read Romans 6:1–4). Those ole boys got away from me—quickly!

Prayer

Lord, I thank You for allowing us to be born again and to start over again by faith in the death, burial, and resurrection of Jesus and through our reenactment of that in water. Thank You for Your spirit, which You gave us at the time of our obedience to the gospel. In Jesus' name I pray, amen.

—Phil

June 20

God's Eternal Rescue Plan

The Lord Jesus Christ, who gave himself for our sins to rescue us from the present evil age, according to the will of our God and Father.

—GALATIANS 1:3–4

I HAVE MADE MANY leaps of faith through the years, especially launching new businesses and agreeing to be on different TV shows. I am constantly asking God to clarify His will for my life. The above verse is a simple reminder of what God wants me to remember the most. God's will is for all men to be delivered, to be rescued from death, to be saved, and to have an abundant, joyful life with Him for eternity. God's will is for us to be in heaven, but also for all to be delivered from the sin that would easily entangle us and make us ineffective in our Christian walk here in this life. I want to remember that God's will is for all people to be rescued and that He has chosen *us* to tell them where to find that rescue. Remembering this helps keep everything in perspective.

Prayer

Father, I want to walk in Your will and tell people every chance I get that there is a Savior Who has done all that needs to be done for them to be rescued. I pray for open hearts, and I pray this in the precious name of Jesus, amen.

—*Willie*

JUNE 21

GOD'S RENEWABLE ENERGY

Do you not know? Have you not heard? The LORD is the everlasting God, the Creator of the ends of the earth. He will not grow tired or weary, and his understanding no one can fathom. He gives strength to the weary and increases the power of the weak. Even youths grow tired and weary, and young men stumble and fall; but those who hope in the LORD will renew their strength. They will soar on wings like eagles; they will run and not grow weary, they will walk and not be faint.

—ISAIAH 40:28–31

AT MY AGE, this passage sounds really good! Not that I'm slowing down—I'm still so fast you can't even see my hands move. But I must admit that running and walking without growing tired has a real appeal—that's what I call "renewable energy," Jack! Renewable energy in our environment is a hot topic because of the expansion of mankind around the planet. There is a constant search for new ways to power our existence and our comfort. Isaiah says that truly a renewable energy source does exists—and the source of it is not in government programs but in the hands of God Almighty! Eternal, renewable energy by the Almighty; now that's good news for any century!

Prayer

Almighty God, we pray for Your power today to soar like eagles. We ask for this in Jesus' name, amen.

—Si

June 22

Test Your Credibility

If anyone thinks they are something when they are not, they deceive themselves. Each one should test their own actions. Then they can take pride in themselves alone, without comparing themselves to someone else.

—GALATIANS 6:3–4

THINKING TOO MUCH of ourselves and bragging to others about what we've done is not an admirable trait. I instantly recognize this weakness in others when I meet them and they start talking about their achievements and accomplishments and start dropping names of famous people they know. I never want to be that guy! I want to be humble and consistent and test my credibility by the life I live and the impact I have on other people. I don't mind telling people how great they are, but I will never say that about myself!

Prayer

Father, I pray that I will remain ever humble before You. Forgive me when I think I am something, because, in reality, I am nothing. I take pride in the fact that I know You, that I am surrounded by people who keep me humble, and that I always try not to compare myself to others. Thank You for Jesus, in whom I *am* something, amen!

—*Al*

JUNE 23

HONOR GOD WITH YOUR BODY

Flee from sexual immorality. All other sins a person commits are outside the body, but whoever sins sexually sins against their own body. Do you not know that your bodies are temples of the Holy Spirit, who is in you, who you have received from God? You are not your own; you were bought at a price. Therefore honor God with your bodies.

—1 CORINTHIANS 6:18–20

THIS CAN REALLY be a scary section of scripture because this really touches the lives of all Christians. With the way our world is today, it is so easy for us or our kids to get caught up in sexual sins. I think we can never be guarded enough when it comes to shielding ourselves, our spouses, or our kids from any kind of sexual temptation. I believe the way for us to overcome these hardships is to be open and honest with those closest to us and to rely on the Holy Spirit to guide us.

Prayer

Lord, I pray for my wife and kids and for myself that You protect us in our daily lives and keep our hearts and minds pure. I pray that we honor You with our bodies, knowing that *You* bought us at a price.

—Jep

June 24

Sweet Forgiveness

The teachers of the law and the Pharisees brought in a woman caught in adultery. They made her stand before the group. . . . When they kept on questioning [Jesus], he straightened up and said to them, "Let any one of you who is without sin be the first to throw a stone at her.". . . At this, those who heard began to go away one at a time, the older ones first, until only Jesus was left, with the woman still standing there. Jesus straightened up and asked her, "Woman, where are they? Has no one condemned you?" "No one, sir," she said. "Then neither do I condemn you," Jesus declared. "Go now and leave your life of sin."

—JOHN 8:3,7, 9–11

I JUST LOVE THIS story, don't you? I counsel a lot of women who have been in all kinds of situations and sin, and the message of Jesus' forgiveness is like a sweet balm to their hurting souls. When sin is exposed, we cringe at the thought of what other people will think and how they will react when they know about our ugliness. Jesus' approach was to remind her accusers that they, too, had sin in their lives. Aren't we glad that Jesus offers forgiveness? With that forgiveness comes a challenge to leave our sinful ways.

Prayer

Father, I thank You for loving us even though we have done rotten things. And thank You for not letting us stay in our sinful ways. Amen.

—*Miss Kay*

June 25

Faith to Get Out of the Boat

And it is impossible to please God without faith. Anyone who wants to come to him must believe that God exists and that he rewards those who sincerely seek him.

—HEBREWS 11:6, NLT

Faith is difficult to understand, and all believers must come to their own faith through their own journey. One way to strengthen your faith is to see the faith of others. Take a minute and read Matthew 14:22–32. Peter's faith is inspiriting. It's what got him out of the boat and into the water. He believed that Jesus could help him do the impossible. Peter "stepped" out in faith. As women, moms and daughters of the king, we have to "step" out in faith. Maybe it's a mission effort of letting go of a loved one or changing jobs—whatever it is, hold God's hand, and He will walk you through. *This* is what pleases the Lord.

Prayer

Dear Lord, as difficult as it is at times to keep the faith, please give me courage to keep on. Strengthen my faith each day by showing Yourself to me, and give me faith like Peter had to step out of the boat and walk to You. In Jesus' name, amen.

—*Korie*

June 26

The Washing of Rebirth

Jesus answered, "Very truly I tell you, no one can enter the kingdom of God unless they are born of water and the Spirit."

—JOHN 3:5

He saved us, not because of righteous things we had done, but because of his mercy. He saved us through the washing of rebirth and renewal by the Holy Spirit.

—TITUS 3:5

PUT THESE TWO texts together and the "when" of your new birth is very clear. Jesus saved us because of his mercy, and not by our good deeds, when we were washed (baptized) and when the Spirit was poured into us! This was all done through our faith in Him and His death, burial, and resurrection.

Prayer

Lord, thanks again for our new birth in Jesus! Amen.

—*Phil*

JUNE 27

PEACE OF MIND

My dear children, I write this to you so that you will not sin. But if anybody does sin, we have an advocate with the Father—Jesus Christ, the Righteous One.

—1 JOHN 2:1

I OFTEN NEED TO hear the message of this verse: I need to be reminded that when I *do* sin—and I will—that I have someone in heaven who is speaking to God on my behalf. Jesus actually comes to our defense! This confirms that He is God and we are not. There's no way we can live without sin; it is only by God's grace that we are saved. We can know for sure that Jesus has taken care of us where we couldn't. Grace . . . forgiveness, that's what brings you peace . . . peace of mind. Relax, you don't have to do anything; He has done it for us. I like knowing that God can do what I can't.

Prayer

Father, I thank You for the peace that You bring. Thank You for the cross. Thank You for Your grace and mercy. Thank You for defending us, and most of all, thank You for Jesus. In His precious name, amen.

—*Godwin*

June 28

Generosity over Judgment

So we fix our eyes not on what is seen, but on what is unseen, since what is seen is temporary, but what is unseen is eternal.

—2 CORINTHIANS 4:18

WE SERVE A God who reminds us when we are getting off track. The question is, are we smart enough to catch the lesson He is trying to teach us? For example, the other day I was at a gas station when a man approached me asking for money. At first I simply blew him off, as I cast judgment that he was probably not going to use the money for what he said he was going to use it for. As soon as he walked away, my stomach became knotted. God was working on me. Finally I realized that regardless of what he used it for, it was not my place to judge, and after all, it is just money. Once I gave him the money, he asked for my info so he could pay me back. I simply replied, "Pay it forward or put it in an offering plate," as I was trying to plant a seed in his heart. The money could be gone tomorrow, but God's love lasts forever.

Prayer

Father, help us to see people and situations as You see them. Help us to err on the side of generosity rather than judgment. Help us to remember that our heavenly reward far outweighs anything this world has to offer.

—Martin

JUNE 29

GOD IS THE REASON

In the same way, let your light shine before others, that they may see your good deeds and glorify your Father in heaven.

—MATTHEW 5:16

DUCK COMMANDER'S GROWTH has expanded our footprint from hunters to yuppies and everyone in between. Through all the changes, the constants have been our faith, attitudes, and respect for the Almighty. The expanse of Duck Commander has allowed us to enter into lives that we could have never reached with our duck calls alone. This was God's plan. Without Him, none of this could have been possible. We recognize this and honor this by trying to show God and His love to all those who care to look our way. We give God glory for what He has done, and He has blessed all who have been a part of this experience. Continuing to honor Him will lead to more blessings. God is the only one who knows where the future of Duck Commander will go; our job is to keep God as the focus of anything we do.

Prayer

God, we give glory to You in all that You have done in our lives. Thank You for Your blessings that You have laid upon us, and never let us lose sight of the meaning for all of this. Continue to let Your light shine through us wherever we go. Amen.

—*Jon Gimber*

June 30

Your Life as Worship

Therefore, I urge you, brothers and sisters, in view of God's mercy, to offer your bodies as a living sacrifice, holy and pleasing to God—this is your true and proper worship. Do not conform to the pattern of this world, but be transformed by the renewing of your mind. Then you will be able to test and approve what God's will is—his good, pleasing and perfect will.

—ROMANS 12:1–2

Most people think that if they "go to church" every time the doors are open, they have fulfilled their duty to God. That is why they refer to "going to church" as "worship services." Read this text carefully, and you will see God is saying that your body, your life—wherever you are—should be lived in totality as your spiritual worship. We, the body of Christ, individually and collectively, worship God whether we are interacting with our wife, our children, in the duck blind, at the supermarket, or at our work place. We are the salt of the earth and the light of the world. Be salt! Be light! Anywhere, everywhere, all the time! *That* is worshipping God in spirit and in truth. Do not be afraid!

Prayer

Lord, help us to glorify You as God wherever we are and whatever we are doing so that all can see Jesus through our lives on the earth. Amen.

—*Phil*

JULY

July 1

Only in God's Strength

Now finish the work, so that your eager willingness to do it may be matched by your completion of it, according to your means.

—2 CORINTHIANS 8:11

How many times have you started a plan to become a better person? Each time you might think that surely this time you are going to beat that one nagging sin, the one trait that just keeps you from being who you want to be. What holds you back? Why can't you conquer it? Perhaps it's because we all try to do big things with our little human strength. In other words, we focus on the problem instead of on the Creator who can solve our problem. Start this day fresh: focus on Jesus and ask Him to be the plan *and* the provider to get you where you need to be. Then you will be able to finish work!

Prayer

Gracious Lord, thank You for sticking with me every time I try to work in my own strength. I love You! Help me to focus on You, so that together, You working through me, we can complete this. In Jesus' name, amen.

—*Korie*

JULY 2

ANGELS AMONG US

Keep on loving each other as brothers and sisters. Do not forget to show hospitality to strangers, for by so doing some people have shown hospitality to angels without knowing it.

—HEBREWS 13:1–2

I HAVE THIS PASSAGE as a plaque on my living room wall. I love it, and I totally believe it. My husband was rescued by an angel in a rough time of his life. I know some folks who seem like angels, dwelling here on earth with us. You never know what someone's story is when you meet them. God sends people to us all the time who either need us or whom we need. I know that everyone I meet is either a current or potential brother or sister in Christ. God gives us our children, and we call them angels. Treat everyone with respect and care. God will send just the right person to you at just the right time. He loves us that much!

Prayer

Father, You give us life, love, and eternal life, and You always give us just what we need when we need it. Father, help us be that type of person to others. Help us to entertain others and show them the light of Your life. Thank You, Lord! Amen.

—*Lisa*

JULY 3

AN ETERNAL VIEW

He has delivered us from such a deadly peril, and he will deliver us again. On him we have set our hope that he will continue to deliver us.

—2 CORINTHIANS 1:10

PAUL WROTE THIS at a time when he was going through great physical trials as his life was being threatened on a continual basis while he preached in Asia. He was certain that he and his friends were going to face death there. Yet he kept preaching. His hope was not in this life but in the hereafter. God does not promise to deliver us from death on this earth, but He does promise to deliver us from *eternal* death. Paul's hope was real in that he knew he would live forever through Christ's sacrifice. What he didn't know was when his time on earth would end. Paul's hope prevailed over every threat, every curse, and every physical beating.

Prayer

Lord, thank You for the hope You gave us through Your Son, Jesus. Because He overcame death here on this earth, we have the hope of living with You forever. Help me to have the same perspective that Paul had, as he risked his life daily to further Your kingdom.

—Missy

JULY 4

THE GOOD IN ME

I say to the LORD, "You are my Lord; apart from you I have no good thing."

—PSALM 16:2

IT IS SELDOM helpful to compare ourselves to others. We feel either inferior or superior, and neither of those feelings is acceptable—and both are usually inaccurate. But when we compare ourselves to God, we *should* feel inferior. He is high above us, and without Him there is nothing good in us. Without Him only evil and selfishness remain. I want to stay humble to the reality of who I am in Christ and always remember that He is God and I am not.

Prayer

Lord, I know that without You I have nothing, no hope and no future. I pray that Your goodness will never leave me. Help me not to choose selfish desires. I thank You, Lord, for living in me; thank You for being all that is good in me.

—*Jessica*

July 5

Service Is Worship

Never be lacking in zeal, but keep your spiritual fervor, serving the Lord. Be joyful in hope, patient in affliction, faithful in prayer. Share with the Lord's people who are in need. Practice hospitality.

—ROMANS 12:11–13

DON'T BE A whiner, griper, or complainer. Be upbeat and joyful about what God has done for you. Through Jesus, you have been chosen to be one of the "eternal ones." Okay, so life is not fair! What else is new? Suck it up! You are a child of God. Bad things happen—to you, me, and the best of them! Be patient! God is with you. Be generous, no matter what—to God and your neighbor. Feed people the best food you can cook! Yeah, it's work, but remember—you are worshipping God by helping some poor soul or feeding your neighbor. Feeding sinners so you can share Jesus with them *is worship*. Practice this continually.

Prayer

Help us, Father, to put this text into practice. Amen.

—*Phil*

July 6

God Knows

Even the very hairs of your head are all numbered.

—MATTHEW 10:30

MY DAD OFTEN repeated this quote: "Some things are unknowable." But humans tend to want answers—especially to situations that do not make earthly sense. If you believe that God knitted you together (Psalm 139:13) and knows how many hairs are on your head, you have to realize that He is omniscient (all-knowing). He knows what would happen if something that didn't happen happened. We don't always know the answers in life, but we know the one Who does.

Prayer

God, You know me better than anyone else. Thank You for creating me and using me to make You known. Through Jesus, amen.

—*Jase*

JULY 7

DO WHAT'S RIGHT

But Daniel resolved not to defile himself with the royal food and wine, and he asked the chief official for permission not to defile himself this way.

—DANIEL 1:8

WHAT WISDOM FROM such a young man. How much trouble would people today save if they followed this example? First of all, he knew from the Word of God what was right and what was wrong. His family was gone, his fellow Israelites had given in—with the exception of three—and he didn't have many to rely on. Daniel and his friends knew what God expected and did it. They weren't rebellious or obnoxious; they were respectful of those in authority but determined to do what was right, and God moved on their behalf.

Prayer

Jesus, help me to be a person who is resolved to do right. Help me be a person who knows Your Word and follows it with an attitude that doesn't drive people away but that draws them to You. Amen.

—*Willie*

FIRM BUT LOVING

Do not withhold discipline from a child; if you punish them with the rod, they will not die. Punish them with the rod and save them from death.

—PROVERBS 23:13–14

I CAN DEFINITELY SAY that my mom and dad practiced this verse. I'm definitely not just talking about spankings; the key word in this text is "discipline." My wife and I try to be very consistent when disciplining our kids and know they will learn and become better kids by doing so. Disciplining with a firm but loving hand is what my parents practiced with me, and I now know that is what God wants me to do with my own children.

Prayer

Heavenly Father, help us look to You when disciplining our kids. Help us be patient and understanding but also firm and consistent. We want our kids to follow You all their lives, so help us guide them toward You.

—*Jep*

July 9

Out Loud and On Purpose

The purposes of a person's heart are deep waters, but one who has insight draws them out.

—PROVERBS 20:5

I HAD A GREAT friend named Charlie Murray who lived by the mantra "Live out loud and on purpose!" The Lord took him home at the young age of thirty-two, so he didn't have that long to live as he challenged others to, but the years he *did* have on earth, he lived his life for God. God has things He wants us to do, but without focus and purpose, we can easily miss what those are. Today, live out loud and on purpose for Christ!

Prayer

Father, we are so blessed to have a purpose to live for. Because You rescued us, we have a blessed mission to help rescue others. Lead us, Father, to live out Your purpose for us today. In Jesus' name I pray, amen.

—*Al*

July 10

The Strong Forgive

Bless those who persecute you; bless and do not curse.

—ROMANS 12:14

WHO IS THE stronger person when they are persecuted? Is it the one who curses the persecutor back? Is it the one who lashes out when offended? No! That is the weak person. The strong Christian forgives with no bitterness. The strong forgive, and they bless and pray for the persecutor. That is what Jesus did. And this is what we will do, if we follow His lead!

Prayer

Father, give us a heart of strength, with Your Spirit's help. Let us bless those who curse us and insult us. Help us understand what real spiritual strength is. Help us to see our actions are spiritual worship. It is through Jesus, our Lord and Savior, I pray, amen.

—*Phil*

July 11

New Things Coming!

And I heard a loud voice from the throne saying, "Look! God's dwelling place is now among the people, and he will dwell with them. They will be his people, and God himself will be with them and be their God. 'He will wipe every tear from their eyes. There will be no more death' or mourning or crying or pain, for the old order of things has passed away." He who was seated on the throne said, "I am making everything new!" Then he said, "Write this down, for these words are trustworthy and true."

—REVELATION 21:3–5

THAT'S WHAT I'M talking about, Jack! When I read the promises of that scripture, I'm amazed that those blessings are for me. This says that we will be physically restored to our living and loving God when our Savior returns. But these words are not written only to encourage us about the future, but also to remind us that we are God's people *now* and He is our God. I wouldn't believe it if I wasn't so sure it is true!

Prayer

Father, we are so excited about the hope of full restoration with You, with our Lord and brother, Jesus, and with the Holy Spirit. We can't hardly wait for the end of the old heaven and earth. Through Christ, with the help of the Spirit, I pray, amen.

—Si

July 12

A Dirty Towel

The evening meal was in progress, and the devil had already prompted Judas, the son of Simon Iscariot, to betray Jesus. Jesus knew that the Father had put all things under his power, and that he had come from God and was returning to God; so he got up from the meal, took off his outer clothing, and wrapped a towel around his waist. After that, he poured water into a basin and began to wash his disciples' feet, drying them with the towel that was wrapped around him.

—JOHN 13:2–5

ISN'T THAT AN amazing scene? Jesus knew that that ole Judas would betray Him, yet look at what He did. He got up and did the "lowly" work of a servant—He washed those disciples' feet, including Judas'! Jesus' best love was shown by serving, not sacrificing! Through His Son, God shows that a dirty towel is actually a more powerful symbol of his love than the cross. Now, I love serving people, but washing the dirty feet of someone I knew was maliciously betraying me—wow! I'm not so sure I could do that, but I hope I could.

Prayer

Father, today I ask for the humility and the ability to serve others rather than to be served. I thank You for the cross that saved me, but also for the dirty towel that shows me how to live a new life. I ask this prayer through Jesus' sacrifice and service, amen.

—*Miss Kay*

July 13

A Happy Life Now

For God so loved the world that he gave his one and only Son, that whoever believes in him shall not perish but have eternal life.

—John 3:16

Since my name is John Luke, I usually sign autographs with John 3:16 and Luke 9:23. John 3:16 is one of those verses that most kids have to memorize in Sunday school. It promises us that if we believe in Jesus, we won't die but will live eternally. But as Christians, we can't just live our lives waiting for the promise of heaven that will come after we die. If we live that way, we will miss the point of God's message. And there's so much more to our Christian walk than that. Jesus also said that He came so that we may have life to the fullest. God's plan for us includes a life that is exciting and full of adventure. If your daily walk with Jesus isn't producing a joyful spirit, you might need to read the scriptures more and be sure you are living your life according to His plans for you.

Prayer

Father, I pray for that joy-filled life that You have designed for me. Help me to face each day knowing You are in control and to show others I am a better person because of this. In His name I pray, amen.

—John Luke

JULY 14

WRITTEN FOR US!

For everything that was written in the past was written to teach us, so that through endurance taught in the Scriptures and the encouragement they provide we might have hope.

—ROMANS 15:4

THOUSANDS OF YEARS, over forty authors, and all the different cultures—that's what was involved in compiling the Bible we have today! There were four hundred years between the time the last prophet died and the New Testament. No Internet or texting or phones—but all those authors wrote in harmony. No incentive of payment, no collaboration, but they all agreed on the message of God. And they wrote it all for our benefit! Can you think of a time when even three people were together in the same room and all agreed with each other? The truth of God's Word is amazing!

Prayer

Father, thank You for verses like this one that let us know You are thinking of us and that Your Word is the truth. Thank You for Your love letter to us. In Your precious name, amen.

—*Godwin*

JULY 15

OTHERS BEFORE OURSELVES

Do nothing out of selfish ambition or vain conceit. Rather, in humility value others above yourselves.

—PHILIPPIANS 2:3

JESUS CHALLENGED US to do two things in our Christian walk: love God and love our neighbor. You can't truly love someone unless you put their best interests ahead of your own. Humans, by nature, are selfish. We have been since the beginning of time and always will be. It is something we have to deal with and overcome by leaning on God in times of struggle. I will say one of my greatest influences in life in this situation is Silas Robertson. The man never has a bad day, and there is truly not one malicious bone in his body. I often say if you were to cut his head open nothing but butterflies and rainbows would come out. Find that example in your life, and do your best to learn everything you can from it. You will be rewarded both on earth and in heaven.

Prayer

Almighty Father, help us to remember we are not here for ourselves, but we are here to serve You and help others come to know You.

—*Martin*

JULY 16

FAITH IN THE UNSEEN

Now faith is confidence of what we hope for, and assurance about what we do not see.

—HEBREWS 11:1

DO YOU EVER go to bed at night and wonder if the sun will rise tomorrow? Do you worry that your next breath will not come, or that the world will end before the day is over? Probably not. Most of us do not go about our lives expecting them to end at any moment. We anticipate tomorrow, next Friday, and the end of the year. The Lord expects this kind of faith in Him. He calls us to be sure, to be "certain of what we do not see." Can we see with our naked eyes distant galaxies? No, but we know they're there. The Lord says this is how our faith should be. Sure, certain, and unwavering. Faith is knowing that our God is working in our lives. Even though we can't see Him, we can see His good works and influence all around us. That is how we can be certain of what our eyes can't see.

Prayer

Lord, open my eyes. Allow me to see evidence of Your love in all things. I am certain You have a plan for my life, though I can't always see it. Thank You for faith and assurance. In Jesus' name I pray, amen.

—Alex Robertson Mancuso

JULY 17

JUMPING FOR JOY

"However, do not rejoice that the spirits submit to you, but rejoice that your names are written in heaven."

—LUKE 10:20

I REMEMBER WATCHING THE World Series when Kirk Gibson of the LA Dodgers hit a home run to beat the Oakland A's basically on one leg. I remember this more than other home runs because it took me a couple of days to get the cobwebs out of my head—I had jumped so high, I went straight into a functioning ceiling fan. Kirk limped around the bases, and the Dodgers went on to win despite that being his only at-bat of the series. It seemed magical, but so many times my team loses or my guy strikes out. If only we had the power of the Spirit and could find a way to summon the inner being of men and women on command. There are ups and downs in every sport, just like in life. Jesus gave His apostles "special powers," and as exciting as that must have been, He reminded them where true joy is found . . . a reserved place in heaven with your name on it.

Prayer

God, I thank You for promising me a place in heaven. Thank You for knowing me by name. Help me to distinguish temporary happiness from eternal joy, and help me keep things in proper perspective.

—*Jase*

July 18

The Love of a Father

Then the man and his wife heard the sound of the Lord God as he was walking in the garden in the cool of the day, and they hid from the Lord God among the trees of the garden.

—GENESIS 3:8

HOW MANY TIMES has this played out since the original sin? When I was a kid and broke one or more of the rules, Mom would tell me, "Just wait till your dad gets home." And in a stroke of genius, I would run and hide. But I always had to come out when Dad came to get me—and I would often try to blame one of the other guys, especially Jase. My kids have done the same thing: hide, then blame. We, like Adam and Eve, forget so quickly the character of a father. The love of a father will always send him into the trees to find his children. Even though the consequences of sin must be faced, we have to remember that our Father loves us.

Prayer

Father, thank You for coming and getting me when I was lost in sin. And even though there were consequences to my sin, You sent Your Son to take the punishment for me. By the blood of Jesus, amen.

—*Willie*

LAW-ABIDING CITIZENS

Let everyone be subject to the governing authorities, for there is no authority except that which God has established. The authorities that exist have been established by God. Consequently, whoever rebels against the authority is rebelling against what God has instituted, and those who do so will bring judgment on themselves. For rulers hold no terror for those who do right, but for those who do wrong. Do you want to be free from fear of the one in authority? Then do what is right and you will be commended. For the one in authority is God's servant for your good. But if you do wrong, be afraid, for rulers do not bear the sword for nothing. For they are God's servant, agents of wrath to bring punishment on the wrongdoer. Therefore, it is necessary to submit to the authorities, not only because of possible punishment but also because of conscience.

—ROMANS 13:1–5

WE CANNOT WILLFULLY break the law, whether shooting too many ducks or anything else. We Christians, based on these texts, have to excel in being law-abiding citizens. Don't forget that!

Prayer

Help us to make Jesus attractive to everyone by the way we live—never by disobedience to law enforcement. Amen.

—Phil

STRIPPED OF PRIDE

Pride goes before destruction, a haughty spirit before a fall. Better to be lowly in spirit along with the oppressed than to share plunder with the proud.

—PROVERBS 16:18–19

ONE OF THE great blessings of twenty-two years in ministry is the opportunity to travel around the world and minister in the third world and developing nations. I was constantly amazed by the commitment and faith among people who had so little compared to what I enjoy in the U.S. Those experiences help me not to be haughty and proud, but to be humble, as I realized that faith does not come from status or possessions. Some of the godliest, most inspirational people I have met around the world had nothing of value except for the most precious things of all—their faith in God, love for people, and commitment to preaching the gospel.

Prayer

Heavenly Father, please help me to *never* be arrogant or haughty. Strip me of my pride, O Lord, and use me to guide others to You. Because of Jesus, I pray this prayer. Amen.

—*Al*

JULY 21

BIGGER THAN THE BOGEYMAN

So we say with confidence, "The Lord is my helper; I will not be afraid. What can mere mortals do to me?"

—HEBREWS 13:6

FROM TORNADOS TO terrorists, we are constantly seeing something on the news that makes us fearful. Fear is one of the ways Satan robs us of the joy God intends us to have. When we spend our time worrying about what might happen, we can't spend our time enjoying what God has given us. I love this verse because it assures me that there is nothing that my God cannot handle. I remember a song from when I was little that told me that God is bigger than the bogeyman. I am so thankful to serve a God who not only handles all my fears but takes them totally away.

Prayer

Father, I thank You for protecting me and for giving me strength when I need to be strong. You are my rock and my hiding place. In His name, amen.

—*Sadie*

July 22

Joyful Always

Be joyful always, pray continually, give thanks in all circumstances; for this is God's will for you in Christ Jesus.

—1 THESSALONIANS 5:16–18

DO YOU KNOW anyone like this? Someone who is always joyful and gives thanks for all circumstances? I know a few people like that, and I try to pattern my life after them. You can't get them down. They seem to always be in prayer and giving God glory, even in tough situations. As I grow older, I have found more joy in being content with what God has blessed me with. I try to pray off and on throughout the day about people and circumstances that are beyond my control. I read prayer requests that are e-mailed, and I try to stop and pray right then. I want to be a person whom others ask for prayers. I want perfect contentment in God and His promises. It's not easy, I know. But when I think back to the time before I gave my life to Christ, then I am grateful for my today. Remembering His redemption always brings me right back to perfect contentment with Christ.

Prayer

I thank You, Jesus, for Your blood. I thank You, God, for Your Son. I thank You, Spirit, for Your encouragement. Make me one with all three. In the name that's above all names, Jesus. Amen.

—Lisa

JULY 23

WHOM SHALL I FEAR?

The LORD is my light and my salvation—whom shall I fear? The LORD is the stronghold of my life—of whom shall I be afraid? Though an army besiege me, my heart will not fear; though war break out against me, even then I will be confident.

—PSALM 27:1, 3

MY DEPLOYMENT TO Afghanistan taught me a lot of things. Mostly that I had always taken what the Lord has blessed me with for granted. I soon realized that life on this earth is a fragile thing and that I should cherish it, no matter the circumstance. I was on edge and fearful the first few weeks there. I then found myself reading Scripture more than usual to combat this. Funny how when situations are at their worst, people realize God is their only way out. This verse brought a sense of calm over me that lasted the rest of the deployment and does to this very day. When your salvation is assured, there is nothing on this earth to fear.

Prayer

Thank you, Father, for this life You have blessed us with. Please help us never to take it and what comes along with it for granted. Help us to fear no evil and be confident in our salvation. In Jesus' name, I pray. Amen.

—Jay Stone

JULY 24

He Has a Place for Us

"Do not let your hearts be troubled. You believe in God; believe also in me. My Father's house has many rooms; if that were not so, would I have told you that I am going there to prepare a place for you? And if I go and prepare a place for you, I will come back and take you to be with me that you also may be where I am."

—JOHN 14:1–4

I'VE TALKED WITH a lot of people about their spiritual lives over the years—I really love doing that. But sometimes the problems they deal with are really serious and so sad—one of the hardest things is when a loved one dies. Jesus offered the above encouragement to His disciples to prepare them for when He left this earth. I'm sure it was a great comfort to them to know that He was only leaving to prepare a place for them to be with God for eternity. That comfort is for us as well. I try to let people know, when they are hurting over losing someone or just feeling sad, that Jesus is always with us and that He has prepared a place for us with Him.

Prayer

Father, we thank You for the hope of eternity with You. The very thought of Jesus waiting to receive us and show us around our eternal home is a great comfort in days of burden and grief. Through Jesus we pray, amen.

—Miss Kay

JULY 25

BE STILL AND KNOW

"Be still, and know that I am God; I will be exalted among the nations, I will be exalted in the earth."

—PSALM 46:10–12

THAT FIRST PART is hard: *be still.* Who has time to be still in this day and age? We are so busy making problems and then solving them. We are rushing here and there for the urgent things, and we forget the important. God's words say, "Be still." When we are still, we can know who He is, and this verse says God is to be exalted by us and the earth. When we see how important He is to us, all the urgent things fall into place. Let's be still and know God and watch Him work—not only in our lives but in all the lives of those we love, just like ripples in a pond.

Prayer

God Who Saves, strengthen my faith today to keep my focus on You and not on all the distraction that can so quickly turn my head.

—*Lynda Hammitt*

JULY 26

CONCENTRATE ON THE POSITIVE

With the tongue we praise our Lord and Father, and with it we curse human beings, who have been made in God's likeness. Out of the same mouth come praise and cursing. My brothers and sisters, this should not be.

—JAMES 3:9–10

MY TONGUE IS so hard to keep in check—even among other Christians. The thing that has helped me with this is right when I'm about to talk negatively about someone, I think of one positive thing I like about that person and focus on that. I've made a ton of mistakes and have so many faults. If people wanted to, they could easily dwell on the negative things about me and point them out. But I pray that people will see the best of me, and that I will see the best in others, as well.

Prayer

Lord, I pray for forgiveness because I know I have fallen short in this area. I pray that I build up my brothers and sisters and treat them how I want to be treated. Help me use my tongue to glorify You in everything I do.

—*Jep*

July 27

Only One Master

Wine is a mocker and beer a brawler; whoever is led astray by them is not wise.

—PROVERBS 20:1

ALCOHOL, LIKE MANY things, is not sinful in and of itself, but it can lead to sinfulness and destruction. When I was in Vietnam, I told myself I would never be like those guys I saw walking into bars and then staggering out hours later. But guess what? With time, I became just like them. Too much alcohol always leads to trouble. Now I know that wisdom, moderation, and, for most, abstinence leads to a much better result. For me, it's been complete abstinence since I left Nam. I decided I'd had enough to drink there for a lifetime! We only need one Master in our life—and that's Jesus. But alcohol, along with other drugs, can quickly become our master! We do have freedom in Christ and shouldn't allow others to take that away, but we should all use our freedoms wisely.

Prayer

Father, I pray that I will use the liberties and freedoms You've given me wisely. I only want to be controlled by Your Spirit. Forgive me when I fall short of Your best for me and when I don't exercise wisdom and restraint. Thank You for Jesus' sacrifice. I pray through Him with the help of Your Spirit. Amen.

—Si

IMAGINE YOUR LIFE . . .

So in everything, do to others what you would have them do to you, for this sums up the Law and the Prophets.

—MATTHEW 7:12

IMAGINE A WORLD where everyone lived by this simple verse—the Golden Rule. Imagine how it would change a nation, a city, a business, a church, or even a family. Too many times, we forget to do this one simple thing: treat others like we want to be treated. Even with the mercy and grace that God displayed to us through Christ on the cross, we still struggle with this simple rule. It's so simple, even a child can understand it, but all too often the evil one's power keeps us from living this one out. Imagine your life lived by this rule, and then set out to live it.

Prayer

Dear God, make me like a child so that I treat everyone the way I want to be treated. Teach me that this kind of life is simply a response to Your love, mercy, and grace. Guide me to think of this rule in my Christian walk. Remind me of Your love for me, and let me show that love to others. Amen.

—Jon Gimber

July 29

Go Forth and Serve!

For just as each of us has one body with many members, and these members do not all have the same function, so in Christ we, though many, form one body, and each member belongs to all the others. We have different gifts, according to the grace given to each of us. If your gift is prophesying, then prophesy in accordance with your faith; if it is serving, then serve; if it is teaching, then teach; if it is to encourage, then give encouragement; if it is giving, then give generously; if it is to lead, do it diligently; if it is to show mercy, do it cheerfully.

—ROMANS 12:4–8

USING YOUR GIFTS from God provides different ways for you to worship Him with your life. Take some time to figure out the gifts you have been given—and we all have been given gifts, every single one of us! Find your gift or gifts! Go forth! Worship with your life!

Prayer

Father, help us, empower us, give us boldness. Help us love our fellow man more than we fear what our fellow man may think of us. Help us to use the gifts You've given us as acts of worship to You. Amen.

—*Phil*

July 30

The Best from Beginning to End

Jesus said to the servants, "Fill the jars with water"; so they filled them to the brim. Then he told them, "Now draw some out and take it to the master of the banquet." They did so, and the master of the banquet tasted the water that had been turned into wine. . . . Then he called the bridegroom aside and said, "Everyone brings out the choice wine first and then the cheaper wine after the guests have had too much to drink; but you have saved the best till now."

—JOHN 2:7–10

By the reaction of the banquet master, we see that saving the best till last was not the wedding tradition. We are blessed by God in that we get the best at the beginning *and* at the end. When I was growing up in the Robertson house, Mom and Granny's meals were always the best, but the food was stretched because our family was large and our budget was small. When Jesus turned the water into wine at this wedding, he showed God's way of provision. When our own efforts have fizzled out, God continues to pour the best into our lives. The *best* is reserved and waiting for you!

Prayer

Father, I thank You for Christ, the best Alpha and the best Omega. Through Him, amen.

—*Al*

July 31

The Heart of the Matter

If I give all I possess to the poor and give over my body to hardship that I may boast, but do not have love, I gain nothing.

—1 CORINTHIANS 13:3

NO MATTER HOW hard we work at giving our hard-earned money or our precious time in service to God, what really matters is the attitude of our hearts. I am often so distracted by what I *should* do or *have to* do or how I *look* to those around me that I miss out on the joy of giving God to others. Grudging obedience is worthless. God does not call us to a life of duty and obligation or a life lived in front of the crowd; He calls us to a life of service that comes from open and loving hearts.

Prayer

Dear God Who Sees, please keep my attitude in check. I seek to live before You today open and honest, not for what others see. I want to make You proud.

—Lynda Hammitt

August

August 1

Faith-Based Fishing

As Jesus walked beside the Sea of Galilee, he saw Simon and his brother Andrew casting a net into the lake, for they were fishermen. "Come, follow me," Jesus said, "and I will send you out to fish for people." At once they left their nets and followed him. When he had gone a little farther, he saw James son of Zebedee and his brother John in a boat, preparing their nets. Without delay he called them, and they left their father Zebedee in the boat with the hired men and followed him.

—MARK 1:16–20

WHAT ARE THE odds that Jesus just happened to pick four fishermen as the first of twelve disciples? These men would spend three years with Jesus being discipled in His ways. Since our family commercial-fished the Ouachita River for the first fifteen years of the Duck Commander business, I think I understand why Jesus chose a third of His group from that profession. Fishing is very much a faith-based business. To keep going out and hoping, and sometimes praying, that those fish moved and swam into your nets really does test your faith. We spent many a morning on our knees on the riverbank praying for a good haul to pay important bills.

Prayer

Father, I thank You for all those fish that paved the way for our success. Through Jesus, I pray, amen.

—*Miss Kay*

LOVE YOUR ENEMIES

Do not repay anyone evil for evil. Be careful to do what is right in the eyes of everyone. If it is possible, as far as it depends on you, live at peace with everyone. Do not take revenge, my dear friends, but leave room for God's wrath, for it is written: "It is mine to avenge; I will repay," says the Lord. On the contrary: "If your enemy is hungry, feed him; if he is thirsty, give him something to drink."

—ROMANS 12:17–20

WHEN I WAS fishing for a living, people would sometimes steal my fish from my nets. At first, I would catch them stealing and scare the daylights out of them by warning them with my shotgun across my lap. They kept stealing. Finally, I applied the above scriptures. I would give them the fish when I caught them stealing the fish. I would ask, "Why steal from me? I'll give them to you—free of charge." Wow, the looks I received! Guess what? They quit stealing my fish. I learned a valuable lesson. God was right, and I had been using the ungodly method of scare tactics. My generosity made them ashamed of themselves. See how it works?

Prayer

Father, help us love our enemies and be good to them. Help us become like You one day at a time, whatever the situation. Amen.

—*Phil*

THE BEST OF THE CATCH

Jesus said to them, "Come and have breakfast." None of the disciples dared ask him, "Who are you?" They knew it was the Lord.

—JOHN 21:12

MY FAMILY WAS known as "river rats" before duck calls and TV shows. We commercial-fished the Ouachita River to make a living. The fish were viewed as one-dollar and sometimes five-dollar bills. Some of the fondest memories I have are of us gathered around the table with family and friends participating in fresh-fish fries. I would sometimes wonder why we ate the best when we could have made more money eating other fish. But it was Dad's philosophy that he should save the best of the catch for his family. Jesus gave His best to His disciples. He not only gave them proof of His resurrection but gave them a glimpse of a forever family.

Prayer

God, I thank You for allowing us to be Your sons and daughters. You are the architect and sustainer of family. The blessings we receive are best when shared with those we love.

—Jase

AUGUST 4

MAKING THE SICK WELL

While Jesus was having dinner at Levi's house, many tax collectors and sinners were eating with him and his disciples, for there were many who followed him. When the teachers of the law who were Pharisees saw him eating with the sinners and tax collectors, they asked his disciples: "Why does he eat with tax collectors and sinners?" On hearing this, Jesus said to them, "It is not the healthy who need a doctor, but the sick. I have not come to call the righteous, but sinners."

—MARK 2:15–17

WHEN JESUS CALLED a tax collector to follow him and be one of his closest twelve, He knew exactly what he was getting himself into. These guys were the bottom-feeders of the Jewish first-century world. Hey, they were kinda like me! They didn't get no *respect*! But Jesus was the kind of guy who hooked up with spiritually sick people so He could make them well. I watched Him make my older brother Phil well many years ago. He calls us to do the same.

Prayer

Lord, please help me to be aware of those around me who need Your healing touch. Help me to take off my "judging vision" and put on my "caring vision" so I can lead people to You, the Great Physician. Through You I pray, amen.

—Si

August 5

Seeking the Lost

"For the Son of Man came to seek and to save the lost."

—LUKE 19:10

IT'S A NEW day, and again I have lost my keys. Not only that, but my son lost his keys too. It's pretty much part of our daily routine. "Have you seen my keys?" And with a roll of his eyes and an "Ugh, no!" Willie asks, "Have you checked your purse? Why don't you hang them up in the kitchen?" We eventually find them, but we are almost always late to where we need to go. In Luke we are told that Jesus came to seek and to save the lost. No, he wasn't sent to find my keys (but I bet he would have helped); He came to seek me! To save me! And He also seeks you, if you are willing to listen to His voice.

Prayer

Dear Lord, thank You for seeking me out! Thank You for not giving up on me and for continuing the saving process each day. Help me to seek You more. I love You, Jesus. Amen.

—*Korie*

AUGUST 6

THINGS CHANGE

Now Joseph and all his brothers and all that generation died, but the Israelites were exceedingly fruitful; they multiplied greatly, increased in numbers and became so numerous that the land was filled with them. Then a new king, to whom Joseph meant nothing, came to power in Egypt.

—EXODUS 1:6–8

JOSEPH HAD RISEN to second in command of Egypt during a terrible famine. He had rescued his family from Israel and brought the seventy of them to Egypt and started a whole new existence. But when new leadership rose up, the prominent place Joseph had held was forgotten. The new leader saw Joseph's descendants only as a threat to his power. Things change! When things change, they often bring about difficulty, and difficulty is exactly what followed the Israelite people throughout the book of Exodus. Things change quickly for us, as well. There will always be new people in charge and with them can come personal difficulty. Our key to survival is trust in a never-changing God, who always delivers His people.

Prayer

We thank You, Father, for always being there for us through changes, both good and bad. Help us to follow You with all of our hearts today. Through Jesus, amen.

—*Willie*

August 7

Ready to Forgive

But do not forget this one thing, dear friends: With the Lord a day is like a thousand years, and a thousand years are like a day. The Lord is not slow in keeping his promise, as some understand slowness. Instead he is patient with you, not wanting anyone to perish, but everyone to come to repentance.

—2 PETER 3:8–9

SOMETIMES I JUST can't understand why God doesn't seem to be answering my prayers. As I've grown more mature in my faith, I realize that I should be patient and trust that God knows what's best for me. I also realize that sometimes when I need to repent, I just don't want to. I could give all my struggles to God, but I'm too often slow to make the change and let go. But God stands ready to change and forgive me, for as the verse above says, He wants "everyone to come to repentance."

Prayer

Almighty God, I pray that I'll be patient with others, just as You are patient with me. And I pray that I won't try Your patience by putting off my repentance. I know You always keep Your promises, and I pray that I will trust Your will for me and my family. Help me to have a repentant heart and have assurance that You continually forgive me.

—Jep

Give Without Hesitation

"So when you give to the needy, do not announce it with trumpets, as the hypocrites do in the synagogues and on the streets, to be honored by others. Truly I tell you, they have received their reward in full. But when you give to the needy, do not let your left hand know what your right hand is doing, so that your giving may be in secret. Then your Father, who sees what is done in secret, will reward you."

—MATTHEW 6:2–4

I'VE LEARNED SO much by watching the women in our church. I've heard of people in need opening their doors to find a porch full of groceries. One person who had no transportation was asked by someone she trusted to sign a form; it was only later that she found out that the form was actually the title to her friend's car, which she was giving to her free and clear. These are only two of many examples I have seen, but they will stick with me always. I want to have that kind of generosity and love for others.

Prayer

Lord, I thank You for all the blessings You have given me. I've never been without shelter and never gone hungry. I hope that I can be as giving as those godly women You have put in my life. Help me to always see another person's need and have the heart to give without hesitation.

—Jessica

AUGUST 9

(AUGUST 9–15 IS A SPECIAL SERIES ON ABRAM)

1: THE FATHER OF THE FAITHFUL

The LORD had said to Abram, "Go from your country, your people and your father's household and go to the land I will show you." . . . So Abram went, as the LORD had told him; and Lot went with him.

—GENESIS 12:1, 4a

WHAT A CALL for Abram! He had to leave the security of family, the comfort of home, and the familiarity and protection of his own people. What is really amazing is that God didn't even tell him where He was sending him. "I'll tell you when you get there," is the essence of what God told Abram. Abram pulled up roots and obeyed God. No wonder we call him "the father of the faithful."

Prayer

Lord, I ask for a strong faith and the courage to leave my own comfort to answer whatever call You give me or my family. Father, we accept Your mission by faith in Your promises to bless and protect. In Jesus, we pray in faith, amen.

—*Al*

AUGUST 10

2: FEAR, THE ENEMY OF FAITH

Now there was a famine in the land, and Abram went down to Egypt to live there for a while because the famine was severe. As he was about to enter Egypt, he said to his wife Sarai, "I know what a beautiful woman you are. When the Egyptians see you, they will say, 'This is his wife.' Then they will kill me but will let you live. Say you are my sister, so that I will be treated well for your sake and my life will be spared because of you."

—GENESIS 12:10–13

EVEN AFTER FAITHFULLY answering God's difficult call, it didn't take long for Abram's faith to be tested. And as we see in this account, it was *fear* that was Abram's downfall. The same can happen to us. When we answer the call of God on our lives, our faith will be tested too. Fear is the greatest enemy of faith, and even the strongest are challenged by that formidable enemy.

Prayer

Father, we pray for strength when we are afraid. There are so many things that frighten us, and we are sorry that our faith is so weak when we don't trust in Your protection. Guard us in Christ. Through Him we pray, amen.

—Al

AUGUST 11

3: The Pitfalls of Success

Now Lot, who was moving about with Abram, also had flocks and herds and tents. But the land could not support them while they stayed together, for their possessions were so great that they were not able to stay together. . . . So Lot chose for himself the whole plain of the Jordan and set out toward the east. The two men parted company: Abram lived in the land of Canaan, while Lot lived among the cities of the plain and pitched his tents near Sodom. Now the people of Sodom were wicked and were sinning greatly against the LORD.

—GENESIS 13:5–6, 11–13

SUCCESS CAN ALSO be a great test of faith. Abram's nephew Lot chose the Jordan plain, where wicked people lived, because it would continue to add to his wealth. The proximity to wickedness would do very costly damage to his faith and the faith of his family. While we all enjoy success and wealth—and they are often blessings from God—if we don't keep our hearts right, those blessings can turn on us and destroy both faith and family!

Prayer

Father, we thank You for our prosperity and our blessings, but we also pray for wisdom and humility, so that we don't lose sight of what is most important. In Jesus' name I pray, amen.

—*Al*

August 12

4: Spiritual Children of Abram

Then the word of the Lord came to him: "This man will not be your heir, but a son who is your own flesh will be your heir." He took him outside and said, "Look up at the sky and count the stars—if indeed you can count them." Then he said to him, "So shall your offspring be." Abram believed the Lord, and he credited it to him as righteousness.

—GENESIS 15:4–6

EVEN IN HIS old age, Abram was childless and without an heir. But God made him a promise: not only would he have a son, but he would have billons of sons in the faith. We who are God's children today are also the spiritual sons and daughters of Abram. His leap of belief in the Almighty started a movement that is still growing today.

Prayer

Father, thank You for giving us the opportunity to leap out in faith to follow You. You give us the chance to find our righteousness in You, and we are honored to follow in our father Abram's footsteps. Through Jesus I pray, amen.

—Al

AUGUST 13

5: WAITING ON GOD

Now Sarai, Abram's wife, had borne him no children. But she had an Egyptian slave named Hagar; so she said to Abram, "The L*ORD has kept me from having children. Go, sleep with my slave; perhaps I can build a family through her." Abram agreed to what Sarai said.*

—GENESIS 16:1–2

PATIENCE! WHY IS it so difficult to wait on God to do what He promises? Abram's wife, Sarai, came up with what she thought was a great plan to fulfill God's word. One problem: it wasn't God's plan! Most of my painful lessons in life have come when I tried to impose my plan onto God's plan. He doesn't need my help, and yet I continue to try to give it!

Prayer

Father, forgive our impatience and our limited vision. Your ways are right, but we keep trying to help You out. Thank You for overlooking our ignorance. Thank You, also, for Christ. In His name, amen.

—Al

6: Judgment Was Coming

Then the Lord said, "The outcry against Sodom and Gomorrah is so great and their sin so grievous that I will go down and see if what they have done is as bad as the outcry that has reached me. If not, I will know."

—GENESIS 18:20–21

IT SEEMS THAT when a certain line is crossed, God can bear it no more and He acts with swift justice. When a certain level of sin is reached, God must act. The people of Sodom and Gomorrah seemed to have reached this point, and God's judgment was enacted. Despite Abram's bargaining for his nephew Lot's family and others, judgment for wickedness was coming! A scary thought in our current climate.

Prayer

Father, we pray for our country and for the wicked among us. We plead and bargain for the souls of men, just like our father Abram. We pray for revival in times of wickedness. We ask this prayer through Jesus, amen.

—Al

AUGUST 15

7: NO JOKING MATTER

"The outcry to the LORD against its people is so great that he has sent us to destroy it." So Lot went out and spoke to his sons-in-law, who were pledged to marry his daughters. He said, "Hurry and get out of this place, because the LORD is about to destroy the city!" But his sons-in-law thought he was joking. . . . Lot's wife looked back, and she became a pillar of salt.

—GENESIS 19:13B–14, 26

WHEN GOD'S JUDGMENT is enacted on mankind it's not a time for joking or looking back! There are times for serious, sober awareness and moving forward toward the arms of God and safety. Lot failed his family even before this fateful day, by not preparing them for God's wrath or the wickedness that surrounded them.

Prayer

Father, we pray for sober judgment in a wicked world. We pray for awareness and leadership of our families in times of trouble and tribulation. Forgive our countrymen who are in rebellion to You; we pray for a return to Your ways. We ask this in Jesus' name, amen.

—Al

August 16

Clothed with Jesus

Let us behave decently, as in the daytime, not in carousing and drunkenness, not in sexual immorality and debauchery, not in dissension and jealousy. Rather, clothe yourselves with the Lord Jesus Christ, and do not think about how to gratify the desires of the sinful flesh.

—ROMANS 13:13–14

THINK BACK TO when you clothed yourself with Jesus (read Galatians 3:26–27). Remember your initial commitment and continue to be that way! Walk in the light! The above scripture tells us not to even *think* about the flesh. You were bought at a price and clothed with the Lord Jesus Himself. Others should see the fruit of your new attire!

Prayer

Father, I thank You for clothing us with Jesus. Let us "wear" Him at all times. You cleansed us and dressed us up with Jesus. Help us look like Him on this earth. Amen.

—*Phil*

August 17

Buzzard Attack

Whenever there is a carcass, there the vultures will gather.

—MATTHEW 24:28

THE BIBLE IS filled with figurative language and gives vivid images that represent pictures of events and circumstances. While specific interpretations can be difficult, principles can be drawn. I remember one year inspecting a duck blind before duck season, only to find that a buzzard had moved in and decided this would be home. The smell was indescribable. After a successful buzzard removal, we could never get rid of the smell, and it continued to be a haven for new buzzards. It led to a full dismantling and relocation of the blind. I found out that a buzzard's defense mechanism is regurgitation. I often think of those who attack the righteousness of God by using buzzard tactics.

Prayer

God, Your righteousness is holy and spreads the aroma of sweetness and life. Help us to withstand the persecutions of those who use words to attack what is good.

—*Jase*

Using Pain for Good

Praise be to the God and Father of our Lord Jesus Christ, the Father of compassion and the God of all comfort, who comforts us in all our troubles, so that we can comfort those in any trouble with the comfort we ourselves receive from God.

—2 CORINTHIANS 1:3–4

EVER WONDER WHY bad things happen to good people? Well, it's mostly because we live in a fallen world where people have free will and can choose to behave in ways that sometimes harm themselves or others. But here in this verse, we see one of the blessings that come out of those bad things that happen to good people: we can help others in their pain.

Prayer

Father, I wish life was always what *I* consider fair, but I'm thankful You are there when it's not. Thank You for the trust You have in me that I will stand firm in times of trials and learn from the experience and be a servant to others who have trials of their own. In Your precious name I pray, amen.

—*Godwin*

August 19

Rescued!

I am the Living One; I was dead, and now look, I am alive for ever and ever! And I hold the keys of death and Hades.

—REVELATION 1:18

THE ONE THING that separates Christianity from most of the world's religions is an empty tomb. The Messiah and Savior for Christians did not stay in his grave! To unlock the gates that imprison humanity—death—is the greatest gift mankind could ever receive. I praise a Living Savior for my hope today!

Prayer

I thank You, Jesus, for rescuing me from my prison of sin and death. The hope I have today is present because You gave it to me. I give my allegiance and commit my heart, soul, mind, and strength to serving only You. I pray by Your name, amen.

—Willie

August 20

Walk the Walk

As the body without the spirit is dead, so faith without deeds is dead.

—JAMES 2:26

WHEN I WAS in high school, our football coach was also my Bible teacher. He would tell his Bible students the same thing that he told his football players: "Don't just talk the talk; walk the walk." In other words, you can talk all day long, but if you don't back it up with your actions, it means nothing. It applied to football, and it applies to our walk with Jesus. If we don't show our faith in God's power by our daily actions, no one will care if we say we are Christians. If we truly love Jesus and appreciate His sacrifice, we will live our lives in a sacrificial way.

Prayer

Lord, thank You for Your sacrifice. Thank You for putting my needs ahead of the comfort of Your Son. Because of Your ultimate act of kindness, I have hope of a resurrected body that I do not deserve. Please help me to live my life in a way that makes me worthy of that sacrifice.

—*Missy*

AUGUST 21

ALONE TIME WITH GOD

Very early in the morning, while it was still dark, Jesus got up, left the house and went off to a solitary place, where he prayed.

—MARK 1:35

I JUST LOVE THOSE times when the house is quiet and I can have some alone time with Jesus. He always fills my soul with His sweetness. Now, Jesus didn't shy away from large crowds—and neither do I—but He showed us that one of the secrets to a successful, large ministry was quiet time alone with His Father. Not only did Jesus need the serenity that being alone with God brings, but He also needed the clear communication line that comes from quiet and introspective prayer. And we can only get that when we withdraw from the hustle and bustle of life.

Prayer

Father, I am so grateful for the quiet moments that You and I are able to spend together. Please bless my busy times by strengthening me through the quiet hours. Help me keep my priorities in order today, and I pray that I may bless someone's life.

—Miss Kay

August 22

God Never Slumbers

I lift up my eyes to the mountains—where does my help come from? My help comes from the Lord, the Maker of heaven and earth. He will not let your foot slip—he who watches over you will not slumber, indeed, he who watches over Israel will neither slumber nor sleep.

—PSALM 121:1–4

We sing a song at church that was written from this verse—and I just love it! The thought that touches me most is that when we need help, the Lord is always there. When we feel we have nowhere else to turn, we can always turn to the Lord. What a comfort! The maker of heaven and earth is all the help you will ever need. He will not slumber or sleep. Anytime, day or night, He is there.

Prayer

Lord, we read this verse, and we believe this verse. Help us in times of trouble to rest in this verse. I believe that You will not let us slip. You will be there for us! Thank You, God, for the comfort this verse brings. In Jesus' name, amen.

—*Lisa*

AUGUST 23

A GRUMBLE-FREE DAY

Do everything without grumbling or arguing.

—PHILIPPIANS 2:14

LADIES AND GENTLEMEN, this is a challenge for each and every one of us. I challenge you to try to go *one day* without doing either of these. It is far more difficult than you may think, but you have to start somewhere. Am I saying that I never grumble or argue? Absolutely not! That would just be a lie, and there are issues with that as well. What I am saying is, make a goal that can be attained. Start with one day—for that matter, start with half a day and work your way up. When you feel a grumble or an argument coming on, say a little prayer and ask God for His help.

Prayer

God, help us to remember there is nothing of this world worth arguing or grumbling about, for we know our time here is limited and that we should put it to the best use possible.

—Martin

PERFECT LOVE

Let no debt remain outstanding, except the continuing debt to love one another, for whoever loves others has fulfilled the law. The commandments, "You shall not commit adultery," "You shall not murder," "You shall not steal," "You shall not covet," and whatever other command there may be, are summed up in this one command: "Love your neighbor as yourself." Love does no harm to a neighbor. Therefore love is the fulfillment of the law.

—ROMANS 13:8–10

YOU KNOW WHY Jesus our Lord never sinned? Because He *loved perfectly*—something we humans have never done. You know what a picture of a "perfect" world looks like? People who love perfectly. Since we don't and He does, we acknowledge our sin of imperfect love. He forgives us, and we are born again and trust Him who is perfect to cleanse us. And He continues to keep us cleansed as we try hard to love as He did. The closer you get to loving your neighbor perfectly, the less you will break the law (sin) and the more you will look like Jesus.

Prayer

Thank you, God, that you view us as 100 percent perfect, even though we are so imperfect in our love for each other. Help us to be like Jesus, more and more, as we learn the toughest skill of them all—loving people like You do! Praise God for His grace! Amen.

—*Phil*

August 25

The Race of My Life

Since we are surrounded by such a great cloud of witnesses, let us throw off everything that hinders and the sin that so easily entangles. And let us run with perseverance the race marked out for us, fixing our eyes on Jesus, the pioneer and perfecter of faith. For the joy set before him he endured the cross, scorning its shame, and sat down at the right hand of the throne of God. Consider him who endured such opposition from sinners, so that you will not grow weary and lose heart.

—HEBREWS 12:1–3

I ALWAYS TELL MY kin that if they ever see me running, they should get a gun and shoot whatever is chasing me, because I ain't running for fun, Jack! One thing about running is that you have to stay focused enough to not want to quit. Maybe if I had a prize to focus on, it would keep me running . . . *nah*! But even though I don't like to run physically, I am running a spiritual race every day of my life. And I know that I have to stay focused on Christ so I can finish the race of my life—the one race I consider worth running, Jack!

Prayer

I pray for spiritual focus, God. I need Christ-vision and the endurance to finish my race without getting entangled with the evil one. I pray this through Christ, my focal point, amen.

—Si

August 26

Our Children Are Watching

Train up a child in the way he should go: and when he is old, he will not depart from it.

—PROVERBS 22:6, KJV

Before I started building duck calls full-time, I was a coach and teacher at my local middle school for twelve years. I would have given my right arm if every parent would have taken this verse to heart! There is so much truth in these words. As parents, we are tasked by God Almighty to plant His seed in our children's minds and hearts. Never forget that part of that training is us as parents living a godly life on a consistent and daily basis. Always be aware that children are watching and learning every second of every day. If we plant a godly seed, there's a good chance it will one day bloom into a godly plant.

Prayer

Father, help me in my daily walk to always be a good example to my children. I pray that they will one day grow into godly men and women. Help me to raise them in a way that will be pleasing to You. Thank You for the blessing of children You have bestowed upon me. May I never take them for granted. In Jesus' name, amen.

—Jay Stone

August 27

Love Your Brother

Anyone who claims to be in the light but hates a brother or sister is still in the darkness. Anyone who loves their brother and sister lives in the light, and there is nothing in them to make them stumble.

—1 JOHN 2:9–10

I REMEMBER TELLING MY dad, "Dad, I just don't like that person; look how they are acting." Dad would always say, "Son, you got to love your brother." Funny thing is, as I was growing up, I'm sure I was the guy other people looked at and said, "I don't like that guy!" I've been on both sides of this issue and now know there is only one way to be: completely loving to all my brothers. I want to be in the light as *He* is in the light.

Prayer

Lord, help us love our brothers and sisters in Christ. Help us show compassion and forgiveness so that we will not stumble. Help us lift up our brothers in prayer so that You will bless them.

—Jep

August 28

Obeying Human Authority

Remind the people to be subject to rulers and authorities, to be obedient, to be ready to do whatever is good, to slander no one, to be peaceable and considerate, and always to be gentle toward everyone.

—TITUS 3:1–2

ALTHOUGH GOD IS our ultimate authority, He also advises us to follow the laws of the land. It can be confusing when those who govern us have little respect for God's authority, but we must do all that God has commanded us, and that includes staying within the parameters set by human laws. Keep in mind that God is master of all things, and everything in existence exists because it is His will. No matter who our leaders are, we must still do what is good and considerate. The Lord values obedience; He mentions it many times throughout the Bible. If you can be obedient to your leaders and the authorities over you, then you can be obedient to Him. Think about that the next time you run a stop sign or fib a little on your tax return. Showing reverence to those who govern us is showing reverence to God Himself.

Prayer

Father, help me to show humility to those who rule. I know that Your will is the ultimate authority and that I must learn to follow You in all things. Thank You for Your divine justice. Through Jesus I pray, amen.

—Alex Robertson Mancuso

August 29

Seeing God

Blessed are the pure in heart, for they will see God.

—MATTHEW 5:8

TOO MANY TIMES in my life, I have allowed myself to be taken from God's path because I worry about stuff. These are the times that I most need God in my life; however, I get lost because I focus on the wrong things. Reading this scripture reminds me that I need to keep my heart focused on what is good and pure, and then I will truly see God as He is working around me.

Prayer

Heavenly Father, slow me down. Make my movements and thoughts direct and precise. Allow me to search for the pure simplicity that can only be found through You. Keep my heart and intentions pure so that I can see Your plans for me. Work me, teach me, and mold me, Lord. Amen.

—Jon Gimber

AUGUST 30

GOD ALONE SATISFIES

Keep your lives free from the love of money and be content with what you have, because God has said, "Never will I leave you; never will I forsake you."

—HEBREWS 13:5

IN TODAY'S WORLD it is so easy to cover up or even ignore discontentment. Our culture tells us we need more, better, faster, newer, *more*. God calls us to be content in Him. Unlike the short-term things of this world, He will always be there for us. We long for something to fill the emptiness we feel, but the things we work to surround ourselves with are passing and can never fill our longing hearts. God alone can fill that longing with His bright and glorious light.

Prayer

Dear God, who provides, keep my eyes on You and not the next thing. I feel so empty and ask You to fill me with Your love and light.

—Lynda Hammitt

AUGUST 31

CONTENT IN NEED AND IN PLENTY

I know what it is to be in need, and I know what it is to have plenty. I have learned the secret of being content in any and every situation, whether well fed or hungry, whether living in plenty or in want. I can do everything through him who gives me strength.

—PHILIPPIANS 4:12–13

AFTER I CAME to Jesus when I was twenty-eight, many problems came at me from a lot of different directions. With financial matters, I would pray, "Father, I pray You bless me in these financial matters, but I want You to know I will follow Jesus whether You bless me or not. I'll make it, Father, with Your help." *God was always there!* I just kept preaching the good news no matter what! He helped me to be content with little or with plenty—we truly can do everything through Him who gives us strength!

Prayer

Father, You blessed me more than I could ask or imagine. I am humbled by it all. I am nothing. You are the mighty God of the cosmos. I praise Your name. Amen.

—*Phil*

September

September 1

Our Weeping Lord

Jesus wept.

—JOHN 11:35

THIS SHORT PASSAGE says a whole lot about our Lord and Savior. He was sent word that His friend Lazarus was dying, and He knew that any delay on His part would result in the death of His friend. But He delayed. He didn't go to Bethany right away because He knew that in four days, He would raise Lazarus from the dead. He also knew this miracle would serve as a sign of His divine power to raise the dead and that He would be raised after His crucifixion. He knew that Lazarus' sisters, Mary and Martha, would feel anger and resentment toward Him because of His delay. But He also knew that, eventually, they would rejoice at their brother's miraculous resurrection. Jesus knew *all* of this, and yet *he wept* when He arrived at their home. He wept because his friends were hurting. I love that about my Lord: that He would care enough to cry, even when He has the ultimate solution for the problem. How beautiful is that!

Prayer

Jesus, I thank You for having emotions for Your hurting friends and family. I thank You for weeping, for laughing, and for loving, and I pray this prayer through You, amen.

—*Missy*

September 2

Loving Confrontation

So watch yourselves. "If your brother or sister sins against you, rebuke them, and if they repent, forgive them. Even if they sin against you seven times in a day and seven times come back to you saying, 'I repent,' you must forgive them."

—LUKE 17:3–4

When Jep was in college, he made some bad choices and started living in sin. But, gratefully, this lifestyle only lasted a short time. One day, Jep arrived at his parents' house to work just like any normal day, only to find that all his brothers' trucks were already there. He walked in to find his brothers and dad—all waiting on him. They confronted him about cutting up and told him he needed to stop. At their loving confrontation, Jep broke down, and they all cried and prayed together. They loved him so much that they couldn't stand there and watch their baby brother follow Satan. They also made the decision to forgive him and continued to help him in his walk with Christ.

Prayer

Lord, I pray that You help me show forgiveness and help me to be there for my brothers and sisters in Christ when they are struggling. I pray that I'm not judgmental but loving in the way I reach out. Give me the strength to always stand up for what is right, acknowledge sin, and call it out.

—Jessica

SEPTEMBER 3

UNSHAKABLE

Those who trust in the LORD are like Mount Zion, which cannot be shaken but endures forever. As the mountains surround Jerusalem, so the LORD surrounds his people both now and forevermore.

—PSALM 125:1–2

THIS VERSE HAS been made into one of my favorite songs. It asks for God to surround his people because we need to be in His presence. This is very comforting to sing and praise God with. Just knowing that God, the Creator of everything, has us, His people, in His presence. His love, His grace, His power, His strength, His forgiveness, His holiness, and His righteousness are all surrounding us and making us like Mount Zion—unshakable.

Prayer

Father, we don't know the words to say that will allow You to know how blessed we feel because You love us, forgive us, and surround us with Your glory. Please, Father, listen to our hearts and know that we are asking to be in Your presence every day and that we yearn to be surrounded by You. In Jesus' holy name, amen.

—*Lisa*

September 4

Watch Your Words

But now you must also rid yourselves of all such things as these: anger, rage, malice, slander, and filthy language from your lips.

—COLOSSIANS 3:8

DO YOU HAVE a hard time controlling your tongue? Does filthy language come from your lips at times? I once had a coach who said to one of his players, "I wouldn't hold in my hand what comes out of your mouth." Wow! Think about that one for a minute. It's a visual image that can help you see that words can be filthy and not pleasant to hold. It can serve as a reminder to guard your mouth. The next time you are tempted to say something that is filthy or unkind, ask yourself, "Can I hold this in my hands? Would I be proud to carry these words around and show them off?" Think about using words that empower others and lift them up—not bring them down.

Prayer

Dear merciful Father, thank You so much for reminders, like these, that we need to rid ourselves of all evil and unkind things. Thank You for sending the Spirit to help us; we can't do it alone. Thank You again for Your mercy! In Jesus' name, amen.

—*Korie*

SEPTEMBER 5

PEACE OF MIND

Rejoice in the Lord always. I will say it again: Rejoice! Let your gentleness be evident to all. The Lord is near. Do not be anxious about anything, but in everything, by prayer and petition, with thanksgiving, present your requests to God. And the peace of God, which transcends all understanding, will guard your hearts and your minds in Christ Jesus.

—PHILIPPIANS 4:4–7

THIRTY-FIVE MILLION PEOPLE in the United States are on drugs for depression. Someone out there is not happy, happy, happy! The rarest of commodities—peace of mind—eludes the masses. While some depression is of a clinical nature and does need medication, many people sink into depression because they feel lost and without purpose. They don't have Jesus in their lives. Jesus can give us the peace of mind we so desperately need. The peace of God guards our hearts and our minds! That is cool, indeed!

Prayer

Father, I thank You for Your peace that stands guard over us. I praise You for giving us peace of mind. Your divine protection is like crawling into our mothers' arms! Thank you. Amen.

—Phil

SEPTEMBER 6

Consider It All Joy

Consider it pure joy, my brothers and sisters, whenever you face trials of many kinds, because you know that the testing of your faith produces perseverance. Let perseverance finish its work so that you may be mature and complete, not lacking anything.

—JAMES 1:2–4

I DEFINITELY ENDURED SOME trials while Phil was in his wild years. I can't say that I considered *all* those trials "joy," but I can say that God was with me every step of the way. Even after Phil came to the Lord, the forty years since he designed the very first Duck Commander duck call have included a lot of tests along the way: Economic downturns, low duck populations, hunting-industry shake-ups, family problems, and more. Of course, none of these were pleasant at the time, but all of them were building perseverance and, ultimately, maturity for our family to be able to handle everything we are dealing with today. God's work in us is a process, and His ways are always best in developing character and integrity—if we are willing to follow.

Prayer

Father, our family considers it pure joy that we have overcome so many trials, and we pray for strength for the work You continue to do in us. Forgive us when we fail to trust You and fall short of Your glory. We pray this in Jesus' name, amen.

—*Miss Kay*

SEPTEMBER 7

(SEPTEMBER 7–16 IS A SPECIAL SERIES ON THE TEN COMMANDMENTS)

1: No Other Gods

"You shall have no other gods before me."

—EXODUS 20:3

When God gave His law to His people, He began with a building block on which all the rest would stand. The exclusivity of His rule and the place He held in His people's lives was critical to establishing their trust in Him so they would listen to everything else He would have to say. When I break this law, the other laws seem that much easier to break! There is only room in my heart for one God, the Almighty Creator of the heavens and the earth!

Prayer

Almighty God, I give all allegiance to You and humbly ask forgiveness when I allow other gods to take precedence in my heart over You. I am far from perfect, which is why I need the constant cleansing of your Son Jesus' blood. I am grateful for His grace and pray this prayer in His name, amen.

—Willie

2: Watch What You Worship

"You shall not make for yourself an image in the form of anything in heaven above or on the earth beneath or in the waters below. You shall not bow down to them or worship them."

—EXODUS 20:4–5

It is ironic, although probably not accidental, that one of the most popular television shows of the past ten years is called *American Idol.* In twenty-first-century America, our attitudes toward celebrities are certainly a form of idol worship. We have to be aware of this phenomenon with our own family's success through *Duck Dynasty.* Our family does not want to be idolized, and more important to us, we don't want to idolize anything except our heavenly Father, His one and only Son, and the indwelling Holy Spirit. God knows our tendencies to worship flesh and blood, wood and stone, precious metals, or currency, and He warns us to stay out of that trap—which will always let you down, by the way. I only want to bow the knee to the one true God of all!

Prayer

Father in heaven, merciful Son and mediator, and interceding Spirit, please accept my worship today and my pledge not to lift up idols or bow down to them. I ask forgiveness in falling short, through the cleansing blood of the Lamb, amen.

—*Willie*

3: BE CAREFUL WITH HIS NAME

"You shall not misuse the name of the LORD your God, for the LORD will not hold anyone guiltless who misuses his name."

—EXODUS 20:7

FOR SOME REASON, Robertson men love to give nicknames to those around us. Some of those names are based on physical attributes (Big Boy, Burly, Curley, Walrus, Red) and others may come from some other family attribute or story (Spaniard, Ace, Hawk, Ham Sammich). Many are simply called by their last name, but hardly anyone is called by their first or preferred name that everyone else calls them by. It is just one of the many quirks we all seem to possess! But there's one name we don't play around with, and that is our Lord's name. We treat it with respect and honor and don't really tolerate anything else in our hearing. I only want to lift up the name of my great God and never do I want to demean it!

Prayer

I honor, today, the wonderful names of my Lord, my Father, my Savior, my Comforter, my Alpha, and my Omega. Father, forgive me when I misuse Your name in any way, and thank You most of all for the name of Jesus Christ and the Holy Spirit, which offer me hope through this prayer, amen.

—Willie

SEPTEMBER 10

4: A Day to Honor God and Rest

"Remember the Sabbath day by keeping it holy. Six days you shall labor and do all your work, but the seventh day is a sabbath to the LORD your God. On it you shall not do any work."

—EXODUS 20:8–10

OUR GOD SET aside a time to be honored and remembered and for us to rest and give Him the credit for our hard work and success. God compared His creative process in Genesis 1 to days of successful work and set aside one day of rest to commemorate and honor His wonderful creation. This shows us the importance of rest and setting aside a time to honor God for our hard work. It is very easy to keep working on through the breaks, thinking that by the sweat of our own brow, we are making our way. Sabbath is all about rest and paying tribute to the true author of our success, our heavenly Father! We give God glory in our work, but also in our ability to stop, rest, and pay tribute!

Prayer

Father, thank You for the success we enjoy from our labors. As we pause to rest and reflect, may we always give You the honor You deserve. We thank You for the redeeming work of Christ on our behalf. Through His sacrifice we pray, amen.

—*Willie*

5: HONOR YOUR PARENTS

"Honor your father and your mother, so that you may live long in the land the LORD your God is giving you."

—EXODUS 20:12

WHEN MY DAD talks to audiences about his sons, one of the things he always mentions is the fact that none of the four of us ever disrespected him to his face. Not once, never. Of course, we did disrespect him at times with some bad choices *out* of his presence, but when we look back, we see that he was gracious, like our heavenly Father, even then. We were all very respectful of Dad and Mom because they disciplined us, but also because we understood the principle God was putting forth with his fifth commandment. We honored them because we saw honor in their relationships with their parents. The greatest example parents can set is how they treat their parents. I honor my earthly parents and my heavenly Father with all my heart!

Prayer

We feel so fortunate to be able to call you Father, and we know this is possible because You loved us first; now we return that love with honor. We so appreciate our lives, our blessings, and our abilities to pay forward Your love to future generations. Thank You for my parents and their love for You and the blessing they are to me. In Jesus' name, amen.

—*Willie*

September 12

6: Respecting Life

"You shall not murder."

—EXODUS 20:13

MY OLDER BROTHER Al, who was a pastor in our church for many years, attended a murder trial involving some of our church members. He was only twenty-six at the time and hadn't had much life experience, but he was eager and excited to be a part of something so dramatic. As he tells it, as the trial went through all the testimony, evidence, and closing arguments, he grew less excited and more melancholy because he started realizing how many lives were hurt because of this murder. He saw the extended wounding of family, friends, and even people who hadn't known this family before the murder. He says that he viewed murder differently from that day until now, and as he's shared the experience with the rest of us, we can say we feel the same. The taking of human life always has a huge effect on all who are connected to it.

Prayer

Father, please help us to respect the life that You breathe into human beings. I pray for all those who have been affected by murder and ask for healing in their lives from this traumatic event. Help us to live this day fully for You, with the help of the Holy Spirit, through Jesus, amen.

—*Willie*

SEPTEMBER 13

7: THE PROMISE TO BE FAITHFUL

"You shall not commit adultery."

—EXODUS 20:14

THE SANCTITY OF faithfulness is the bedrock of God's promise to His people. His promise to never fail us or leave us gives sinful humans a standard to live by. This same promise extends to the marital bonds of a husband and a wife. While men and women fall short of God's perfect standard, the challenge to honor a vow of marriage with emotional and physical faithfulness is the bedrock for a solid and long-lasting relationship. Some marriages never overcome infidelity, but many others do because of the blessing of forgiveness, even from this relationship-challenging sin. The ten most meaningful words in a wedding sermon are "I promise to be faithful until death do us part."

Prayer

Heavenly Father, we ask for the strength to maintain our commitment to faithfulness, to both You and our spouses. For those who have violated this law and vow to their spouses, I ask for forgiveness and healing and the hope of reconciliation. Thank You for your never-ending faithfulness to Your promises. Thank You for Christ, who gives us hope. In His name, amen.

—*Willie*

September 14

8: Don't Steal!

"You shall not steal."

—EXODUS 20:15

THIEVING, AS MY dad called it, was a big no-no when the Robertson boys were growing up. Dad was hard on us for tearing up perfectly good equipment, and he was quick to tell us never to take anything that belonged to someone else. I remember that a young boy once took some of Dad's rods and reels out of his truck, and when Dad found out about it, he went to their apartment to get them back. The boy's dad rebuked Dad for leaving them "unprotected and easy to steal" and didn't seem surprised or disappointed in his son's theft. He did give back the fishing tackle, but Dad was none too happy about the lesson that man had taught his son and chose to use the incident to hammer home a familiar theme to us: don't steal! Thanks, Dad, we got the point!

Prayer

Father, thank You for all of the great things we own and possess. I pray that we will respect other people's property and, most of all, that we will respect You as the ultimate owner of all things. Forgive us when we forget this important principle and take what does not belong to us. Thank You for the gift of Jesus, as we pray through Him, amen.

—*Willie*

September 15

9: Speak the Truth About Others

"You shall not give false testimony against your neighbor."

—EXODUS 20:16

I'M GOING TO tell!" Giving "testimony"—false or true—against our "neighbor" begins when we are small children. Honesty and telling the truth is usually the very first moral issue that children grapple with. In this verse, God commands us not to give *false* testimony about our neighbor—saying that someone did something wrong when they didn't. This was such a serious offense to God that in the Old Testament (Deuteronomy 19:17–19) the punishment for someone who gave false witness was that whatever the witness intended to happen to the party he accused would be done to him. Talk about motivation to tell the truth! Our God is very patient and long-suffering with His dishonest children, but He calls us to a higher standard!

Prayer

Father, we ask for forgiveness for our far too many transgressions of dishonesty. We pray for courage to face the consequences of our actions when we are tempted to be dishonest and less than truthful—especially in accusing others wrongly We praise You for Your constant truthfulness and integrity. We thank You for the truth of the risen Christ and pray in His name, amen.

—*Willie*

10: Keep Your Eyes on Your Own Stuff

"You shall not covet your neighbor's house. You shall not covet your neighbor's wife, or his male or female servant, his ox or donkey, or anything that belongs to your neighbor."

—EXODUS 20:17

MASTERING THE ART of contentment is a difficult thing to do, especially in the bountiful country of the United States of America. So many people have accumulated wealth and possessions, especially compared to the rest of the world. The Robertsons were raised without very many possessions, but we didn't know to compare ourselves to others, so we were content and didn't realize we were poor. Even if ignorance is bliss, there will always be something around to covet, so the key to obeying this principle is to find that comfort level in being content with what we have.

Prayer

Lord, we pray for the elusive art of contentment. We pray for the ability to trust in You for the possessions we have and to avoid the temptation of coveting the things that belong to other people. Thank You for the blessings of our great country and help us to keep all of our wealth in perspective and to be generous in our help to others. We pray through the selfless sacrifice of Jesus Christ, amen.

—*Willie*

September 17

Don't Give Up on People

Be merciful to those who doubt; save others by snatching them from the fire; to others show mercy, mixed with fear—hating even the clothing stained by corrupted flesh.

—JUDE 1:22–23

JUDE IS SUCH a cool little book of the Bible. "Save others by snatching them from the fire." That phrase really inspires me to get out and share Jesus with others. Jude also tells us to show mercy, which I think is really important. It's so easy just to give up on someone who doesn't want to follow Jesus right away. We need to be the people who never give up on potential Christians and are there for them when they are ready.

Prayer

God, help us to be Your ambassadors. Help us point people to You so that they will make You Lord of their lives. We love You with all our hearts and give You all the glory, amen!

—Jep

AWED BY COURAGE

When the members of the Sanhedrin heard this, they were furious and gnashed their teeth at him. But Stephen, full of the Holy Spirit, looked up to heaven and saw the glory of God, and Jesus standing at the right hand of God. "Look," he said, "I see heaven open and the Son of Man standing at the right hand of God." At this they covered their ears and, yelling at the top of their voices, they all rushed at him, dragged him out of the city and began to stone him.

—ACTS 7:54–58

I TAUGHT AND PREACHED for twenty years, and I have had both great and not-so-great reactions to lessons I have presented. Since I am writing this, I obviously never got the reaction Stephen did to this barn-burner sermon! Stephen said what needed to be said to people who were threatened by the gospel of Jesus. He was the first of many martyrs after Christ's death in the first century. I am awed when I see the courage of men and women who say what needs to be said on behalf of Almighty God.

Prayer

Father, I am forever grateful for the example of courageous men and women in the past and the present who proclaim Your word at the risk of persecution and death. In their honor, I pray through Jesus, amen.

—Al

SEPTEMBER 19

ALWAYS AT THE READY

But in your hearts revere Christ as Lord. Always be prepared to give an answer to everyone who asks you to give the reason for the hope that you have. But do this with gentleness and respect.

—1 PETER 3:15

PEOPLE WHO KNOW me know that I love to talk—and this verse gives me guidance on how to use my gift of gab. Peter says that if I truly revere the Lord, I must be ready at all times to tell others why. I have to admit that I don't always wait for someone to ask me about my hope—I usually just start telling them about Jesus. But this verse also reminds me of what my attitude should be when I share this good news—I am to be respectful and use gentle care. The worst witness I could give is one of harshness, smugness, or self-righteousness.

Prayer

Father, I pray today for an opportunity to tell someone about the hope that You have instilled in my heart. I pray for the right attitude, the right tone, and the right heart as I have the privilege of pointing people to Your love and salvation. I am so grateful for the hope that I have and look forward to spending eternity with You! I praise You for Your Son and the Holy Spirit. It is through Jesus I pray, amen.

—Miss Kay

September 20

No Condemnation—None!

Therefore, there is now no condemnation for those who are in Christ Jesus, because through Christ Jesus the law of the Spirit of life who gives life has set you free from the law of sin and death. For what the law was powerless to do because it was weakened by the flesh, God did by sending his own Son in the likeness of sinful flesh to be a sin offering.

—ROMANS 8:1–3

DO YOU HEAR that? There is no condemnation for us—absolutely none! No matter how many rotten, filthy things we did in the past, all have been removed and forgotten by God! All the things we could have been condemned for, all of those evil things were put on the back of Jesus. We are free! We are free! Jesus paid it all. Our response to this outlandish gift? Crucify the flesh and live by the Spirit. The victory is yours—here and *now*.

Prayer

Praise our mighty Lord because He sees us as flawless in light of what Jesus *has* done (the cross) and what He *is* doing (the mediating work). Thank You, Father, for *fixing us*! Glory to God! Amen.

—*Phil*

SEPTEMBER 21

BRINGING GOD GLORY!

As [Jesus] went along, he saw a man blind from birth. His disciples asked him, "Rabbi, who sinned, this man or his parents, that he was born blind?" "Neither this man nor his parents sinned," said Jesus, "but this happened so that the works of God might be displayed in him."

—JOHN 9:1–3

EVEN AFTER ALL that Jesus has done for us, many folks still think that bad things only happen to bad people—that every harmful or evil thing that happens is God's direct punishment. Hey, people! We live in a broken world—bad things happen to all of us! In the verse above, Jesus gives us a different take. He explains that *some* bad circumstances (not all, mind you) exist simply to display the greatness of God and to impact watchers with His glorious power! This concept helps me to be patient while He is doing His work—on and through me.

Prayer

Father, I want to live through the hard times in a way that brings glory to You. Please help me to see Your hand at work in me—always. Through Jesus, amen.

—Si

SEPTEMBER 22

THE BIRTHPLACE OF HUNTING

The fear and dread of you will fall on all the beasts of the earth, and on all the birds in the sky, on every creature that moves along the ground, and on all the fish of the sea; they are given into your hands. Just as I gave you the green plants, I now give you everything.

—GENESIS 9:2–3

MY FAMILY HAS enjoyed the pursuit of the five food groups that God outlined to Noah after the flood. This is the birthplace of hunting. It also is a responsibility given to humans by God to manage the animal kingdom. My family has lived off of the land, but we also have spent our time, energy, and money managing the habitat and the environment where these creatures roam. God made animals to be wild and developed a food chain that, I'm happy to say, humans are at the top of.

Prayer

Thank You, Lord, for the wilderness and all the animals that reside in it. Give us wisdom in managing our environment and a respect for the creatures that live in the wild. Guide us in our responsibilities in managing the animal kingdom, and may we always give You thanks for the tasty meals these creatures provide.

—*Jase*

September 23

Jesus Is Supreme Over All

The Son is the image of the invisible God, the firstborn over all creation. For by him all things were created: things in heaven and on earth, visible and invisible, whether thrones or powers or rulers or authorities; all things have been created through him and for him. He is before all things, and in him all things hold together. And he is the head of the body, the church; he is the beginning and the firstborn from among the dead, so that in everything he might have the supremacy.

—COLOSSIANS 1:15–18

TAKE A MINUTE to meditate on all the things the above scriptures say about Jesus! I just love how they show how supreme Jesus is. It is so awesome to me to realize that with of all the power and knowledge that Jesus has, He still cares for and loves little old me. It's cool to think that Jesus spanned that big gap between God and us little old humans.

Prayer

Lord, we are so grateful that You sent Your Son down here so that we could be saved. We know that He is the head of the church; help us to be faithful servants of His. Help us be confident knowing that He is *in* everything and *holds all* things together!

—*Jep*

September 24

Let God Lift You Up

Humble yourselves before the Lord, and he will lift you up.

—JAMES 4:10

One of the many life lessons that my dad has taught me through the years is the sentiment behind this passage. He told me early in life never to tell people how great I was at anything, but let others tell you if you were good at something. That always stuck with me. I now understand that he was teaching me humility to deal with the gifts and talents that God has given me, and he was teaching me to avoid the pride and narcissism that can come when we're not humble. I never want to lift up myself; I want to allow God to do that as I kneel before Him!

Prayer

I am so grateful for my gifts and abilities, and I attribute them all to You, Father. I humble myself before You and ask that You get glory from my life and my actions. Remove my pride, dear Lord, and cleanse me of selfishness. I want to grow in You today and every day. I make this request with hope in Christ and His ability to save, amen.

—Al

September 25

Man Up!

But whatever were gains to me I now consider loss for the sake of Christ. What is more, I consider everything a loss compared to the surpassing worth of knowing Christ Jesus my Lord, for whose sake I have lost all things. I consider them garbage, that I may gain Christ and be found in him, not having a righteousness of my own that comes from the law, but that which is through faith in Christ—the righteousness that comes from God on the basis of faith.

—PHILIPPIANS 3:7–9

We will never appreciate the suffering of our Lord until we experience a small measure of it ourselves. Suffering happens. When it does, our task is to be like Paul here in these verses. Paul teaches us that everything but Christ is rubbish—*rubbish*! Learn from your difficulties—grow from them—move on!

Prayer

Father, help us through our momentary sufferings. Help us not to whine or blame You when they come. Teach us, Father, not to run from suffering but to relish it and to man up in the face of it! Give us the power to stand up under it. Amen.

—Phil

SEPTEMBER 26

LAWS ARE FOR OUR BENEFIT

Then he said to them, "The Sabbath was made for man, not man for the Sabbath. So the Son of Man is Lord even of the Sabbath."

—MARK 2:27–28

THE PHARISEES JUST loved to find fault with Jesus—like a few people I know! One day, after some of their typical yammering, griping, and complaining, Jesus reminded them of an important lesson about the law: God made the law to *protect* people, not *enslave* them. Those ole Pharisees actually tried to keep things right with God by perfect obedience! Absolute nonsense! But even when we know the truth about this, we sometimes fall into the trap of thinking the *law* is supreme—instead of *Jesus*. Now, don't get me wrong, Jack. I'm not saying anything negative about the law—it is for our *good*. Obeying it makes life and relationships sweeter. But I'm no slave to the law; I'm a slave to Jesus!

Prayer

God, I am grateful for Your law, even though I can never obey it flawlessly. I'm so thankful that Jesus took care of the law's demands, but I live by Your principles because they are just and make my life better. Forgive me when I fall short of Your standard and think more highly of myself than I should. I pray this through Jesus, amen.

—*Si*

SEPTEMBER 27

BECOME LIKE JESUS IN BETWEEN

I want to know Christ—yes, to know the power of his resurrection and participation in his sufferings, becoming like him in his death, and so, somehow, attaining to the resurrection from the dead.

—PHILIPPIANS 3:10–11

I REMEMBER AS A kid my dad telling me that the key to being a great duck hunter is to do what ducks do. I realized that I needed to observe and listen to real ducks to know how to imitate them. Jesus became like us to connect with us and reconcile us to the Father. The Bible is a love letter from God to humans, not a rule book. Jesus was a real being who died to selfishness every day on His journey to death on a cross for the sins of the world. Christ's resurrection not only showed God's power but spread hope to the world. One bit of advice I got was to start my day with a prayer focused on the cross and to end each day with a focus on the resurrection. You become like Jesus in between.

Prayer

Father, I thank You for the cross and second chances. Help me die to self daily and never to forget Your burial and resurrection.

—*Jase*

September 28

Healing Confession

Therefore confess your sins to each other and pray for each other so that you may be healed. The prayer of a righteous person is powerful and effective.

—JAMES 5:16

In the context of praying for physical healing, James reveals a wonderful truth about the healing power of confessing our sin. He enlists us to seek out someone to confess to in order to find healing. I have known this tremendous feeling when I was bold enough to do what God instructed me to do. To take the risk of revealing weakness and enlisting the assistance and accountability of another can be a scary thing, but also a cleansing thing, as well. When we risk confession of weakness, we are rewarded with healing. When we respond God's way, He shows us that when we trust Him to handle our sin, we always come out feeling strengthened and confident!

Prayer

Father, I am so blessed to have clear answers to life's biggest questions. I know that I gain that insight from You, and I ask forgiveness for the times I try to "go it alone" and don't listen to Your guidance. Thank You for the people You have put in my life to hear my confession and help me find healing in You. I thank You most of all for Jesus, amen.

—Al

SEPTEMBER 29

EXITING PLANET EARTH

But the Scripture declares that the whole world is a prisoner of sin, so that what was promised, being given through faith in Jesus Christ, might be given to those who believe. Before this faith came, we were held prisoners by the law, locked up until faith should be revealed. So the law was put in charge to lead us to Christ that we might be justified by faith. Now that faith has come, we are no longer under the supervision of the law.

—GALATIANS 3:22–25, NIV 1984

THERE ARE TWO kinds of people on earth. You are either under the Law or you are in Jesus and under grace. Under the Law there is no provision for sin (violations); the Law demands perfection. Grace demands trusting and trying, and the provision for sin is the blood of Jesus. In Jesus, we have grace; outside of Jesus, we have sin and death. No one gets off planet Earth alive without Jesus. No one. I'll take Jesus, hands down.

Prayer

Father, I thank You for Your grace that saves us through faith. Thank You for providing the ultimate sacrifice for our violation of Your law—namely the blood of Jesus. Help us to trust You to forgive us, and help me to try not to sin, but when I do, help me always to know that You are ready to forgive us through the blood of Jesus. Amen.

—*Phil*

SEPTEMBER 30

THE DAYS OF OUR YOUTH

Remember your Creator in the days of your youth, before the days of trouble come and the years approach when you will say, "I find no pleasure in them."

—ECCLESIASTES 12:1

BEING THE YOUNGEST of the Robertson boys, I sometimes get ribbed for being the "baby." But now I have babies of my own—four of them. And I am so thankful for the spiritual example that my children have in my teenage nephews and nieces—Reed, Cole, John Luke, and Sadie. They struggle like any teenager, but they stay connected and involved with other Christian teens at our church. They also use the platform given them because of the success of *Duck Dynasty* to speak to groups about their faith. I suppose one of the reasons I admire them so much is because I made a real mess of some of my teenage years, so I enjoy seeing them do the right thing. They bring joy to a proud uncle's heart—even if I am the "baby."

Prayer

Father, I thank You for all the youth who remember their Creator in their younger years and for the example they set. I thank You for delivering me through my teen trials and guiding me to my Lord, Jesus Christ, in whom I pray. Amen.

—*Jep*

October

October 1

What You Don't Say

Those who consider themselves religious and yet do not keep a tight rein on their tongues deceive themselves, and their religion is worthless.

—JAMES 1:26

As you know, I love to tell stories! But stories about people coming to Jesus are the best kind of stories of all. There was a sound engineer who worked on one of our shows a few years back who was converted to Christ by what he *didn't* hear. He told Phil that he heard *everything* as a sound guy. But after listening to everyone on our crew for several days, he was perplexed because he couldn't figure out when we used profanity. He knew we had to, but when did we do it? When Phil told him we didn't curse, he asked why. That question was just the one Phil was looking for, and he shared with him the good news about Jesus, which led to his acceptance of Christ and a new destiny. What we don't say, and then what we say to explain what we don't say, can turn around the lives of those who are listening!

Prayer

Father, help me be aware of everything I say today as well as everything I don't say. Forgive us for being flippant with words and our coarse joking or anything that doesn't have good purpose. I pray this through Christ, amen.

—*Si*

October 2

Pure Religion

Religion that God our Father accepts as pure and faultless is this: to look after orphans and widows in their distress and to keep oneself from being polluted by the world.

—JAMES 1:27

IN MY COUNSELING and teaching, I come across a lot of single women and fatherless children. My heart always goes out to them because I remember the days I took care of my boys by myself—and those were hard times. There is nothing more Christlike than helping someone who can't survive without help. Widows and orphans certainly fit into that category. But in the same verse, James also reminds us our culture can pollute our vision. One of the biggest pollutions of our culture is *selfishness*. I have a hard time seeing the needs of others if I am only focused on what I want.

Prayer

God, I want to be pure and faultless in Your eyes, and I know that can only happen when I get the focus off myself and see the needs of the helpless that you put in my path. Please help me to be generous, loving, and available for widows, orphans, and anyone who needs me. I pray through Jesus, with the help of Your Spirit, amen.

—*Miss Kay*

October 3

Because I Have Suffered

We have peace with God through our Lord Jesus Christ, through whom we have gained access by faith into this grace in which we now stand. And we boast in the hope of the glory of God. Not only so, but we also glory in our sufferings, because we know that suffering produces perseverance; perseverance, character; and character, hope. And hope does not put us to shame, because God's love has been poured out into our hearts through the Holy Spirit, who has been given to us.

—ROMANS 5:1–5

WHAT A POSITION to be in! We have access to the Creator of the cosmos, and we are under grace by faith to boot! So let the sufferings come—and they will come! But look at what suffering produces! Perseverance, character, hope! Those are great qualities to have and each one is *produced* by suffering—of all things. Make a pact with God: "I will be a better man or woman because I have suffered, Lord"!

Prayer

Thank You, Father, for the lessons we learn by suffering. Help us to grow and do good things *because* of suffering. Help us learn perseverance from suffering. Help us all to stand firm when suffering comes. Amen.

—*Phil*

October 4

Saved from Sure Death

My brothers and sisters, if one of you should wander from the truth and someone should bring that person back, remember this: Whoever turns a sinner from the error of their way will save them from death and cover over a multitude of sins.

—JAMES 5:19–20

I REMEMBER SITTING ON a curb when I was eighteen years old in Kenner, Louisiana, bleeding and broken from my latest scrap. I was in service to an evil lord. I was estranged from my family and living just like the prodigal son in Luke 15. But on that fateful Sunday morning, one of NOPD's finest, who "happened" to be a Christian, saw an opportunity to guide an errant son back home to his family—and more important, back home to his heavenly Father. I was saved from spiritual death and a sure early physical death by one person who took this verse to heart. I can't wait to see him again in heaven.

Prayer

Father, I am grateful for that brother who helped turn this sinner from his wicked ways and guided me home to the Ouachita River. There I reunited with my earthly family and became a son of Yours in my death, burial, and resurrection from that watery grave of baptism. Thank You for my Savior, Jesus; through Him I pray, amen.

—Al

The Blessing of Freedom

But our citizenship is in heaven. And we eagerly await a Savior from there, the Lord Jesus Christ.

—PHILIPPIANS 3:20

IF WE ARE born in the USA, then we are automatically citizens of this country. When we are born of Jesus, we automatically become citizens of heaven. In the country we live in, we usually take our freedoms for granted. We do not realize what a great gift we have in the freedom to worship, work, and play where and how we like. But just as we take those freedoms for granted, we also take our freedom in Christ for granted. We usually don't live like we are eternal beings; we sin and take God's grace in stride. We need to keep our eyes looking ahead to the home in heaven waiting for us; our hearts must be eagerly set on the day our Savior comes back. Let's live with a view to His coming so we will be included in His glory.

Prayer

Father, please help us to appreciate the sacrifices that our soldiers have made for our earthly freedom, and also help us know that the sacrifice of Your Son is what saves us eternally. I thank You, Father, for your sacrifice for our sins. We await Your return. In Your Son's name, amen.

—*Lisa*

October 6

The Beginning and the End

"I am the Alpha and the Omega," says the Lord God, "who is, and who was, and who is to come, the Almighty."

—REVELATION 1:8

When I think about the implications of this verse, my mind short-circuits. The beginning and the end? The past, present, and future? Jesus' description of Himself begins a remarkable revelation to the apostle John. Even though I can't comprehend it, it gives me tremendous comfort to know that my Lord spans time and, in fact, exists beyond it. Everything I've ever done or will do can be handled by Jesus. With this promise, I can have peace for yesterday, today, and tomorrow.

Prayer

Father, I have so much peace knowing that You were there, are there, and will be there for me and for those I love. Please help me in my weaker moments of doubt and increase my faith. Through Jesus I pray, amen.

—Willie

OCTOBER 7

OUT OF HIDING

He said to them, "Do you bring in a lamp to put it under a bowl or a bed? Instead, don't you put it on its stand? For whatever is hidden is meant to be disclosed, and whatever is concealed is meant to be brought out into the open. If anyone has ears to hear, let them hear."

—MARK 4:21–23

LIGHTS ARE MEANT to shine, and the Bible tells us we shine like stars in the universe! In a world that is scary, it is so easy to try to pull back, hunker down, and hide out to avoid evil and persecution. Jesus never meant for His followers to hide. We are called to be out there shining, loud and proud, and engaging our culture where it lives and breathes. Be cautious but unafraid, as our Lord protects the hearts and souls of His chosen ones.

Prayer

Father, we are so honored to be the lights that reflect Your wonderful glory. We are the moon to Your sun, and we relish shining as Your examples of how to live in this depraved generation. Please give us ears to hear and listen to Your directive. We pray this in Jesus' name, amen.

—*Korie*

October 8

Heirs of God!

Now if we are children, then we are heirs—heirs of God and co-heirs with Christ, if indeed we share in his sufferings in order that we may also share in his glory.

—ROMANS 8:17

DID YOU HEAR that? Jesus died for *you*; He was buried and raised from the dead! Do you *believe* it? Have you repented and confessed Him as Lord? Have you been baptized and given the Spirit of God? If so, relax! You will inherit everything your Father has! Your Father has and owns everything there is. He made the cosmos, and you have inherited all of that. You are an heir of heaven! You inherit what your earthly father has (when he dies), but all that inheritance is temporary. Just look at what you inherit from your heavenly Father! Wow!

Prayer

Father, I am speechless because of what I will inherit! I am absolutely speechless. I can say no more except *amen* to that!

—*Phil*

October 9

My Favorite Deposit

Having believed, you were marked in him with a seal, the promised Holy Spirit, who is a deposit guaranteeing our inheritance until the redemption of those who are God's possession.

—EPHESIANS 1:13–14, NIV 1984

I USED TO HANDLE all the duck call orders for Duck Commander—most on any scrap of paper or napkin I could find. I also handled all the bills—that was the hard part. I'm glad my boys take care of all of that now! It took me a few years to fully appreciate bank deposits versus bank withdrawals. It was so much easier to take out and spend than put up and save, but I had to learn to be frugal in order to balance the budget. The Holy Spirit is a wonderful deposit given to us by God to remind us of the real prize in store for us when we get our glorified bodies and eternal life. It's hard to comprehend His power to actually regenerate flesh and bone and bring our bodies back to life, but that's our ultimate promise!

Prayer

Father, we are so excited about the possibilities with You in eternity, and we are blessed to have Your Spirit as a deposit toward our future reward. We anticipate living forever, with the help of Your Spirit and because of Your Son, Jesus, amen.

—Miss Kay

October 10

Around the Dinner Table

Better a dry crust with peace and quiet than a house full of feasting, with strife.

—PROVERBS 17:1

I JUST LOVE THE family dinner scene on *Duck Dynasty*, and it has become one of the iconic parts of the show. People around the world continue to tell us how much they love that scene. The prayer, the voice-over of Willie recapping what he learned, and just the smiling faces gathered for a meal all bring joy and blessings to those who watch. A feast that includes love and peace is so important to our family, and we are proud to show that to the world and encourage others to do the same.

Prayer

Father, I thank You for the blessings of food, family, and faith. Because of Your love in our lives, our family strives to love each other, enjoy each other, forgive each other, and bless each other. I thank You for Your grace and peace, which flows through us. Because of Christ, I offer up this prayer, amen.

—*Jep*

The Legacy of Faith

I have no greater joy than to hear that my children are walking in the truth.

—3 JOHN 1:4

JEP STILL HAS notes Kay wrote him through his teens. The impact she had on him is evident, as well as the impact she had on all her boys. Phil and Kay didn't falter in their love for Christ or their love for their boys. They are all believers, and my greatest accomplishment will be my family following Jesus Christ. I look forward to the day each one of my children comes to follow Jesus to make Him Lord of his or her life. That is the legacy I want to leave. What peace that will be.

Prayer

Lord, I thank You for blessing me with a large family. Having four children has brought so much joy into my life. I pray they will come to know You and follow You from an early age. I pray they won't make the mistakes I've made in my life. Help me to be the best mom I can be and help them come to know You, Lord.

—*Jessica*

OCTOBER 12

SPIRITUAL BURIAL GROUNDS

For all of you who were baptized into Christ have clothed yourselves with Christ.

—GALATIANS 3:27

IT IS INTERESTING that three-fourths of our planet is made up of water. Where there is no water, life doesn't last. Baptism through faith in Jesus Christ is an act of submission and a relinquishing of self. Baptism into Christ is an opportunity granted by God. Our family lives on the Ouachita River, and it provides the perfect backdrop for those who hear the good news of Jesus Christ. Some of my favorite hunting and fishing spots have become spiritual burial grounds for many and give an opportunity to new believers to be born again.

Prayer

God, I thank You for new creations. Thank You for the opportunity and privilege of being clothed with Your Son. Help us to realize our powerless position and to submit to the grace and hope found in Christ.

—Jase

October 13

Choose Your Companions Wisely

Do not be misled: "Bad company corrupts good character."

—1 CORINTHIANS 15:33

When the boys were little, I was very attentive to the friends they chose. They were not allowed to spend time in anyone's home whom I did not know well and whose lifestyle I did not approve of. That resulted in their spending lots of time at home and at their cousins' house. Because of this, once they got older and their world widened, they started choosing friends who had lifestyles and values that mirrored our family's. Have they ever chosen the wrong friend in the past? Yes, but they learned quickly from the consequences. It doesn't take long to recognize ungodly behavior in someone whom you spend lots of time with. I'm very proud of them for making the adjustments and seeking godly relationships.

Prayer

Lord, thank You for making our home a refuge. The gift of Your Spirit in our home brings peace and joy to our entire family as well as to our friends and neighbors. I pray that my children will continue to bring friends into our home who serve You as their God and who encourage them daily to live a life of gratitude and service to You.

—Missy

Energized and Raised

We know that the whole creation has been groaning as in the pains of childbirth right up to the present time. Not only so, but we ourselves, who have the firstfruits of the Spirit, groan inwardly as we wait eagerly for our adoption to sonship, the redemption of our bodies. For in this hope we were saved. But hope that is seen is no hope at all. Who hopes for what they already have? But if we hope for what we do not yet have, we wait for it patiently.

—ROMANS 8:22–25

THIS TEXT TELLS us that our bodies will be energized and raised to live. Jesus proved that can happen. You are not *you* unless you are body, soul, and spirit. If you fall asleep (die) before Jesus comes back, He will bring your soul back with Him. Your body will be in the cemetery when your body, soul, and spirit are united again to live eternally. I have never heard a greater story anywhere or from anyone. I believe!

Prayer

Thanks, Father, for the great hope, our final adoption as sons when our bodies are raised from the ground. Thanks, Father, for keeping us alive, apart from our body, during the interim until Your Son returns. What a hope, Father! Thanks forever! Amen.

—*Phil*

October 15

Iron Sharpens Iron

When I saw that they were not acting in line with the truth of the gospel, I said to Cephas [Peter] in front of them all, "You are a Jew, yet you live like a Gentile and not like a Jew. How is it, then, that you force Gentiles to follow Jewish customs?"

—GALATIANS 2:14

TWO THINGS ALWAYS strike me about this verse. The first is the fact that Paul was bold enough to challenge Peter, who was really the father of the early church. Paul must have believed the verse in the Old Testament that says that iron sharpens iron! He felt strongly enough that Peter was hurting the church with his favoritism that he called him out on it. The second thing that strikes me about this verse is more of a general observation that when we try to bind traditions on people, we are out of line with the Good News message. We must have the gospel message of Christ as our core and not try to add in traditions to rule over people's lives.

Prayer

Heavenly Father, we thank You for the gospel and the boldness to challenge each other when we don't act in line with it. I am so grateful for the people You have put in my life who keep me focused. Through Jesus, I pray, amen.

—*Jase*

October 16

The Art of Listening

Fools find no pleasure in understanding but delight in airing their own opinions.

—PROVERBS 18:2

ROBERTSONS DO LOVE to argue. It is sort of a rite of passage in our family to get old enough to enter the fray of voicing your opinion. When we were young, we listened to my pa, granny, mom, and dad talk about politics, religion, and other topics, and then one by one we began to inject our own thoughts. When Si or one of our other uncles or aunts was visiting during the holidays, it really got lively! I'll admit we all have to work on listening and understanding the other person!

Prayer

Father, please help me listen today and understand someone else, so that I may bless them. Forgive me when I am only concerned about my own opinion. Help me bring You glory today, through Jesus, amen.

—Willie

October 17

I'm Holy!

As obedient children, do not conform to the evil desires you had when you lived in ignorance. But just as he who called you is holy, so be holy in all you do; for it is written: "Be holy, because I am holy."

—1 PETER 1:14–16

As I've lived out my faith over the years—and I've lived quite a few years—I've sometimes made the mistake of trying to be "holy" all on my own. But, hey, I can safely say that has never worked. I'm a bit of a lost cause when it comes to perfection! My only hope for "holiness" is through my Savior, Jesus. And, Jack, it's your only hope too. It's a good feeling to let go and let God do His work in me—because I sure can't do it on my own!

Prayer

Father, I thank You for helping me see that I could never achieve holiness and godliness by my own goodness. Now I understand that only when I submit my life to You and take on *Your* holiness can I be made holy! You continue to amaze me by Your grace and Your goodness. Now I can safely say that I am holy today, because *You* are holy. In Christ I pray, amen.

—Si

OCTOBER 18

HE UNDERSTANDS!

In the beginning was the Word, and the Word was with God, and the Word was God. . . . The Word became flesh and made his dwelling among us. We have seen his glory, the glory of the one and only Son, who came from the Father, full of grace and truth.

—JOHN 1:1, 14

THE MORE I read the Bible, the more I am amazed at what God did for us and what He went through just to be near us. He became one of us so He could walk among us, experience what we experience, and let us know that we mean everything to Him. He gave up so much to come down here to be with us—I can't even comprehend that level of love. Now that He has walked among us, we know that He *understands* what it's like to be human. How cool is that?

Prayer

Father, I lift You up and praise You! Thank You for all the things You do to help us understand Your love for us. May we take nothing in this life for granted, always be conscious of our actions, and always try to reflect You. In Your precious name, amen.

—*Godwin*

October 19

God's Likeness

With the tongue we praise our Lord and Father, and with it we curse human beings, who have been made in God's likeness. Out of the same mouth come praise and cursing. My brothers and sisters, this should not be.

—JAMES 3:9–10

HOW MANY TIMES have we sat in church, sung praise, heard a sermon from God, then gone to lunch to talk about how horrible someone's children were or how bad their outfit looked? We all do it. It's an easy trap to fall into, because it's so simple, and, well . . . it's human nature. Sometimes we don't even notice ourselves doing this! The Lord tells us we must be pure in thought, and the book of James tells us we must be pure in speech as well. James says, "Fresh water and salt water cannot flow from the same spring." We are all made in God's image, so speaking ill of anyone else is speaking ill of God Himself. We should leave all judgments to God, the author and perfecter of our faith. He is much better able to judge than we are.

Prayer

Father, make my heart and my words a spring of fresh, flowing water. Help me to act like You by seeing in everyone else Your likeness. Let not my mouth bring poison or evil to others. Thank You for Your consistent mercy. Through Jesus, amen.

—Alex Robertson Mancuso

October 20

When I Am Weak, Then I Am Strong

I was given a thorn in my flesh, a messenger of Satan, to torment me. Three times I pleaded with the Lord to take it away from me. But he said to me, "My grace is sufficient for you, for my power is made perfect in weakness." . . . That is why, for Christ's sake, I delight in weaknesses, in insults, in hardships, in persecutions, in difficulties. For when I am weak, then I am strong.

—2 CORINTHIANS 12:7–10

WOW! THE APOSTLE Paul reveals a great truth to us that is born from his own pain and disappointment. Who would blame him for so earnestly and persistently pleading with God to remove a painful torment of Satan? Christ's response to Paul really gives us something to think about—He doesn't always say yes. Knowing this gives me strength to power through difficult times and the mindset to tolerate the thorns that cause me grief. Jesus says His grace is more than big enough to handle our weaknesses. Ultimately, we find that while still in our weakness, God provides a heavenly strength!

Prayer

Father, I am so glad I can delight in Your grace for carrying me—even when my troubles don't go away. In Jesus, I pray, amen.

—Al

October 21

Working Together for Good

And we know that in all things God works for the good of those who love him, who have been called according to his purpose. . . . What, then, shall we say in response to these things? If God is for us, who can be against us?

—ROMANS 8:28, 31

THESE VERSES, IN their context, describe faith to me. As our lives on earth unfold, we have to know that things are happening according to God's plans. Notice that the verse says that God works in "all things" for our good. While certain events may not be so great, God, the master weaver, will weave them all together to make a beautiful tapestry. This understanding drives us to keep on moving, knowing that He is in control of our futures and already has made a plan for us. This faith is what allows us to go into the path of our lives, knowing that the Almighty has a plan—and that is enough.

Prayer

Father, I stand firm knowing that You have a plan for me. While I don't know Your exact plan or the path that will get me there, my faith in You gives me plenty of preparation for the journey. Lord, I eagerly join this journey knowing that there is nothing that cannot be done through Your plan and Your mighty power. Amen.

—*Jon Gimber*

October 22

Living Eagerly

Our citizenship is in heaven. And we eagerly await a Savior from there, the Lord Jesus Christ.

—PHILIPPIANS 3:20

THE KEY WORD in this verse is "eagerly." As we wait on our Savior to return for us, it is important to remain eager. We must be eager to spread the gospel of Jesus. We must be eager to help and love others. We must be eager to go to God in prayer. We must be eager to serve Him in any capacity. It is very easy to become lackadaisical in our Christian walk and let the status quo be good enough. I know I am guilty of this from time to time, as I am sure we all are. But I like to keep this word in my mind and use it as a frequent reminder to be *eager* to serve Him.

Prayer

Father, help me stay eager as I serve You and spread the message of Your love for all of us.

—*Martin*

OCTOBER 23

A CASE STUDY IN FAITH

You yourselves are a case study of what he does. At one time you all had your backs turned to God, thinking rebellious thoughts of him, giving him trouble every chance you got.

—COLOSSIANS 1:21, *THE MESSAGE*

DID YOU KNOW that? That you are a "case study," I mean. Our very lives are a case study in the redemptive power of Christ! We all start out with our backs turned to God and, as the verse says, "giving him trouble every chance" we get. Even after we accept the salvation He offers through Jesus, we still fight battles with His Spirit in our minds. Our human nature lives on in our minds, fighting against what we know is right. But the good news is that we can choose to let His power take hold of our thoughts, and then we can be a case study in what happens to a person who is truly changed by the power of Christ in us.

Prayer

God of Forgiveness, keep my face turned toward You. Make Your Spirit strong in my heart so that my rebellious nature is brought under Your control.

—*Lynda Hammitt*

October 24

Taking Care of One Another

If one part [of God's body] suffers, every part suffers with it; if one part is honored, every part rejoices with it.

—1 CORINTHIANS 12:26

EACH TIME OUR daughter, Mia, enters the next phase of her physical challenge that accompanies a cleft lip/palate, it mentally overwhelms me. I become an emotional wreck. Not in front of her, mind you, but alone in my quiet time. I've come to rely on a small group of women who have become my spiritual support group. They are my rocks, my shoulders, and even my punching bags. They get me. They cry with me and then make me laugh the very next minute. They support me and hold me up to the Father in prayer for strength and endurance. These are also the same women who are proud of our success as a family. They brag on Facebook about us and tell all their friends about our funny little TV show. I'm convinced that they love me just as much as I love them, no matter what.

Prayer

Lord, thank You for my true friendships in Your kingdom. I know that my true friends have the same goal of serving You as I do. Because they love You so much, they love me. They are such a blessing in my life, and I pray that You bless them in everything.

—*Missy*

October 25

The Lord Bless You

" ' "The Lord bless you and keep you; the Lord make his face shine on you and be gracious to you; the Lord turn his face toward you and give you peace." ' "

—NUMBERS 6:24–26

I HAVE A SWEET friend who has said this blessing over her son ever since he was a baby. He is now a grown man, and when she gets the chance, she still does it today. She has blessed me before by touching me and whispering this blessing to me. It is just so special to have someone love you so much that they will pray God's blessing upon you. It is very comforting to think that the Lord will turn His face to shine on you and be gracious to you and give you peace. This blessing is for you, as well.

Prayer

Thank you, Father, for Your unfailing promises and the blessings You so richly give us. Please, Father, always let Your face shine upon us. In Jesus' name, amen.

—Lisa

October 26

Spur One Another On

Let us consider how we may spur one another on toward love and good deeds, not giving up meeting together, as some are in the habit of doing, but encouraging one another—and all the more as you see the Day approaching.

—HEBREWS 10:24–25

One of the great blessings of my years of ministry was that I was always expected to meet when the saints met at our church. I never really had an option to go or not go, because it was my job to be there—to encourage the church and to edify and "spur on" the body of Christ. I never wanted "going to church" to be the ultimate goal for the forever family. Instead, I wanted meeting together to be the encouragement and training center to send out our local missionaries to their jobs, schools, and surrounding culture. Sort of like college isn't where you want your young adult to stay, but just to be trained and equipped to make their way in the job world. Even though I no longer work for the church, I am still grateful to get encouragement there to grow where God plants me in this world.

Prayer

Father, I am so thankful for my church family and the help they give me to walk this Christian walk and live out the mission You called me to. Through Jesus I pray, amen.

—*Al*

October 27

All God's Creatures

The Lord is trustworthy in all he promises and faithful in all he does. The Lord upholds all those who fall and lifts up all who are bowed down. The eyes of all look to you, and you give them their food at the proper time. You open your hand and satisfy the desires of every living thing.

—PSALM 145:13B–16

EVEN AS A believer, I sometimes forget how big God's love is. Since I am usually surrounded by other believers, I forget that God's love is for *all* of His creation, not just those who have made Him Lord. Of course, He doesn't love evil or sin, but He does love His created beings and He provides for all of humanity and creation.

Prayer

Father, I thank You so much for all You give me and my family. Help me to have a clear vision of those around me, to appreciate them as my fellow human beings, and to tell them about the gospel and Your plan for their salvation. Thank You for Christ and His salvation; through Him I pray, amen.

—Jep

October 28

Nothing Can Separate Us!

Who is the one who condemns? No one. Christ Jesus who died—more than that, who was raised to life—is at the right hand of God and is also interceding for us. Who shall separate us from the love of Christ? Shall trouble or hardship or persecution or famine or nakedness or danger or sword? As it is written: "For your sake we face death all day long; we are considered as sheep to be slaughtered." No, in all these things we are more than conquerors through him who loved us. For I am convinced that neither death nor life, neither angels nor demons, neither the present nor the future, nor any powers, neither height nor depth, nor anything else in all creation, will be able to separate us from the love of God that is in Christ Jesus our Lord.

—ROMANS 8:34–39

Oh the glorious gospel! Read it again—especially notice the questions and answers. *Who condemns us?* Is it Christ? *No.* Christ *intercedes* for us. *Who can separate us from Christ's love?* Can death? Danger? *Anything? No.* It is too grand for me, too good for any of us—but it is all true. I am overwhelmed by it all. We don't deserve this, Father, but . . . we'll take it!

Prayer

Father, thank you that we are more than conquerors through Jesus. Help us to shout from every roof that Jesus lives! Amen.

—*Phil*

October 29

Not Ashamed

I am not ashamed of the Gospel, because it is the power of God that brings salvation to everyone who believes: first to the Jew, then to the Gentile.

—ROMANS 1:16

THERE IS POWER in the message of Christ. Never doubt it. It not only changes *your* life, but it changes the lives of the people around you. When they know where you came from and the change the gospel has made in you, they have to realize it took divine intervention to do something like that. That's what gives you the ability to not be ashamed of the gospel!

Prayer

Father, help us to proclaim You and what You did for us. Help us to be humble and to realize it's not about us but You. In Your precious name, amen.

—*Godwin*

OCTOBER 30

STRONG AND COURAGEOUS

Be on your guard; stand firm in the faith; be courageous; be strong.

—1 CORINTHIANS 16:13

OUR FAITH IS sometimes clouded with melancholy thoughts and the "blahs." Growing up Robertson, we never had any doubt about what was manly and macho. In this scripture, God calls us to be strong and courageous. He knows that we have times of weakness and don't always feel this way—but God is always calling us upward, to be the men and women He created us to be. He wants us to be strong and defend our faith. He wants us to have the gumption to spread the good news of the gospel through the world. We honor God when we honor His design of our nature.

Prayer

God, strengthen me. Empower me. Use me in my family, my church, and anywhere I go as a soldier for You. Keep me firm and steadfast as I shine in the world. Let all who see me know that the boldness of Christ lives in me and strengthens me. Let this radiate to the world so that others can see You through me and my actions. Amen.

—Jon Gimber

October 31

I Can Do All Things

I can do all things through Christ who gives me strength.

—PHILIPPIANS 4:13, NKJV

THIS VERSE WILL always hold a special place in my heart. As a child, this scripture was forever ingrained in me by my parents and grandparents. At the time I would use this verse in sports when I was struggling. It was written everywhere I spent any significant amount of time. Now I find myself using this scripture for completely different reasons. When God places any challenge before me or when I feel tempted not to be His best, this scripture pops into my mind. It is truly a blessing to have the power of Christ to help us in everything we do.

Prayer

God, I thank You for sending Your Son to give us a way out of this wicked world and also for the strength He provides while we are still here.

—*Martin*

November

November 1

Godly Anger

In the temple courts [Jesus] found people selling cattle, sheep and doves, and others sitting at tables exchanging money. So he made a whip out of cords, and drove all from the temple courts, both sheep and cattle; he scattered the coins of the money changers and overturned their tables. To those who sold doves he said, "Get these out of here! Stop turning my Father's house into a market!"

—JOHN 2:13–16

JESUS WAS *ANGRY* in this scene in the Temple courts. Jesus showed that taking advantage of others under the banner of being God's appointed servants really gets God riled up! I recently learned of a Scottish Gaelic clan called Clann Dhònnchaidh, which is also known as Clan Robertson; the meaning of this term is "fierce when roused." That seems to make perfect sense to me! We are not easily riled, but when we are, look out! Jesus showed His own fierce side when people made a mockery of God by using His worshippers to make a profit. We need to reserve our anger for the kind of things that anger God and be forgiving and gentle the rest of time.

Prayer

We pray for good, positive attitudes today, Father, but we also pray for fierce passion when we need to be zealous for what is right. In Christ's name, amen.

—*Willie*

November 2

Hanging with the Right People

Blessed is the one who does not walk in step with the wicked or stand in the way that sinners take or sit in the company of mockers, but whose delight is in the law of the Lord, *and who meditates on his law day and night.*

—PSALM 1:1–2

HEY, WHEN I read this scripture, I know what kind of person I *don't* want to be! I don't want to run with the wicked, I don't want to hang around where sinners hang, and I don't want to make friends with those who look down on others! When I think about it, these are three big ways that people serve evil instead of good. I'm sorry to say that I have been all three of those guys, but I repented and never want to be like any of them again! Ever!

Prayer

Father, forgive me for my days of hanging around with those who don't respect You and don't respect others. And forgive me for judging or mocking others, as well. I want to be like the guy in the scripture above—the blessed guy who doesn't do any of these things. I'd like to be like one of those trees planted by the great Ouachita River—making You look good by the life I live. I pray all of this through Jesus, my Lord, amen.

—*Si*

NOVEMBER 3

NO ROOM FOR STINGINESS

Remember this: Whoever sows sparingly will also reap sparingly, and whoever sows generously will also reap generously. Each of you should give what you have decided in your heart to give, not reluctantly or under compulsion, for God loves a cheerful giver.

—2 CORINTHIANS 9:6–7

THINK ABOUT ALL that God has done for you! The best gift of all? The blood of God for you and me. Inconceivable! Therefore, let none of us ever be stingy with God. I have learned a valuable lesson since I met Jesus—the more I give, the more I am blessed. You will never out-give God—never! And when you give, give it freely, out of your own choice! God doesn't want a gift given grudgingly. What He did can never be repaid by any of us. Hey! Be generous and cheerful in your generosity!

Prayer

Father, Your giving Jesus should motivate us all to be generous with our money, time, and energy to serve God. Help us to live up to that calling. Amen.

—*Phil*

DISCIPLINED FOR OUR GOOD

Endure hardship as discipline; God is treating you as his children. For what children are not disciplined by their father? . . . Moreover, we have all had human fathers who disciplined us and we respected them for it. How much more should we submit to the Father of spirits and live! They disciplined us for a little while as they thought best; but God disciplines us for our good, in order that we may share in his holiness. No discipline seems pleasant at the time, but painful. Later on, however, it produces a harvest of righteousness and peace for those who have been trained by it.

—HEBREWS 12:7, 9–11

I HAVE SAID MANY times that I never received discipline from my dad that I did not deserve, but I did get away with some things that I could have used some discipline for. Having raised two daughters and now watching my granddaughters grow up, I fully appreciate what my dad and mom did for me in disciplining me to be a better man, a godly man. I know my heavenly Father will never make a mistake in making me a better man.

Prayer

Father, I praise You for the discipline You have used to make me a better man. Help me to grow in being a man who is full of respect, grace, truth, and integrity. Through Jesus I pray, amen.

—Al

NOVEMBER 5

SEARCH ME, O GOD

Search me, God, and know my heart; test me and know my anxious thoughts. See if there is any offensive way in me, and lead me in the way everlasting.

—PSALM 139:23–24

I JUST LOVE THIS scripture. Every time I pray it, God pops something into my head that I need to work on. Every time. That part that says "See if there is any offensive way in me" gets me every time. Ever since our ancestors Adam and Eve made that poor choice in the Garden of Eden, we have been trying to hide our bad actions, bad thoughts, and bad intentions from our Creator and Father. But He always sees and He always knows. If we'll just ask Him to reveal what He sees in us, He'll do it. The devil wants us to be dishonest *with* ourselves *about* ourselves, but self-examination and openness to God's leading is the key to being a changed person and to a restored relationship with our Father.

Prayer

Father, please search my heart today and reveal to me anything that displeases You. I want to give you every thought, every desire, and I ask You to lead me to Your will and purpose in everything I think and do. I thank You for Jesus and His ability to save, secure, and settle my eternal future. Through Him, I pray. Amen.

—Jep

November 6

(November 6–12 is a special series on the Gospel of Christ)

1: Our Desperate Need

There is no one righteous, not even one. . . . For all have sinned and fall short of the glory of God. . . . For the wages of sin is death, but the gift of God is eternal life in Christ Jesus our Lord.

—ROMANS 3:10, 23; 6:23

THERE'S NO MESSAGE more important on planet Earth than the gospel of Jesus Christ. But the message starts out with a pretty bleak picture of our condition. Ever since that fateful day in the Garden of Eden that you read about in Genesis 3—when Eve and Adam decided they knew better than their Creator—we have had to deal with sin and its terrible consequences. God told the first man and woman that death, both spiritual and physical, would result from sin, and His word has been true about that for all of the years since, for all of humanity. With no answer for sin, humanity needs something, or someone, to bring them hope.

Prayer

Father, we are so damaged by the ravages of sin. Our enemy Satan has been selling a lie from the beginning of our existence, and we keep buying it and trying to be our own god. O God, we need the hope that only You can provide. Through Jesus, I pray, amen.

—*Jase*

November 7

2: God Incarnate

The next day John saw Jesus coming toward him and said, "Look, the Lamb of God, who takes away the sin of the world!" . . . For God so loved the world that he gave his one and only Son, that whoever believes in him shall not perish but have eternal life. For God did not send his Son into the world to condemn the world, but to save the world through him.

—JOHN 1:29; 3:16–17

THINGS ARE LOOKING up! In response to our desperate sin condition, God sent His only Son, Jesus Christ, to be born in a manger in the hills of Bethlehem, Judea, over two thousand years ago. Jesus' coming was so powerful that human beings have been counting time by Him for more than a thousand years, and everything else before He came is marked as time *before* He came. This man was also God and lived a perfect, sinless life for thirty-three years and did many miraculous signs and brought a message of love, hope, and faith in God's ability to save humanity.

Prayer

Father, we thank You for sending a part of Yourself to this earth embodied in a man named Jesus. We acknowledge His ability to show us the answer for sin and death, and we are grateful for the hope we now have because of His life. We are sorry for the cost. Amen.

—*Jase*

3: THE PERFECT SACRIFICE

And being found in appearance as a man, he humbled himself by becoming obedient to death—even death on a cross!

—PHILIPPIANS 2:8

God made him who had no sin to be sin for us, so that in him we might become the righteousness of God.

—2 CORINTHIANS 5:21

FOR THOUSANDS OF years, the Hebrew people had sacrificed animals in an effort to take away the stain and guilt of sin, but the Hebrew writer tells us in Hebrews 10 that those animals never had the ability to remove sin from the people. The only sacrifice that would suffice for humanity's sin was the perfect sacrifice of a perfect man who also had the power to connect a redeemed humanity to God. Jesus Christ, the Son of the Almighty God, was that perfect man, and He gave himself up to die on a Roman cross for the sins of all humankind.

Prayer

Father, the sacrifice of Yourself and Your Son has given us all a chance to be redeemed from sin and its consequences, and we can't fully tell You how grateful we are and how awesome it is to be free from the stain of rebellion. Please bless us to live in a way that honors Your sacrifice. We offer this prayer through our rescuer, Jesus Christ, amen.

—*Jase*

NOVEMBER 9

4: Overcoming Death

On the first day of the week, very early in the morning, the women took the spices they had prepared and went to the tomb. They found the stone rolled away from the tomb, but when they entered, they did not find the body of the Lord Jesus. . . . "Why do you look for the living among the dead? He is not here; he has risen!"

—LUKE 24:1–3; 5–6

Regarding his Son, who . . . was appointed the Son of God in power by his resurrection from the dead: Jesus Christ our Lord.

—ROMANS 1:3–4

EVEN THOUGH JESUS' sacrifice on a Roman cross cleansed us from sin, humanity still faced the specter of physical death because of the physical consequences of sin. Even for redeemed people, the grave still loomed large! But not after Jesus showed mastery over death by rising from the dead three days after being laid in a tomb. This divine power answered the greatest fear that humans know: how do I survive beyond my physical death?

Prayer

Father, we no longer fear death because of the resurrection of Jesus from the grave. Thank you! We now live like men and women who have hope of a forever home with You. Through Christ, amen.

—*Jase*

November 10

5: Exalted in Heaven

God has raised this Jesus to life, and we are all witnesses of it. Exalted to the right hand of God, he has received from the Father the promised Holy Spirit and has poured out what you now see and hear.

—ACTS 2:32–33

After he had provided purification for sins, he sat down at the right hand of the Majesty in heaven.

—HEBREWS 1:3

After Jesus was raised from the dead, he appeared to over five hundred witnesses and then left planet Earth like Superman! Without a rocket booster, He literally flew up, up, and away. He reentered heaven to take a seat at the right hand of the Father, where the Bible tells us that He now mediates for us, His brothers and sisters, until He will return at the end of all days.

Prayer

Father, we feel such confidence knowing that all of our sins have been forgiven, that we are living without condemnation, that we are indwelled by your Spirit, and that our brother Jesus successfully advocates our eternal future with You. We thank You through Him, amen.

—*Jase*

November 11

6: He's Coming Again!

God is just: He will pay back trouble to those who trouble you and give relief to you who are troubled, and to us as well. This will happen when the Lord Jesus is revealed from heaven in blazing fire with his powerful angels.

—2 THESSALONIANS 1:6–7

Christ was sacrificed once to take away the sins of many; and he will appear a second time, not to bear sin, but to bring salvation to those who are waiting for him.

—HEBREWS 9:28

NOW WE WAIT until the times reach their fulfillment and our Lord will return the same way he left—in the clouds! We eagerly wait for that day with full knowledge that our forever home will always be there with God.

Prayer

Father, we have a hard time waiting, and so many days we ask for Your coming! We do trust Your timing in all things and know that every new brother or sister appreciates that You waited one more day before Your return. Please help us to live each day like it might be the day that You return. We eagerly await our Lord and pray through Him until His coming, amen.

—*Jase*

7: A NEW LIFE!

"Therefore let all Israel be assured of this: God has made this Jesus, whom you crucified, both Lord and Messiah." When the people heard this, they were cut to the heart and said to Peter and the other apostles, "Brothers, what shall we do?" Peter replied, "Repent and be baptized, every one of you, in the name of Jesus Christ for the forgiveness of your sins. And you will receive the gift of the Holy Spirit. The promise is for you and your children and for all who are far off—for all whom the Lord our God will call."

—ACTS 2:36–39

TO OBEY GOD is to *believe* the wonderful story of His Son, to *commit* to a new life with God in control, to *confess* our weakness, to *glory* in His strength, and to be *renewed* with a new birth. This new birth brings us into a forever family of like-minded brothers and sisters who serve God with everything they have. God's Spirit indwells His family and bears fruit; the Holy Spirit guides lives, counsels hearts, and intercedes for prayers to the Father and Son. What a life we have in Christ!

Prayer

Father, we praise You in newness of life and worship You in spirit and in truth. Thank You for the redemption and the hope we now have because of Jesus and Your Spirit. With their help, we pray, amen.

—*Jase*

November 13

Refreshing Hearts

I always thank my God as I remember you in my prayers, because I hear about your love for all his holy people and your faith in the Lord Jesus. . . . Your love has given me great joy and encouragement, because you, brother, have refreshed the hearts of the Lord's people.

—PHILEMON 1:4–7

I JUST LOVE PAUL'S description of his friend Philemon in this letter. It reminds me of a group of women I work with. I call them my "Muffins and Mentoring Group." We meet once a week in the morning, and everybody brings delicious breakfast food to share. I feel about these women like Paul felt about Philemon: their love has definitely encouraged me, and they refresh the hearts of many others. As part of a church family, it's so important to develop relationships beyond the few minutes you have on Sunday morning or Wednesday night. Relationships with Christian brothers and sisters will encourage you, and you will encourage them. Take a little time to write someone today and remind them what they mean to you and encourage them by refreshing their spirit.

Prayer

God, we are so blessed to have close friends who help us in this journey of life. I praise you for my friends and pray blessings upon them. Amen.

—Miss Kay

November 14

Milk and Meat

Anyone who lives on milk, being still an infant, is not acquainted with the teaching about righteousness. But solid food is for the mature, who by constant use have trained themselves to distinguish good from evil.

—HEBREWS 5:13–14

EVERY MOTHER KNOWS that infants need milk to grow until they get their teeth and are able to join the rest of the family in enjoying solid food. The bigger our children get, the more food they need, and by the time they become teenagers, you can't seem to fill them up! This is natural and just as God intended. In our spiritual growth, we experience a similar process. When we are new Christians, we can only handle spiritual milk—basic teachings and easy concepts. But as we grow in Christ, we should naturally get hungrier for the "meatier" food. It takes some spiritual maturity to digest the deeper teachings and grow in them. As time passes, we need to progress in our spiritual diet.

Prayer

Father, we are grateful for the early days of our Christian walk and Your patience with us. Help us move past the spiritual milk and grow to maturity so we can feed on the rich essence of Your Word. We thank You for Jesus, the Bread of Life, and pray through Him, amen.

—Korie

November 15

Rich in Good Deeds

Command those who are rich in this present world not to be arrogant nor to put their hope in wealth, which is so uncertain, but to put their hope in God, who richly provides us with everything for our enjoyment. Command them to do good, to be rich in good deeds, and to be generous and willing to share. In this way they will lay up treasure for themselves as a firm foundation for the coming age, so that they may take hold of the life that is truly life.

—1 TIMOTHY 6:17–19

THIS IS A great text for people who have done well financially on this earth. God says wealth is uncertain, at best. God is right. God says He richly provides everything for our enjoyment. God wants us to be happy, happy, happy, according to this text. Therefore, God says you are to be generous and willing to share. Tightfistedness is out! The treasure waiting on us far outweighs anything we can have down here.

Prayer

Father, You have blessed us richly. Let us bless others with our good deeds. We know that the life to come far outweighs anything here on earth now. Help us to practice the teaching that it is more blessed to give than receive. Amen.

—*Phil*

November 16

Why Do You Boast?

For who makes you different from anyone else? What do you have that you did not receive? And if you did receive it, why do you boast as though you did not?

—1 CORINTHIANS 4:7

IN THIS VERSE, Paul is addressing the Corinthians, who are struggling with being prideful. They are comparing themselves to each other as to who has more gifts. Sound familiar? How many times a week do you compare yourself to your friend, a stranger, a co-worker, etc.? Whether it is material possessions, education, children's accomplishments, or physical beauty, we must remember that we did not accomplish any of this on our own. The Lord God decided to bless us with these things. Do you think He blessed you because He likes you better than His other children? He chooses to bless us because He desires us to give Him the glory. Use the blessings God has given you to make Him look good—not to make yourself look good.

Prayer

Lord, why You choose to bless us so abundantly is sometimes hard to comprehend. Please help me to remember that all good things come from You and that You chose to give them to me so that I may glorify You. Thank You for the enjoyment of these blessings. I will always strive to use them to serve You.

—*Missy*

NOVEMBER 17

THE WAYS OF GOD

"For my thoughts are not your thoughts, neither are your ways my ways," declares the LORD. "As the heavens are higher than the earth, so are my ways higher than your ways and my thoughts than your thoughts."

—ISAIAH 55:8–9

TAKE A SECOND to think about your thoughts throughout the day. What do you think about the most? Homework, schedules, kids, girlfriends, boyfriends, practice? Compare how much time you spend thinking about those things to how much time you spend thinking about our Lord and Savior. In today's busy life and culture, our Lord is often forgotten and He knows this. Let's look at this from a different viewpoint: This verse compares God to us—and the main comparison is that He is *way* bigger than we are and is *far* above us. He is the Supreme Being, and we are nowhere close to Him. Even when we sin and turn our backs on Him, He still loves us. We serve an amazing God!

Prayer

Lord, I am sorry for my wandering thoughts. Help me to focus on You throughout this day and the days to come, so that it will become a habit and I will become closer to You. Help me always to be aware of how great and powerful You are and to have the proper respect for You. In Your Son's name, amen.

—*Cole*

BUT IF YOU DO SIN. . .

I write this to you so that you will not sin. But if anybody does sin, we have an advocate with the Father—Jesus Christ, the Righteous One. He is the atoning sacrifice for our sins, and not only for ours but also for the sins of the whole world.

—1 JOHN 2:1–2

I FIND THIS PASSAGE so intriguing. John starts off by saying he's writing this book to us so that we will not sin, and in the very next breath, he says, "But if anybody *does* sin . . ." I think part of what he means is: "After I've just told you all I've told you, how can you ever be the same and sin like before?" He's right! The more I learn about God, the more I want to be like Him. I want to please God, and the best way to please God is to live a holy life. Will I ever live a totally sinless life? No! But John assures me that if I do sin, I have an advocate with the Father. Jesus is our atoning sacrifice—not just for the "godly," but for the whole world. I want to live each day as holy as possible so that I can please God and show Him that I cherish His sacrifice, but I am so thankful He's made a provision for the many times that I blow it.

Prayer

Father, although we know we will not ever live a perfect life, help us to live each day in Your light and be a light for the world You sacrificed Your son for. In His name, amen.

—*Lisa*

November 19

Wise Relationship Choices

Do not be yoked together with unbelievers. For what do righteousness and wickedness have in common? Or what fellowship can light have with darkness? What harmony is there between Christ and Belial? Or what does a believer have in common with an unbeliever?

—2 CORINTHIANS 6:14–15

As followers of Jesus, we strive for balance in many areas, and one of those areas is our interaction with people who aren't Christians. Our desire, always, is to be a light to any we come in contact with, but we must wisely be aware that we are all susceptible to bad influences. So as we share our faith and mingle with people from every background—like Jesus did—we need to constantly watch our own hearts and make sure that *we* are the influence and not the other way around. Though we have friendships with non-Christians, we must choose fellow believers as our *best* friends. We want to share Jesus with everyone but don't want our vision to become clouded or our hearts to grow numb.

Prayer

Lord, protect me from the evil one. Guard my heart from all wickedness. I pray that when I'm out in the world You will help me keep my focus on You. Help me to spread the gospel to everyone and to always live in Your will.

—*Jessica*

NOVEMBER 20

ALL TANGLED UP

"People are slaves to whatever has mastered them." If they have escaped the corruption of the world by knowing our Lord and Savior Jesus Christ and are again entangled in it and are overcome, they are worse off at the end than they were at the beginning. . . . Of them the proverbs are true: "A dog returns to its vomit," and, "A sow that is washed returns to her wallowing in the mud."

—2 PETER 2:19–22

WHOA! THIS IS a scary scripture—probably one of the scariest in the entire Bible! I guess sometimes we need to be a little shook up to remind us that this Christianity business is serious! I know how bad habits can become bad behavior, and before long you're a slave to that behavior. When I was in Nam, I got involved in some pretty heavy drinking even though I had promised myself I wouldn't. So I guess I was like that dog returning to its vomit. Not a pretty picture, Jack! Thank God, I was able to get untangled from drinking, and I've never gone back. I want to live for Christ and never turn my back on all the blessings He's given me!

Prayer

Father, we thank You for cleansing our dirty lives and habits with the blood of Jesus. Deliver us from anything that entangles us or takes our eyes off of Jesus. Through Him we pray, amen.

—Si

November 21

Two Simple Principles

"Teacher, which is the greatest commandment in the Law?" Jesus replied: " 'Love the Lord your God with all your heart and with all your soul and with all your mind.' This is the first and greatest commandment. And the second is like it: 'Love your neighbor as yourself.' All the Law and the Prophets hang on these two commandments."

—MATTHEW 22:36–40

I LOVE IT WHEN Jesus simplifies things for me. In the scripture above, He boils down all of the Old Testament law into two simple principles—loving God and loving others. When I think of my everyday actions that aren't in line with God's will, one of these two principles is always violated. Just because something is simple doesn't mean it is easy, but at least I know how to live today . . . and every day!

Prayer

Lord, I want to love You with all my heart, soul, mind, and strength today, and I want to love others as I love myself. Forgive us for falling short of these noble goals. We are so appreciative of the saving grace of Jesus that covers our sins. In Him, amen.

—Jep

MADE RICH IN EVERY WAY

Now he who supplies seed to the sower and bread for food will also supply and increase your store of seed and will enlarge the harvest of your righteousness. You will be enriched in every way so that you can be generous on every occasion, and through us your generosity will result in thanksgiving to God.

—2 CORINTHIANS 9:10–11

THIS IS THE Word of God. *Everything* you have is from Him. He says here that He will enlarge the harvest of your righteousness. You will be enriched in every way so that *you* can be generous on every occasion! I have applied this over and over, and the blessings keep pouring in. Do it—be generous. Turn on; tune in; be generous!

Prayer

Father, You are the giver of all things. You give life itself, our breath and everything else! Therefore, Father, let us never be stingy toward You or our brothers and sisters. Help us to help others. Let us never be lazy or unproductive in our livelihoods or toward You. Amen.

—*Phil*

November 23

Citizens of God's Kingdom

You are no longer foreigners and strangers, but fellow citizens with God's people and also members of his household.

—EPHESIANS 2:19

ABOUT TWENTY-TWO YEARS ago, when I was just starting my ministry at our church, I went on my first mission trip to Romania. The country was only about two years removed from communist dictatorship, and it was dark and scary. We had a pretty frightening incident with some coal miners who were revolting against the current government, and we were more than a little on edge. I will never forget how great I felt when I visited the U.S. embassy and was allowed in behind those armed marines standing watch over sovereign U.S. soil! I was a citizen of the United States, and that gave me special privileges. For the rest of the trip, I gained confidence because I knew there was a place that would recognize my blue passport and to which I could retreat if we got into trouble. As citizens of God's kingdom, we are blessed and protected.

Prayer

Father, I am grateful and proud to be a citizen of Your kingdom and am so appreciative for the protection afforded me in this culture. I pray through Jesus, amen.

—*Al*

NO BITTER ROOT

See to it that no one falls short of the grace of God and that no bitter root grows up to cause trouble and defile many.

—HEBREWS 12:15

IN A BIG family like ours, there are plenty of chances for bitterness to pop up between family members like an ugly weed. The verse above tells us that bitterness can become a problem when we fall short of the grace of God. I think that part of the meaning for us is that when we don't live in an attitude of grace toward others, bitterness can take root in our hearts. Bitterness is a cancer of the soul and hurts everything it touches—and it offers *nothing* of value. Since the Hebrew writer starts off by saying "See to it," I take that to mean we have control over what makes us bitter, and even more, *grace* seems to be the magic tonic that helps cure the sour nature of bitterness.

Prayer

Father, please help us to embrace Your grace and release the bitterness that is so destructive to our souls and the souls around us. Forgive us when we don't allow You to cleanse, heal, and bless us with Your grace.

—Miss Kay

November 25

God's Promised Protection

He will cover you with his feathers, and under his wings you will find refuge; his faithfulness will be your shield and rampart.

—PSALM 91:4

THE SCRIPTURE ABOVE is both gentle and powerful. It portrays God as having feathers and wings—both of which provide gentle protection. It also talks about a "shield" and a "rampart." A rampart is an embankment or wall that is meant to protect. There will always be times in our lives when we feel fear and hopelessness, but it is during these times when we must put our trust in God. It may seem as if the weight of doubt has surrounded us, but if we put our trust in God, He will not let us down.

Prayer

Dear God, be with me as I walk down the road of life. Wrap Your arms around me and help me grow strong in the faith. Please make me the person You would have me be. I love being wrapped up in You. Thank You, Lord, and in Jesus' name, amen.

—*Godwin*

IT'S QUITE SIMPLE

But he's already made it plain how to live, what to do, what GOD is looking for in men and women. It's quite simple: Do what is fair and just to your neighbor, be compassionate and loyal in your love, and don't take yourself too seriously—take God seriously.

—MICAH 6:8, *THE MESSAGE*

I OFTEN WONDER WHAT life would be like if everyone (believer or unbeliever) would follow this one verse. There would be no need for lawyers or prisons. Teachers would actually be able to teach, and moms would have quiet, peaceful days. That sounds nice! But, in reality, it's hard to always be compassionate, fair, and loyal. Our humanness gets in the way. To achieve this discipline, we might have to bite our tongues or count to ten before we speak. We might have to simply ignore some comments or some "looks" we get. But if you want a more pleasant life experience, these little changes will help that happen. God is never wrong, and He declares this to be the best way to live!

Prayer

Father, I thank You for my friends and family. Please forgive me for not being as loving and forgiving as I should be. Help me to look through Your eyes and see souls who need Your grace and mercy, just as I do. In His name I pray, amen.

—*Korie*

NOVEMBER 27

BE PREPARED

Preach the Word; be prepared in season and out of season; correct, rebuke and encourage—with great patience and careful instruction.

—2 TIMOTHY 4:2

HUMANS IN ALL walks of life are always preparing for the next season. Getting ready for whatever comes next is a valuable part of life. The hunter prepares for the next game season, the farmer prepares for the next planting or harvesting season, the athlete prepares and trains for the next sports season. We Robertsons are always preparing for the next hunting season. However, the Lord says that even more than hunting, we should always be prepared to share His Word. Unique opportunities to share the Word of God can present themselves anytime, so prepare yourself every day to be an instrument of the Lord. He also says to do this with great care and love. Avoid presenting His message in a way that will make people not want to be open to it. God's Word should inspire love, trust, and faith in us all.

Prayer

Lord, prepare me to be Your instrument on earth. Create in me a desire to share Your love and wisdom with all I encounter. Help me to be vigilant in all seasons and ready to show Your grace, mercy, and patience to everyone I meet. In the name of Jesus I pray, amen.

—*Alex Robertson Mancuso*

November 28

God Will Provide

Do not be anxious about anything, but in every situation, by prayer and petition, with thanksgiving, present your requests to God.

—PHILIPPIANS 4:6

GOD WILL PROVIDE what we need; all we have to do is ask Him. Prayer is a part of our life that is often overlooked. I struggled with a relationship in my life for a while because I was only concerned about what I wanted it to be—not what God wanted it to be. I will never forget the night I prayed and told God that I wanted nothing more out of this relationship than what He wanted it to be. Since that day, it has done nothing but gotten stronger and stronger. It is so awesome that we serve a God who wants us to talk to Him and ask Him for things. He will always provide!

Prayer

God, it is such an honor to be able to talk to You and know that You *want* me to talk to You. I know You will provide everything I need!

—Martin

November 29

The Downside of Riches

Those who want to get rich fall into temptation and a trap and into many foolish and harmful desires that plunge people into ruin and destruction. For the love of money is a root of all kinds of evil. Some people, eager for money, have wandered from the faith and pierced themselves with many griefs.

—1 TIMOTHY 6:9–10

MONEY CAN BE a snare to us all. God said it, and I have seen it happen to many—just like He said! I went from poor to rich, so I, for one, had better realize what the *love of money* can do to a man. Miss Kay told me she has been poor with me and rich with me; then she said, "Rich is better, Phil." Though it's not wrong to enjoy our blessing, our focus needs to be on blessing God and others with the riches He's given us. If we love money, we can be cursed because of it. Let us allow God to control us—not money!

Prayer

Father, You made me rich, and I thank You for what You've given me. But please let me be consumed with You and never with riches. Help us to remember the downside of wealth and wrong priorities. Let our priority on earth be You and You alone! Amen.

—*Phil*

November 30

People Are Watching

Remember your leaders, who spoke the word of God to you. Consider the outcome of their way of life and imitate their faith.

—HEBREWS 13:7

ONE OF THE most intimidating things about being a leader in your church is the accountability that comes with the position. To think that people watch you and follow your example keeps you both humble and cognizant of your tremendous responsibility when it comes to leading God's people. Some people avoid leadership because of these factors, but this is a God-appointed position. As a leader, I know that He will guide me in the right ways to lead others to Him.

Prayer

Father, as a leader of Your people, I am humbled that You chose me to lead, and I pray that my example will always follow Your Word and Your will. I embrace Your calling to be a positive influence in the lives of people. I love my Lord, Who is my ultimate example of what a leader is supposed to look like. In His name I pray, amen.

—*Al*

December

DECEMBER 1

PRAY FOR US!

Pray for us, too, that God may open a door for our message, so that we may proclaim the mystery of Christ, for which I am in chains. Pray that I may proclaim it clearly, as I should. Be wise in the way you act toward outsiders; make the most of every opportunity. Let your conversation be always full of grace, seasoned with salt, so that you may know how to answer everyone.

—COLOSSIANS 4:3–6

I HAVE HAD SO many people tell me that they are praying for our family. They realize that we have been given a huge platform to bring God glory and reach people, and they pray for our protection, our witness, and our success in a world that Satan has owned far too long. These friends-in-prayer are praying the charge from Paul to the Colossian church—and my family *feels* the power of it. We will continue to speak of grace and spice it up with the style God has blessed us with—all to impact people with the gospel of Christ! Please keep the prayers going!

Prayer

Lord, we are so blessed by the opportunity You have given our family. I pray for every child of Yours out there who is proclaiming Your glory and grace every day in their lives, as well. Through Christ we pray, amen.

—*Miss Kay*

DECEMBER 2

RINGING OUT THE MESSAGE

You became imitators of us and of the Lord, for you welcomed the message in the midst of severe suffering with the joy given by the Holy Spirit. And so you became a model to all the believers in Macedonia and Achaia. The Lord's message rang out from you not only in Macedonia and Achaia—your faith in God has become known everywhere.

—1 THESSALONIANS 1:6–8

THE WHOLE ROBERTSON family has been changed by God—in a big way! We've been encouraged by a great church family, and now we have taken on the task of ringing out the message of Christ to the U.S. and the world. When Phil and I were kids running the woods in Vivian, Louisiana, we had no idea what God had in store for our future. We've come a long way since that log cabin in the woods—but the most important thing we do now is share God's message of hope. We want to be like the Thessalonians in the scripture above and let our faith be known everywhere!

Prayer

Father, I thank You for my beginnings, and I thank You for where You've taken us today. I pray that our family always makes You look good. Keep us humble as we live before You. May our faith in You become known everywhere. Thank You for Your cleaning power and for Jesus, our Lord, in whom we pray, amen.

—Si

DECEMBER 3

LET YOUR LIGHT SHINE

You are the light of the world. A town built on a hill cannot be hidden. Neither do people light a lamp and put it under a bowl. Instead they put it on its stand, and it gives light to everyone in the house. In the same way, let your light shine before others, that they may see your good deeds and glorify your Father in heaven.

—MATTHEW 5:14–16

MY SWEET SON Little Will sleeps with a light on in his room every night. It isn't because he's scared; he just likes to be able to see when it's dark. If you have ever attempted to walk through your garage in the dark, you quickly realize a flashlight would have been a good idea. Light is valuable! Followers of God *have* to light the way for the world to see. Our light is shown in the way we treat our family, how we speak to the checkout person, and how we handle an angry parent at a sporting event. When you shine your personal light of joy, you show the world that God lives in you.

Prayer

Father, it's hard to consistently shine in such a dark world. I get discouraged and wonder if it's making a difference, but I trust that if I shine, You will make the difference. In His name I pray, amen.

—*Korie*

New Mercies

Because of the Lord's great love we are not consumed, for his compassions never fail. They are new every morning; great is your faithfulness.

—LAMENTATIONS 3:22–23

Sometimes we feel like the pressures and challenges of life just might swallow us up. But this verse *promises* that we will not be "consumed." Why? Because of the Lord's great love for us. What a comforting concept to know that every morning when we wake up, the mercies of our Lord have been refreshed in our lives. How wonderful to know that His compassions *never* fail. Just repeating this verse to myself instantly calms my spirit and gives me new strength. The Lord's power never diminishes in its ability to cleanse, heal, forgive, and renew. How blessed are we!

Prayer

Father, we are grateful for this new morning and pray for refreshing and cleansing as we face this day. May we face the opportunities of this day with confidence and the knowledge of Your unending love for us. We pray this through Jesus, with the help of Your Spirit, amen.

—*Missy*

December 5

The Progression of Love

And this is my prayer: that your love may abound more and more in knowledge and depth of insight, so that you may be able to discern what is best and may be pure and blameless for the day of Christ, filled with the fruit of righteousness that comes through Jesus Christ—to the glory and praise of God.

—PHILIPPIANS 1:9–11

I LOVE ALL OF Paul's prayers in his letters, but this one is just *rich.* He shows an amazing progression. It starts with *love,* then it moves to *knowledge* to *insight* to *discernment* to *purity* to *fruit* to *glory* to *God.* If we don't build the matrix of our lives in this progression, we will not bring glory to God the way He intends. In other words, no step skipping! It all begins with love for God and continues with love for others and then progresses to a place of maturity and praise to our Lord.

Prayer

Lord, we thank You for showing us the clear path to living for You. You are the great example of purity, reverence, and love. May we follow Your example and live out this beautiful prayer of our brother Paul. In Christ we offer this prayer, amen.

—*Jase*

DECEMBER 6

SNAP TO ATTENTION

They were looking intently up into the sky as [Jesus] was going, when suddenly two men dressed in white stood beside them. "Men of Galilee," they said, "why do you stand here looking into the sky? This same Jesus, who has been taken from you into heaven, will come back in the same way you have seen him go into heaven."

—ACTS 1:10–11

WATCHING JESUS FLYING away from the planet Earth must have been an amazing and unbelievable sight! Even more shocking must have been two angelic types who appeared out of thin air to basically snap them out of wonder and put them to work! I love the exhilarating moments of realizing God's greatness, but I have to be snapped to attention from time to time and reminded that there are people around me who don't even know the God I worship.

Prayer

Father, I marvel today at Your awesome greatness and the genuine love and mercy You have for me. I could stay here and praise You all day, but there is work to be done before Jesus comes back. Please give me focus today to help another see You. Through Jesus I pray, amen.

—*Willie*

FACEDOWN

After the Philistines had captured the ark of God, they . . . carried the ark into Dagon's temple and set it beside Dagon. When the people of Ashdod rose early the next day, there was Dagon, fallen on his face on the ground before the ark of the LORD! They took Dagon and put him back in his place. But the following morning when they rose, there was Dagon, fallen on his face on the ground before the ark of the LORD! His head and hands had been broken off and were lying on the threshold; only his body remained.

—1 SAMUEL 5:1–4

DON'T YOU JUST love this story? Here the Philistines thought they had done such a powerful thing—stealing the Israelites' sacred ark—and when they put it in the same temple as their false god, the god was found facedown on the ground, as if worshipping the ark! The power of God overpowers false idols every time! The very first of the Ten Commandments is "You shall have no other gods before me"—the very first one! I never want to follow a god whose feet you have to nail to the floor to keep him upright! I will continue to choose true power over false promises.

Prayer

Almighty God, I praise You for being the most high and powerful force in the universe and beyond. I never want to settle for false gods that are of this world. Through Jesus, I pray, amen.

—*Jep*

DECEMBER 8

LIVING IN ME

But very truly I tell you, it is for your good that I am going away. Unless I go away, the Advocate will not come to you; but if I go, I will send him to you.

—JOHN 16:7

THE DISCIPLES MUST have been scared to death at the thought of their leader leaving them. But Jesus insisted that it was a good thing. Jesus comforted his disciples by promising something greater than His physical presence—the indwelling Holy Spirit. God's brilliant plan of salvation offered not only the perfect sacrifice for sin through the death of His Son but the empowering presence of His own Spirit in the lives of all of His children. What an honor and a blessing to have a living guide, comforter, advocate, and counselor living in my very own heart. God's Spirit helps us follow the path God has laid out for us, and He is the deposit for my eternal life. I am in awe!

Prayer

Father, we thank You for Your Son's sacrifice of Himself, and we also thank You for the Holy Spirit that lives in us while You are in heaven interceding for us. We thank You, Holy Spirit, for Your guidance, comfort, counsel, and intervention on our behalf, and we pray today that we will follow Your lead as we live for God. Through Jesus, with the help of the Spirit I pray, amen.

—*Jessica*

DECEMBER 9

A WONDER LIKE NO OTHER

I will praise you, O Lord, with all my heart; I will tell of all your wonders.

—PSALM 9:1, NIV 1984

I AM NOT A talented singer, but I do love to sing praises to our Lord. So many times I have gone to Wednesday worship (where we mostly sing and praise God) out of obligation. After I leave, I am so glad that I went to meet and worship with my brothers and sisters. When you look outside at the landscape, what do you see? What about when you look at the stars and the heavens? Wonders! God created these wonders for us. When my older daughter had her two daughters, I witnessed a wonder like no other! There are no words. I was amazed. When my daughters were baptized, it was even a greater wonder. I know that when the resurrection happens, we will all think it is the most wonderful wonder of all. Think back in your life and see what wonders God has put there. You will be amazed!

Prayer

Thank You, Father, for the wonders of Your mighty love! We will praise You until we see Your face—and then we will praise You for eternity! In Jesus' name, amen.

—*Lisa*

DECEMBER 10

LIVE DURING THE DAY

You are all children of the light and children of the day. We do not belong to the night or to the darkness. So then, let us not be like others, who are asleep, but let us be awake and sober. For those who sleep, sleep at night, and those who get drunk, get drunk at night.

—1 THESSALONIANS 5:5–7

I WON'T LIE TO you, most of the trouble I have had in my life has come during the wee hours of the night and early morning. From drinking and carousing in my young years to Internet pornography in later years, I have come to understand exactly what Paul was trying to encourage me to do in this passage from 1 Thessalonians 5. I have learned and subsequently counseled others to sleep at night and live during the day. I realize some people struggle with insomnia or work the night shift, but for most of us, we can decide to be up at night or down, and I maintain that the better course of action is to sleep when your family sleeps and go full board for Christ when they are awake!

Prayer

Father, I thank You for the light of day and the newness of mornings. Thank You for forgiving me and leading me daily in light. Through Jesus, amen.

—*Al*

December 11

Never in Vain

Therefore, my dear brothers and sisters, stand firm. Let nothing move you. Always give yourselves fully to the work of the Lord, because you know that your labor in the Lord is not in vain.

—1 CORINTHIANS 15:58

When you were a kid, did your siblings beg you to do things for them, promising that they'd make your bed or wash dishes for a whole month in return? How did that usually work out? They probably never did the first chore on your behalf; it was all in vain. Your labor for the Lord is never in vain. He has promised that we will be rewarded for our faith in Him, and He never breaks promises! If God is with us, no one can be against us. With that in mind, stand firm and do not be moved on your principles and love of righteousness. No one else in the world can offer us what God can offer us! Give yourself fully to the will of the Lord, and you will not be disappointed with the treasures stored up for you in heaven.

Prayer

Father, I want to work harder for You. I know that my labor in Your name will not be in vain. Help me to stand firm, to be strong like the man who built his house upon solid rock. Through the name of Jesus, I pray, amen.

—*Alex*

A SPIRIT OF POWER

Do not be ashamed to testify about our Lord, or ashamed of me his prisoner. But join with me in suffering for the gospel, by the power of God.

—2 TIMOTHY 1:7–8, NIV 1984

THE WORST SHAME I could ever bring upon myself is to be ashamed to testify about the Lord Jesus. Far be it from us to be ashamed of the one who has given us eternal life. God forbid any of us ever shrink back from proclaiming Jesus. I will not—I must not—I cannot help but proclaim Jesus, and I don't care who is standing against me, period!

Prayer

Father, I pray I am never ashamed of Jesus, my Lord. I pray You give me great boldness to proclaim Him anywhere I am. Help us all to roar like lions as we share the great gospel of Jesus! Amen.

—*Phil*

DECEMBER 13

HATERS ARE GONNA HATE

Everyone will hate you because of me. But not a hair of your head will perish. Stand firm, and you will win life.

—LUKE 21:17–19

WHEN I READ this verse, I always think of one of my best friends. Every time someone would joke with her or make fun of her, she would just shrug her shoulders and say, "Haters are gonna hate." She's so right. That's just how the world is. Those who hate God will also hate those who love Him. But our reward is not having other people like us; our reward is heaven. All we have to do is stand firm.

Prayer

Dear Lord, help me to be more focused on You and not care what the world thinks of me. Thank You for loving me and giving me the gift of Your Son. It's in His name I pray, amen.

—*Reed*

December 14

Building Up People

Your love has given me great joy and encouragement, because you, brother, have refreshed the hearts of the Lord's people.

—PHILEMON 1:7

IF THERE'S ONE thing I noticed when I came to work with the Robertsons, it was the positive impact they seem to have on everyone. Building up people is their norm. That's something I wasn't used to, but it sure made me feel good. I know that it wasn't them but God in them, but I sure appreciate how they all seem to let God work so positively through them.

Prayer

Father, thank You for the hearts You have touched and changed. Help us to think of others and to keep building each other up in our words and prayers. I thank You for the Robertson family and how close they are to me and my family. In Your precious name I pray, amen.

—*Godwin*

DECEMBER 15

NEVER GIVE UP

But we're not quitters who lose out. Oh, no! We'll stay with it and survive, trusting all the way.

—HEBREWS 10:39, *THE MESSAGE*

LIFE IS HARD, both for the saved and the unsaved alike. The difference is that those of us who trust in the Lord have help and hope when things get tough. We do not give up but continue on, knowing that God is with us and that we will be victorious. We have a hope that keeps our hearts alive even when others would give up. God is our strength.

Prayer

Beloved Father, thank You for the victory. It is so good to know I am not alone. You see and care about my life. I am safe with You! I am hopeful because of You. I pray to You for strength and courage.

—Lynda Hammitt

December 16

Make the Time

Where two or three gather in my name, there am I with them.

—MATTHEW 18:20

ONE OF THE toughest struggles for the Robertsons is scheduling. But one thing they always make time for is assembling with our forever family—our church. Scheduling issues affect everyone, because there are always so many people and things bidding for our time. It would be so easy to sacrifice worship time because of busy schedules and demands. This is exactly what the devil wants. His desire is for us to put something, anything, before our time for God. Reading this scripture reminds me that God is always there. He walks with us and protects us from a world that is fighting for our time, money, and efforts. Gathering to worship is a commandment of God. There is no greater way to honor Him than to meet with the brothers and sisters and sing praises, worship, and study how to serve and spread the gospel of Christ.

Prayer

Father in heaven, never let me forsake gathering to worship You. Guard my thoughts, and remove the obstacles I use to try to justify not gathering to worship with my brothers and sisters. Bless our gatherings, and never let us forget to assemble to worship and serve You.

—Jon Gimber

December 17

Choose Wisely

Be very careful, then, how you live—not as unwise but as wise, making the most of every opportunity, because the days are evil. Therefore do not be foolish, but understand what the Lord's will is.

—EPHESIANS 5:15–17

I GET A LOT of experience being "very careful"—as this verse says—when I make the reeds for the Duck Commander duck calls. They have to be done just right, and I'm the *master* of duck call reeds. I don't get involved in the business end of things much—hey, I can't do it all! But one thing I know is that for every opportunity there is a cost. For everything I decide to do, I pay the cost of what I could have done instead. The same principle works in spiritual things. When we choose things that are evil and stupid, then we pay the cost of lost opportunities to do something good—something wise and unselfish. I may not have a lot of business sense, but I can figure that one out! God wants us to choose the opportunities that allow us to give the max to help others and lead them in the right direction. You've got some choices to make, Jack!

Prayer

Lord, I am so grateful that You took the opportunity to come to earth and die for my sins. Today, help me bless someone else and be wise in my walk. Through Jesus, amen.

—*Si*

A BEAUTIFUL THING

Husbands, love your wives and do not be harsh with them.

—COLOSSIANS 3:19

BOYS, DID YOU get that? I have worked hard on that simple statement from God for fifty years with Miss Kay. I only wish I could have figured that one out earlier—from the beginning. I am now ashamed of my past treatment of my woman. But thank God, I am finally putting that text into practice. It is a beautiful thing when your woman is your best friend, your wife, your sister, and your fellow worker in the Lord. Again, it is a beautiful thing and *it can be done*! Love her, and do not be harsh with her. God is watching and so are your kids—closely!

Prayer

Father, I confess I make many, many mistakes. I was a scumbag jerk in this area for years, but You, Father, showed me how to love my woman, Miss Kay, and not be harsh with her. I am truly grateful to You. And I am sure Miss Kay is really grateful to You for straightening me out on this. Amen.

—*Phil*

DECEMBER 19

STAND BY YOUR MAN

Wives, in the same way submit yourselves to your own husbands so that, if any of them do not believe the word, they may be won over without words by the behavior of their wives, when they see the purity and reverence of your lives.

—1 PETER 3:1–2

I HAVE ALWAYS TRIED to be submissive to Phil, but during the first ten years of our marriage, many in my family—and even Phil's family—told me I was too submissive and needed to leave Phil because he was never going to change his ways. But my precious grandmother had instilled the theme of this verse in my heart, and with time and much prayer, Phil was finally won over by the grace of God. Sometimes Phil compares me to Sarah, whom Peter describes later in this text as a woman of great spiritual beauty and a model for women to emulate. He's a joy to submit to now.

Prayer

Father, I thank You for giving me the strength to stick it out through the dark hours and to keep loving Phil while he found his way to You. Our lives and destinies were changed because You gave me perseverance, and I thank You for the joy of being married to man who truly loves me. Through Christ I bring this praise, amen.

—*Miss Kay*

Personal Application

Wives, submit yourselves to your husbands, as is fitting in the Lord. Husbands, love your wives and do not be harsh with them. Children, obey your parents in everything, for this pleases the Lord.

—COLOSSIANS 3:18–20

I WANT TO SHARE another take on the above teaching than Mom and Dad just shared. I am always amazed at how many people, including me, go to a passage like this and quote it for *someone else* to be reminded of! One of the great epiphanies of my life was in the early years in our family when I realized that I desperately needed honesty from my wife and children. But it took me a while to figure out that I wasn't receiving it because I was not a good receiver of truth, even though I kept asking for it! When I adjusted my response, our relationships got a lot more honest and improved dramatically. That epiphany helped me learn to read verses like this one and ask how they *apply to me,* before I ask how they apply to someone else.

Prayer

Lord, forgive my ignorance, which is all too often on display. I thank You for wisdom and insight and especially for learning to be a better receiver of other people's honesty. Through Jesus, I pray, amen.

—*Al*

DECEMBER 21

LOVE IN ACTION

Love must be sincere. Hate what is evil; cling to what is good. Be devoted to one another in love. Honor one another above yourselves. Never be lacking in zeal, but keep your spiritual fervor, serving the Lord. Be joyful in hope, patient in affliction, faithful in prayer. Share with the Lord's people who are in need. Practice hospitality.

—ROMANS 12:9–13

IF WE COULD practice this one passage, we could conquer the world. My father-in-law, Phil, always says, "Love God, and love your neighbor." That sounds pretty simple, doesn't it? But putting it into practice is another matter. This passage teaches how love looks when it's put into action. There's some real power in the words of this scripture: "love," "cling," "honor," "zeal," "serving," "joyful," "patient," "faithful," and "hospitality." All these actions work together, flowing back and forth in our hearts as we implement them. The more I love others, the more joy I have. The more I cling to good, the more patient I become. The more faithful I am in prayer, the more zealous I am for the Lord. The more I practice hospitality, the more my desire to serve others grows. It's no wonder that it all begins with love.

Prayer

Father, help me to continue to grow in these qualities for the rest of my life. In His name, amen.

—*Lisa*

A Dangerous Descent

When tempted, no one should say, "God is tempting me." For God cannot be tempted by evil, nor does he tempt anyone; but each person is tempted when they are dragged away by their own evil desire and enticed. Then, after desire has conceived, it gives birth to sin; and sin, when it is full-grown, gives birth to death.

—JAMES 1:13–15

I ALWAYS THINK OF this passage as the opposite of Led Zeppelin's famous song title "Stairway to Heaven." The above verse actually describes a "stairway to hell"—a self-induced descent into darkness that begins with desire and winds up with destruction. So many times we follow this path to our own demise. I am grateful that my God can reach down those stairs and rescue us from ourselves when our desires are mixed up with the devil's. I want to learn to instantly recognize the very first step of that stairway—desire—before taking that next dangerous step down!

Prayer

Father, please forgive me for following the desires of my heart when they are not of Your will. I pray for recognition today of every step, every motive, and every thought. Please give me awareness when I start a dangerous descent into evil and put someone in my life to warn me and hold me accountable. I thank You for Jesus, whose sacrifice for sin saves me from the evil one; in His name I pray, amen.

—*Willie*

December 23

God's Beautiful Handiwork

For it is by grace you have been saved, through faith—and this is not from yourselves, it is the gift of God—not by works, so that no one can boast. For we are God's handiwork, created in Christ Jesus to do good works, which God prepared in advance for us to do.

—EPHESIANS 2:8–10

I LOVE BEING CALLED God's handiwork, and I love being saved by His grace. It is so easy to fall into that age-old trap of thinking that somehow we can make our own spiritual way through our good works and our own power. Nothing could be farther from the truth. We are only saved by the grace of our good God and *He* has done the prep work for all the good things that we now accomplish in Him! That leaves absolutely *no* room for me to take credit for goodness or claim I somehow have managed my salvation. I have only our Father and His Son to thank.

Prayer

Father, we are so blessed to be awash in Your grace. I pray that the good works You planned for me today will bring You glory, help others see You more clearly, and allow me to appreciate You more. I pray this through Jesus, with the help of Your Spirit, amen.

—Jessica

December 24

An Eternal Plan

For he chose us in him before the creation of the world to be holy and blameless in his sight. In love he predestined us for adoption to sonship through Jesus Christ, in accordance with his pleasure and will.

—EPHESIANS 1:4–5

You have to love it when a plan comes together! What's incredible about God's plan of salvation is that God thought it all through before we were ever even created! Talk about advance planning! Of course, you have to have the divine ability to exist outside of time to come up with a plan like this, but that is the God we serve—He's omnipresent! I just consider myself fortunate to have had my God think of me and provide me with the opportunity to become His son when I embraced my Savior, Jesus.

Prayer

Lord, we are so appreciative to be included in Your plan for humankind. We are forever grateful to be called sons and daughters of the Almighty! Your will is our will, through Jesus, amen.

—Jep

December 25

By His Wounds We Are Healed

He was despised and rejected by mankind, a man of suffering, and familiar with pain. . . . He was pierced for our transgressions, he was crushed for our iniquities; the punishment that brought us peace was on him, and by his wounds we are healed.

—Isaiah 53:3–5

On this day of December 25—the day we celebrate the birth of our Jesus—I want to think about Him as a man and what He came to this earth to do. We've talked a lot about Jesus in this collection of devotions, and that's because He is the one the Robertson lives are centered around. This poignant prophecy is a haunting picture of our Lord hundreds of years before He actually came and died for all humanity. He is portrayed as a broken man who offered hope to a broken humanity! He was *pierced,* He was *crushed,* and He was *punished.* But by His wounds we are *healed.* I am humbled to call on such a Lord to be my Savior, redeemer, and friend.

Prayer

Father, I am always split between sorrow and joy when I grasp what Jesus had to go through for my sin. Thank You for sending Him to our planet two thousand years ago. I pray through His sacrifice, amen.

—*Jase*

December 26

Lift Your Hands!

Praise the Lord, all you servants of the Lord who minister by night in the house of the Lord. Lift up your hands in the sanctuary and praise the Lord. May the Lord bless you from Zion, he who is the Maker of heaven and earth.

—PSALM 134

As you bask in the afterglow of Christmas Day, take some time to simply give glory to God and praise His holy name for all that He has done and continues to do for His people. God gave the unimaginable gift—His only and very beloved Son. And He gave Him so that we—though we are rebellious and often unappreciative—could be reconciled to Him. I want to live my whole life as a song of praise to Him. Today especially, I lift my heart, my hands, and my eyes to the heavens to praise our wonderful God and Father.

Prayer

Father, we acknowledge Your greatness and praise Your name! May glory, honor, and praise be lifted up to You. May we offer our lives as a sacrifice of praise to You today. We love You and thank You through Christ, our Lord and Savior, amen.

—Al

December 27

Comfort for the Fearful

For God has not given us a spirit of fear and timidity, but of power, love, and self-discipline.

—2 TIMOTHY 1:7, NLT

THIS IS A verse that my wife and I prayed with our daughter. It helped her and us to learn to control fear and not to lash out when we are frightened. We learned, instead, that God has given us a spirit of *power, love,* and *self-discipline.* It is important to learn good things with your whole family. Paula and I are proud of the daughter we raised, but we know we couldn't have done it without God's Word and His Help.

Prayer

God, please give me the strength to go forward when all odds are against me. Give me the wisdom to know and see Your will for my life and the courage to live it. I thank You for my daughter and our family. In Your name I pray, amen.

—*Godwin*

HAPPY WITH WHAT WE HAVE

I have learned to be content whatever the circumstances. I know what it is to be in need, and I know what it is to have plenty.

—PHILIPPIANS 4:11–12

THESE DAYS THERE are so many things to have! Phones, tablets, iPods, online shopping. The world is literally at our fingertips. It's easy to be discontent with our lives. Early Christianity experienced tremendous growth without the aid of technology. Many of those Christians were murdered, persecuted, hunted, and even forbidden from gathering together, so they had no church buildings. They had no cars, computers, or phones to make their secret meetings easier, and many of them eventually lost their lives because of their faith. How dare we be discontent with our soft lives and freedom of worship? God tells us that He is in control of all things, that we should be happy with what He gives us. We are sinners and truly deserve nothing. God, in His perfect grace and mercy, gives us every moment and every breath.

Prayer

Lord, help me to see that You have given me all I need and more. You are my sustenance; You quench my thirst and ease my hurt and hunger. Help me to be content with the life You've graciously given me. Through Jesus I pray, amen.

—*Alex Robertson Mancuso*

DECEMBER 29

BEARDS WITH BLESSINGS

A wife of noble character who can find? She is worth far more than rubies. Her husband has full confidence in her and lacks nothing of value. She brings him good, not harm, all the days of her life.

—PROVERBS 31:10–12

I'M THE ONE brother without a beard, but I'm always asked by folks around the country, "How did those bearded guys get hooked up with all of those beautiful women?" When I ask my brothers about it, they always say, "Must have been the money!" We laugh at that in the family, because we know how little money we all had when we got married. And none of the guys had a beard in those days; they looked like me! The truth is, our wives say they married us because they saw Christ in us and saw the potential for spiritual leadership. Of course, we saw the love of the Lord in our wives, as well. Our marriages were forged in love for our Lord, and the success has come because God decided to pour out His blessings on us. We have not been perfect, but we have all managed to stay together—serving God and raising our families to serve our God, from generation to generation.

Prayer

Father, I am so grateful for the spiritually beautiful women You brought into my and my brothers' lives. We praise You for Jesus, amen.

—*Al*

December 30

Seventy Times Seven

Then Peter came and said to Him, "Lord, how often shall my brother sin against me and I forgive him? Up to seven times?" Jesus said to him, "I do not say to you, up to seven times, but up to seventy times seven."

—MATTHEW 18:21–22, NASB

On this earth, we are bound by our nature, and our earthly nature often has trouble with forgiveness. Sometimes it's because we have been wronged in the same way before by the same person. Our nature wants to hold grudges and exchange forgiveness for retribution. This verse reminds us that forgiveness is something we must give as God forgives us. We will never run out of chances with the Lord. Knowing that we have been forgiven so much is the first step in giving forgiveness to others.

Prayer

Heavenly Father, teach me to forgive others as You forgive me. Teach me to let go of things that are limiting my forgiveness. Soften my heart and open my mind to loving others as You love me. Remind me of the mercy and grace that You gave me. Show Your mercy and grace to others through me, as I practice forgiveness. Amen.

—Jon Gimber

DECEMBER 31

RISE, KILL, AND EAT!

The next day, as they went on their journey and drew near the city, Peter went up on the housetop to pray, about the sixth hour. Then he became very hungry and wanted to eat; but while they made ready, he fell into a trance and saw heaven opened and an object like a great sheet bound at the four corners, descending to him and let down to the earth. In it were all kinds of four-footed animals of the earth, wild beasts, creeping things, and birds of the air. And a voice came to him, "Rise, Peter; kill and eat."

—ACTS 10:9–13, NKJV

YEAH, I KNOW this passage is about the Gentiles being brought into the kingdom, but the bottom line is this: if it walks, crawls, flies, or swims, God says we can whack it or stack it!

Prayer

Father, thank You for Your creation. The animals, birds, and reptiles are delicious. We enjoy Your creation very much, and we are looking forward to our new heaven and our new earth! Amen.

—*Phil*

Permissions Acknowledgments